Instructor's Guide

Managing
School Districts
for High Performance

Instructor's Guide

Managing
School Districts
for High Performance

Editors

Stacey Childress

Richard F. Elmore

Allen S. Grossman

Susan Moore Johnson

Harvard Education Press
Cambridge, Massachusetts

Library of Congress Control Number 2007932117

Paperback ISBN 978-1-891792-76-2

Published by Harvard Education Press,
an imprint of the Harvard Education Publishing Group

Harvard Education Press
8 Story Street
Cambridge, MA 02138

Cover: YayDesign

The typefaces used in this book are Bembo and Univers.

Contents

MODULE I
Making Coherence Concrete

MODULE II
Finding and Supporting Personnel

MODULE III
Building a High-Performing Organization

MODULE IV
Managing Schools across Differences

MODULE V
Sustaining High Performance over Time

Introduction

This collection of cases is an outgrowth of a unique partnership between the Harvard Business School, the Harvard Graduate School of Education, and a number of large school districts. Dubbed the Public Education Leadership Project (PELP), this four-year endeavor explored a set of issues related to the challenge of implementing a districtwide strategy for improving the performance of all students in large public school districts.

The university faculty recruited a number of districts to participate in the design of a knowledge-generation and executive-development program aimed at senior administrators who have general management responsibility. The process of developing the cases in this volume was iterative. Faculty members met with administrators and other stakeholders in our partner districts and questioned them about the leadership and managerial challenges they faced in implementing their districtwide strategies to improve student performance. We then focused our attention on finding concrete manifestations of those problems in real urban districts and on writing cases to demonstrate the complexity of the design and implementation decisions that actual leadership teams were facing.

Some of these cases are drawn from PELP partner districts and some from other districts that came to our attention. We taught the cases in the PELP executive program, in other practitioner programs, and in academic degree programs at both the education and business schools at Harvard. We then revised them to reflect what we had learned in the process of teaching them.

We returned to our partner districts to discuss how effectively the cases helped them sharpen their practices, and we also developed new cases to reflect the most current problems the district partners were facing. As a result, the cases in the course book reflect a productive four-year dialogue among academics, practitioners, and students in graduate professional programs.

Based on the collective teaching and learning experience of the faculty members, practitioners, and students who have used these cases, we are interested in bringing the case method more centrally into the preparation and ongoing development of education administrators. Though the case method is not the only way to teach current and future practitioners, it is a powerful and transformative approach. The chief constraint thus far to using the case method in the preparation of educational administrators has been the lack of a critical mass of good material and a dearth of people willing to try case teaching. We hope this book will address both of these needs.

Teaching and the Case Method: Why Cases?

The case method of teaching embodies a particular point of view about the relationship between theory and practice and between the classroom and the world in which practitioners operate. The fundamental idea behind case teaching is that the case—a real-world situation almost always derived from actual events—serves as the focal point for discussion among teacher and students. Participants in case discussions are typically asked to take the role of one of the protagonists in the case, thus making them confront the real choices, constraints, and opportunities of the people in the case. In this sense, case teaching situates teacher and students in an environment midway between the classroom and the world at large. The theory—in this case the PELP framework and whatever other theoretical material instructors wish to introduce—provides the backdrop for concrete discussions about what to do in the situation defined by the case.

Case teaching is also meant to alter the traditional relationship between student and teacher by creating a common focus on problem-solving in the classroom, rather than putting the teacher in the position of "delivering" the content. The expectation that underlies case teaching is that all participants bring something to the discussion, and that the resultant learning is a product of the collective knowledge of the group, rather than the knowledge of a single person. In this spirit, case method pedagogy is often referred to as participant-centered learning.

Case teaching embodies four basic principles:

1. A discussion class is a *partnership* in which students and the instructor share the responsibilities and power of teaching, and the privilege of learning together.

2. A discussion group must evolve from a collection of individuals into a learning *community* with shared values and common goals [for learning].

3. By forging a primary (although not exclusive) *alliance with students,* the discussion leader can help them gain command of the course material.

4. Discussion teaching requires *dual competency:* the ability to manage content and process.[1]

Case discussions often begin with, and always include, a question that forces action: "What should 'X' (the case protagonist) do?" It proceeds through an analysis of the problems confronting the protagonist, the context in which those problems occur, and the alternatives available for addressing the problems. Teacher and students construct their understanding of the case from the case itself, from their background knowledge, from the theoretical framework underlying the content, and from individuals' unique perspectives and value orientations. No two case discussions are ever identical, though they may have a basic structure in common.

Good case discussions also typically involve some kind of closure or summing-up of the main learning and lessons gleaned from the discussion. Again, the product is created jointly by the instructor and the students, with students usually taking the lead in drawing conclusions and the instructor helping to manage the flow of ideas.

Case teaching is an exercise in mutual trust. The instructor trusts the students' capacity to draw important facts and conclusions from the case. The students trust the instructor's capacity to sustain the flow of the discussion and to model a safe and productive learning environment. Students ultimately develop and manage their competencies in productive group learning. The most important quality for participants in case discussions is the capacity to listen and respond to the comments and views of others, not simply to argue a position.

Using the Instructor's Guide and Student Text

This volume is designed to be a companion to the student text. It includes only materials designed to support teaching the cases, not the cases themselves. It is designed to help instructors use the cases and to adapt their use to various audiences—primarily graduate professional students and practitioner participants in leadership-development programs. Each case in the student text is accompanied by a teaching note in this volume that provides basic guidance in how to initiate and organize the flow of the case discussion. The function of a teaching note is not to dictate how the case should be taught, but to distill the experience of instructors who have previously taught the case into a form designed to be useful those who are teaching it for the first time. The teaching notes are the product of extensive work by faculty members and research assistants in the development and teaching of the cases. The notes grow out of several iterations of teaching and revising cases. Still, they represent only one group's experience, and they should be seen as opening a conversation about how to teach the case rather than providing a definitive recipe. Fluency in case teaching comes from practice. Not all case discussions are smooth and graceful, and as with many things in life, some of the most productive learning comes from experiences that are far from perfect. The point is to build competence and fluency over time. As with any kind of teaching, the best way to master case teaching is to try it out and reflect on the consequences of trying. There are resources that can help both novices and the experienced alike prepare to use these cases and to practice case teaching.[2]

The student text can either stand on its own or be used in conjunction with other course materials that reflect the instructor's own ideas and point of view. Each module begins with a brief introduction that is designed to set the focus for that collection of cases. Taken together, the modules represent the critical organizational components of how to implement a districtwide strategy for improvement, as outlined in "Note on the PELP Coherence Framework." We designed the module sequence based on our own experiences teaching the material in a number of environments to graduate students and practitioners, so the flow reflects our point of view about the logical progression of the ideas. However, the modules can be used separately for

distinct topical discussions, they can be reorganized to accommodate instructors' own course designs, or they can be used as the overall design for a single course or sequence of professional-development activities. Since the case modules are quite extensive, instructors might want to schedule review and consolidation sessions at the end of each module.

The first case in most of the modules comes from outside the field of education. Our practitioner partners have told us that they find these cases very useful in introducing the key ideas in the PELP Coherence Framework; they help the instructors focus on core concepts and problems rather than immediately translating the ideas into a familiar context. The noneducation cases also open participants up to the idea that the problems of the education sector are shared by other public and private organizations, and that knowledge drawn from those sectors can be useful to educators.

The education cases in each module are meant to draw out the complexities involved in designing, communicating, and implementing a districtwide improvement strategy across an entire school system. They are typically written in what we call action-forcing mode. That is, they require the instructor and the participants to focus a major part of the discussion on the actual decisions that real people have faced, rather than assuming an arm's-length attitude toward the problems in the cases. We have found it useful to hold participants in the action-forcing mode long enough so they can appreciate how difficult the problems in the case are and how important it is to be knowledgeable and reflective about their own practice in similar situations.

Each case is designed to be taught in a 75- to 90-minute segment. The time can vary according to the needs of the instructor and the participants. It is also useful to program in some time to reflect explicitly on the cumulative learning up to that point in the course and on the progress of the group in managing participation and discussions. We have found that explicit discussion of group norms for participation creates broader participation and greater engagement from students. Instructors may also want to create smaller groups to discuss the action-forcing questions, and then reconvene to share in the large-group setting, since some participants are more willing to participate in smaller groups than in large groups. Overall, though, cases work best when the entire group is engaged in cooperative problem-solving around the problems presented in the case.

Modeling Coherence in the Classroom

The student volume stresses the importance of coherence in the organization and management of school systems. It provides a framework for developing coherent improvement strategies in school systems and a set of cases that demonstrate the successes and pitfalls of systems that have tried to develop such strategies. It is important that the design and the pedagogy of the courses and programs that flow out of this volume attempt to model the main message of the framework and the cases: coherence counts.

We have found in our work with participants that it is relatively easy for them to become immersed in the details of specific cases and in their own anecdotal experiences and miss the point of the framework, which is to organize their thought and action into a coherent strategy for improvement. The work of educational administration is fraught with attractive nuisances—distractions that appear to be urgent and necessary but that have no material relationship to the overall purposes of the organization. One of the main messages of the PELP framework and the accompanying cases is the importance of discipline and focus in the process of framing a strategy and then using it to transform the culture of the organization and the actions of the people in it.

The challenge facing instructors who

choose to use this material is how to model this kind of coherence in the pedagogy of the classroom. If the message is about coherence but the pedagogy does not model that message, then participants are likely to take away what the pedagogy tells them, not what the content says. Here are a few ideas about how to model coherence in the classroom:

1. **Revisit the Framework Regularly.** The PELP "Note on the Coherence Framework" is meant to be both a guide for action and a framework for organizing discussion of the cases. Participants will find that the framework develops increased depth and meaning the more they learn about specific strategic issues and the more opportunity they have to share their ideas with others in case discussions. Instructors will also find opportunities to bring their own ideas into the framework as discussions progress. The framework will not support this cumulative understanding if there isn't specific time set aside to return to it and discuss how one's understanding of strategy and coherence is developing in light of the learning and discussion.

2. **Explore Relationships among the Pieces.** It is true, as the saying goes, that "the devil is in the details." The cases provide an opportunity to see how the specifics of the design of a strategy of improvement can affect the overall success of that strategy. But if the discussion focuses only on the pieces, the strategy will disappear into the background and cease to be a major organizing force in analysis and discussion. So it is incumbent on the instructor to ask questions that force participants to return to the larger picture: How does so-and-so's teacher-compensation plan relate to the purposes that the district is trying to accomplish? Do the individuals in "X" district understand the superintendent's vision? If not, what would help to make that

happen? How would you get "Y" and "Z" to work together to get a better, more coherent result?

3. **Can You See the Strategy in the Details?** One major insight the PELP faculty took away from our work with districts is the need to help the leaders see that the strategy they are pursuing must be visible to the people who are carrying it out. School systems are accustomed to implementing programs and projects, not strategies. So it is important for people to learn to see the big picture in the details of the organization. One question that helps to surface this issue is: If you were to walk into a random classroom (or school) in "X" district, could you see the strategy of the district in action? What would you expect to see?

4. **Reflect, Act, Reflect.** Participants consistently tell us that their most powerful learning occurs when they have time to reflect on the learning from case discussions and to cycle their learning through a new understanding of their own work. Coherence emerges from repeated cycles of reflection and action. In order to model this in the classroom, participants must have time to think about their responses and recommendations in any given case and to modify them in light of what they have learned from analysis and discussion. Ideally, they would also have an opportunity to try out ideas in their workplace, or to observe others trying them out, and to reflect on what they have learned from observation.

5. **Keep a Running Record of Insights and Reflections.** To overcome the centrifugal tendencies of the discussion of a series of cases, it is important for participants to feel that there is some continuity and cumulative learning over time. This can be accomplished by having individuals keep a running account of their own theories of action growing out of case discussions and by asking the group to record their main insights cumulatively over time. Introducing the expectation of cumulative learning does a great deal to reinforce the idea of coherence.

Using the Material in Executive Development Programs

The PELP experience been a powerful influence on the authors and our colleagues in shaping our ideas about how to design, organize, and carry out powerful practitioner learning in the service of coherent strategies of improvement in local school districts. In addition to the preceding discussion about case method pedagogy and course design that are relevant to both graduate and practitioner programs, we believe that some of the lessons we have learned about structuring executive-development experiences may have some relevance to our colleagues who intend to use these cases for practitioner programs.

In the PELP executive programs, we required participating districts to bring teams of senior administrators. We felt that a team-based program was essential to demonstrating that the work of designing and implementing a coherent improvement strategy is a *collective,* not an individual, effort. Consistent with that view, we provided ample time during our programs for participants to work in their district teams to refine and deepen their understanding of and commitment to their own strategies, and to address obstacles they predicted they would face when they returned to their districts. We also invested time in activities specifically designed to build a shared identity and cohesiveness among the members of the district teams. Participants uniformly said that they valued this time.

During large-group case discussions, we found it useful to ask participants to reflect on how the problems presented in a particular case or content module occur in their own setting. In general, we have found it more effective to set aside a separate time to talk about the problems that practitioners might bring to the sessions, rather than trying to integrate the discussion of these problems into the case discussion. It is difficult enough to sustain a strong discussion of a case without burdening it with the myriad examples of similar problems that arise in each practitioner's setting.

We also used multiple learning environments to provide opportunities for participants to try out their ideas and to discuss their learning outside of the classroom. We organized participants into more or less randomly constituted small discussion groups to prepare in advance for case discussions, in order to provide them with an opportunity to interact with people in different roles from other districts. We also occasionally put people with similar roles into groups—superintendents, assistant superintendents, curriculum supervisors, etc.—to talk about common problems across district lines. Multiple learning environments allow people to engage more comfortably in learning that draws on their strengths and to develop competencies in areas where they are less strong.

While the PELP model is only one among many ways to use the materials in these volumes, we feel that there is much to be gained by creating multiple settings in which teams of practitioners can learn.

An Invitation

We view this collection of cases and supporting materials as an invitation to case teaching in educational administration for those who have not used the method before, and a stimulus to further thought for those who have. Following is an article about case teaching by our departed colleague, C. Roland "Chris" Christensen, whose work has deeply influenced all of us. We hope this is the beginning of a much longer conversation among fellow scholars and practitioners.

Notes

1. "Teaching and the Case Method: Premises and Practices," in *Teaching and the Case Method,* ed. Louis B. Barnes, C. Roland Christensen, and Abby Hansen (Boston: Harvard Business School Press, 1994), 24, emphasis in original.

2. See, for example, C Roland Christensen , David Garvin, and Ann Sweet, eds., *Education for Judgment: The Artistry of Discussion Leadership* (Boston: Harvard Business School Press, 1991), and *Participant Centered Learning and the Case Method: A 3-CD Case Teaching Tool,* (Product #9–904–421) (Boston: Harvard Business School Publishing, 2004).

C. Roland Christensen

Premises and Practices of Discussion Teaching

As Alexander Pope reminds us, "'Tis with our judgments as our watches, none go just alike, yet each believes his own." This essay, which describes some basic hypotheses about discussion pedagogy, is offered in the hope that other teachers will consider my reflections, and then consult their own "watches."

The most fundamental observation I can make about discussion teaching is this: however mysterious or elusive the process may seem, it can be learned. Through collaboration and cooperation with friends and colleagues, and through self-observation and reflection, teachers can master both principles and techniques of discussion leadership. But the task is complex. Discussion teachers' responsibilities are as varied as their rewards. With greater vitality in the classroom, the satisfaction of true intellectual collaboration and synergy, and improved retention on the part of students, the rewards are considerable. The responsibilities may be difficult to appreciate at first. For example, effective preparation for discussion classes takes more time, because instructors must consider not only *what* they will teach, but also *whom* and *how*. And the classroom encounter consumes a great deal of energy; simultaneous attention to process (the flow of activities that make up a discussion) and content (the material discussed) requires emotional as well as intellectual engagement. Effective discussion leadership requires competency in both areas; it can be achieved only with patience.

The discussion teacher is planner, host, moderator, devil's advocate, fellow-student, and judge—a potentially confusing set of roles. Even the most seasoned group leader must be content with uncertainty, because discussion teaching is the art of managing spontaneity. Nonetheless, a good chart can help a mariner navigate safely even in fog. The premises and associated operational practices described here are my personal chart, tested over years of practice and found dependable in groups that range in size from twenty to eighty or even a hundred participants. Four premises seem fundamental:

1. A discussion class is a *partnership* in which students and instructor share the responsibilities and power of teaching, and the privilege of learning together.

2. A discussion group must evolve from a col-

lection of individuals into a learning *community* with shared values and common goals.

3. By forging a primary (although not exclusive) *alliance with students,* the discussion leader can help them gain command of the course material.

4. Discussion teaching requires *dual competency:* the ability to manage content and process.

A Partnership between Teacher and Students

Lecturing, which emphasizes the instructor's power over the student, is a master-apprentice relationship of great power when the transfer of knowledge is the primary academic objective. But when the objective is critical thinking (in the liberal arts setting, for example) or problem-solving (in the professional school milieu), and the development of qualities such as sensitivity, cooperation, and zest for discovery, discussion pedagogy offers substantial advantages. To achieve these complex, value-laden educational goals, both teachers and students must modify their traditional roles and responsibilities.

In discussion teaching, partnership—a collegial sharing of power, accountability, and tasks—supplants hierarchy and asymmetry in the teacher-student relationship. The discussion process itself requires students to become profoundly and actively involved in their own learning, to discover for themselves rather than accept verbal or written pronouncements. They must explore the intellectual terrain without maps, step by blazing trails, struggling past obstacles, dealing with disappointments. How different from simply following others' itineraries!

Such creative activity cannot be ordered or imposed upon the unwilling. Teachers can police attendance and monitor the memorization of theory and fact by tests. But we cannot order our students to be committed to learning and willing to risk experimentation, error, and the uncertainty of exploration. Such attitudes are gifts from one partner to another.

Professor McGregor of MIT used to tell a story to illustrate the true dependency of superior on subordinates. A young executive arrived at a unionized textile mill and told the union officer, "I am the new manager here, and when I manage a mill, I run it. Do you understand?" The union agent nodded and waved his hand. Every worker stopped; every boom stopped. Then the agent turned to the manager and said, "Go ahead, run it." Students, at least in North America, are not unionized, but they possess the power to turn a discussion class into an academic charade by withholding involvement.

Another force mandating partnership in the teacher-student relationship is the fundamental need for students' input to the leadership of a group—a fact of life that lucky instructors discover in the adolescence of their teaching careers. Students not only teach themselves, and one another, they participate in leadership tasks traditionally counted as the teacher's—such as setting the discussion agenda and determining pacing and emphasis.

When students are unaccustomed to discussion pedagogy, the instructor must take practical steps to promote partnership. Students may greet the notion of sharing power and responsibility with skepticism based on years of contrary experience. To the instructor's promise that "we're all partners here," hardened skeptics may silently respond, "Fat chance!" But even they may feel a twinge of hope: "What if he really means it?" This twinge can prompt further questions: "I know the rules of the regular classroom game. But now the professor's changing them. To what?"

When students feel uncertain about the rules of the game, they try to resolve their doubts by testing the instructor. They ask—explicitly or indirectly—does this teacher genuinely want my contributions? Is she interested in knowing me as a special person, and will she keep my individuality in mind when she listens to my comments? Does he receive my suggestions with a positive attitude (there are some fascinating ideas here), or a negative bias (I'll find something wrong)? Does she really listen at all, or just pause while I talk? Does he ask for my help, work with my suggestions, demonstrate respect for my judgment? How does she react when I question her methods or conclusions? When we teachers repeatedly pass these tests, we communicate respect and validate our students' role as co-teachers. Our confidence in them encourages cooperation and friendship—and friendship is a marvelous ingredient in partnership.

Partnership is fragile and difficult to regain once lost. It needs continual nourishment, which can be provided in part by operational rituals and procedures. How a professor starts the day's session, for example, sends a message about the working relationship of the whole class. If the instructor lays out a step-by-step outline for the discussion—orally or on the blackboard—the class picks up a clear signal: follow my lead or be lost! Any partnership between a leader and followers is clearly a limited one.

In contrast, when the instructor invites students to set the agenda for the day's discussion, the openness of the invitation communicates a different message: you, the students bear the responsibility for this discussion. It belongs to you. As the classroom dialogue evolves, the instructor can further underscore the principle of joint ownership by asking students to summarize points or lines of argument, or to suggest the next question the group should discuss.

Direct participation in the leadership of their class enhances students' self-esteem—essential for effective learning—and gives them an opportunity to consolidate what they know by teaching others. Instructors can increase the value of students' input by publicly acknowledging its importance. We all tend to exert our best efforts when we feel appreciated.

Instructors can also benefit from the sharing inherent in partnership. By bringing unexpected points of view and creative, upsetting questions to material that has become extremely familiar to the instructor, fresh and energetic students play a particularly useful role in class: they wake us up. Moreover, when students function as co-teachers, their growing mastery of discussion leadership permits the instructor to step back—mentally, and sometimes even physically—to observe the class from their perspective. This opportunity to focus on how students listen, react, make notes, prepare to pounce, or perhaps "tune out" is invaluable. Such observation provides instant feedback on the progress, or lack thereof, of individual students as well as the group as a whole. By watching our own classes unfold, we can assess our performance from the most meaningful point of view: that of the students. And when students become skilled partners, their after-class comments can help us answer every teacher's inescapable question: How am I doing?

Partnership is both a window through which students can observe the teaching/learning process and a mirror that reveals them to themselves (surely a major element in any education). In deepening their personal involvement, taking responsibility for the quality of the discussion, and making an emotional investment in the outcome of the course, students claim ownership of their own education. This ownership not only stimulates them to excel, it also enhances our effectiveness as instructors.

Finally, partnership makes teaching more joyful. We teachers trade the aloneness and distance of hierarchy for the cooperation and closeness of colleagueship. Partnership with students gives us an incentive to be students again—and what are great teachers if not great students?

A Learning Community

Quality of context—the milieu in which the collective dialogue takes place—is fundamental to effective discussion. Where the context supports rigorous intellectual analyses and group collaboration, where an operational contract defines how teacher and students work together, and where there is mutual respect among all participants, a community dedicated to learning emerges.

Even a casual observer can tell when a group lacks the spirit of community. "If the tone of a class is confrontational, critical, and acerbic," a colleague once noted, "students will retreat—all except those who are 'red in tooth and claw.'" Gresham's Law (bad money drives out good) applies to the class that lacks community: the vocally aggressive and personally superconfident "drive out" the contributions of their measured and reflective, but perhaps less articulate, fellow students. In the absence of understood, trustworthy boundaries for appropriate behavior, attack—not exploration—often becomes the predominant activity. When participants compete to score individual points rather than collaborate to build group themes, they damage the fabric of discussion. In such a milieu students resist modifying early conclusions even when contrary evidence emerges—a particularly dangerous practice for intellectual growth.

In a true learning community, by contrast, diverse backgrounds blend and individuals bond into an association dedicated to collective as well is personal learning. The students seem interested in one another and the academic assignment of the day. And their dialogue has the open-ended quality of exploration. Speakers not only present points of view but test and modify their ideas; instead of doggedly defending personal conclusions, they listen to one another with interest, not fear. Differences of opinion produce inquiries, not disputes. Working as a unit, the class Icarus to value measured progress without expecting instant gratification.

The basic academic drive to master a body of knowledge, and its application to practice, power all education ventures, including solo study. But what turns a collection of students

into a learning community.' Not the mere assignment to the same room and time slot. The instructor must take concrete steps to promote collaboration and comradeship. He or she needs to develop strategies that will reflect the values that enable a group of individuals to work together productively. Here are the basic values I endorse for this purpose.

Civility—courtesy in working with one's associates—is a simple but powerful virtue. In class as elsewhere, politeness sets a cooperative tone and encourages the openness that lets people help one another by sharing experience and insight. *Willingness to take risks,* both individual and collective, not only helps students understand the topic of the day, but encourages daring and innovation. Finally, *an appreciation of diversity*—in backgrounds, personalities, questions posed, learning styles, frames of inquiry, and spectrums of interpretation—ensures that the group will avoid the rigidity of single-track paths to single-point destinations. Instead, the group will feel free to venture into intellectual terra incognita, where explorers need one another's help and support. The totality of these values can determine the tone of the group's discussions, and their collective impact creates an ethos that can activate, permeate, and enrich a group's minute-by-minute dialogue.

Instructors who build community reinforce these values by their own behavior. It helps simply to welcome the class to each session before plunging into the business of the day, or to greet individual students by name as they arrive. We can demonstrate our commitment to honest sharing by helping discussion participants who run into difficulties, and by asking for students' help when we find ourselves in an intellectual or procedural quandary.

Reinforcing the values of community can also take the form of being candid about ourselves. Hugh Prather puts the point pragmatically when he notes, "In order to see, one must be willing to be seen."[1] To promote openness in students, we must reveal our own areas of certitude and uncertainty, our dreams and our defeats. And, if we want our students to take the risks that make creativity possible, we must show we are willing and able to assist them when they stumble. To make independence practical and enfranchise all the members of the group, we must support students when their comments depart from the consensus of the moment or their proposals collide with firmly held convictions of the class. One way I do this is by explicitly including the iconoclast in a "majority of two" to make it clear that I will abet honest exploration, even when the group finds it unorthodox.

When the instructor both endorses and models a set of positive common values, the group will usually adopt them. Physical attendance then is transformed to academic belonging, and the group can achieve high quality in its discussions and its relationships.

We instructors can also strengthen the sense of community by paying attention to our teacher-student learning contracts. As Abby Hansen notes elsewhere, a pedagogical contract is a pattern "of understood and accepted ground rules that guide the protocols, rituals, mutual obligations, and standards of behavior of a class." We teachers build contracts with our words and our behavior. As we ask questions and respond to students' contributions, we give them material with which to form judgments of our leadership style and values. To communicate our genuine appreciation for the knowledge and judgment of our students, we can invite them to join us in defining the terns of our academic collaboration—and then make sure to honor their terms with our practice.

Implementing the teacher-student learning contract is complicated, for three reasons. First, since teaching contracts are set both explicitly (by statements) and implicitly (by the often inadvertent accretion of precedents), instructors must attend to both dialogue and behavior. Second, because much of our behavior originates on the

intuitive or preconscious level, it can be difficult to know what contract we are promulgating. (A hint: students' readings of our actions provide important clues.) Third, since contracts are organic, they change. Untended, they can either grow wild or decay. As students' interests and command of the course materials evolve throughout the semester, the contract must reflect these sometimes subtle changes.

When we let students share in the governance of their own course, they are less likely to feel like second-class citizens. And since people who contribute to setting standards often feel moved to surpass them, the best teacher-student learning contracts can also transcend themselves. When this happens, they evolve beyond formal procedures, legality, and details of enforcement to become covenants rather than mere contracts: solemn compacts among members of a group to pursue common goals for mutual benefit. Covenants promote the deep commitment that encourages accountability and mutual responsibility. They nurture true community, for who will reveal his innermost beliefs, dreams, doubts, and most adventuresome ideas in an atmosphere of distrust?

One can be a good lecturer without giving these matters much thought. But in the extemporaneous face-to-face dialogue of discussion teaching, all parties are vulnerable, and students in particular feel their exposure keenly. Learning means leaving the known for the unknown—an exhilarating, but scary venture. In a discussion class, students often feel they are undergoing a private, even intimate, recreation of their personae in public view. A mature student speaks poignantly about this experience:

> It is extremely important for me to be in a classroom where there is acceptance and hospitality, and absolute hospitality of teacher and classmates that will allow ideas to be born for the first time. I feel very vulnerable. The teacher is in the privileged position of knowing me before I

change and after. In a way it is similar to being a parent. The teacher holds my continuity because he or she knows me before, yet sees me leave my earlier self behind. School needs to be a safe place to leave my old self behind and change.

While discussion classrooms will never be perfectly safe, instructors can minimize students' vulnerability by promoting trust and respect. It is not enough to espouse these worthy goals in the abstract, for students readily detect empty idea-worship; they believe our actions more than our words. Two skills are especially valuable as teachers attempt to make the discussion classroom hospitable.

First, we can *listen* to students' comments with discipline and sensitivity; second, we can *respond* to them constructively. When discussion participants realize that the instructor treats their comments seriously and takes pains to build them into the discussion, they feel valued. And when this respect is maintained over time, students develop a sense of trust, a sine qua non for a true learning community. Disciplined listening elevates students' comments to the status of contributions. A wise instructor once commented that we should give—not pay—attention to what students say. Paying implies a cold, impersonal commercial transaction; giving communicates colleagueship, sharing, community.

As disciplined listeners, we try to hear the unspoken. Perhaps Bob's terse "Boston isn't moving very fast to integrate public housing" carries a message about his ghetto youth, repeated difficulties in getting good housing for his own family, and aggressive leadership of a tenants' union. If Betty, who has held forth often and forcefully against sending arms to Central America, fails to speak out in today's emotional discussion of the same issue, a disciplined listener will hear her silence and wonder about its cause. Does she expect the teacher to hear yesterday's comments again today? Has she changed her views? The sharpness of questions and responses

and the vividness of language employed are useful clues to the intensity of students' feelings.

Treating students' comments with respect does not necessarily mean accepting them at face value. Discussion participants sometimes float verbal trial balloons filled with hot air. When we spot such bloated assertions, the trick is to suppress the tendency (ours or the students') to sarcastic harpoonery and let the discussion bring these balloons gently back to earth.

As teachers, we also build community with our constructive responses to students' comments. If we view all comments as potentially positive contributions to the group's learning process, our task as teachers is to integrate this raw material so as to further the discussion. I have found certain practical mechanisms useful in putting these ideals to work. For example, one can honor participants' contributions by giving speakers time to complete their arguments. Although teachers feel pressed to keep dialogue moving quickly (doodling can spring up at a moment's notice), haste can produce damaging cutoffs that belittle and stymie speakers. A suggestion after a student finishes talking, watch her eyes. Do they indicate that her thought is now complete? If you feel unsure, wait a few seconds and recheck. A five-second pause often produces a contributor's most insightful thought.

At the most elementary level, an instructor shows respect for a student's statement by making sure that the group has understood its basic analysis. To promote a true community of learning, however, it is also valuable to ensure that a spirit of colleagueship characterizes the way the group will test and explore that analysis. How? By taking care that our comments convey appreciation for the time and effort the student expended to prepare the contribution—and for his or her courage, if the contribution espoused an unpopular view. A learning community needs brave, as well as adroit, students.

Community is strengthened when we put

students' comments to work, immediately if possible. We can use their questions to subject conclusions (both students' and the instructor's) to scrutiny. We can link their contributions from earlier classes to the current dialogue; we can follow their leads for next-step inquiry; we can build summaries around their formulations and use their words.

Community-minded instructors will be cautious in introducing their personal judgments into the classroom dialogue, and will state such judgments in a manner that clearly invites students to differ. "Ruth, many experts disagree on the question of increasing the federal gasoline tax. I'm in favor of it, but where do you come out on this question, and why?"

Constructive response appreciates the conditional tense. *Would* this approach seem right? *Might* this be the route to take? *Should* the evidence lead us to this conclusion? Such an approach leaves maneuvering room for students and instructor alike. It eschews false absolutes such as "This is the way to lay out the factory work flow," or "It is wrong to subsidize low-cost housing." It encourages the cultivation of balanced judgment and lets disagreement flourish without confrontation.

Shared values, a mutually understood teacher-student learning contract, and a relationship of mutual trust and respect all nurture community. When discussion groups become communities, instructors can transcend their own uncertainties and vulnerabilities and enter into genuine covenants with their students. Doing so, they can unleash, and then slowly harness, a powerful energy of experience and creativity that students often did not know they possessed.

Alliance with Students

Effective discussion leadership, unlike lecturing, requires instructors to forge a primary alliance with students. We do not bring the material to them, but rather help them find their own ways

to it. The subject matter defines the boundaries of the intellectual territory, but the students' intellects, personalities, learning styles, fears, and aspirations shape the paths they will take. Students hunger for wholeness. They want recognition, not just as novice learners, but as persons with the competence to contribute to their own education and that of their fellow students. Alliance with them means learning about them. Students' family, social, and institutional affiliations affect both the style and content of their discussion contributions. Our personal reward for getting to know students is obvious; the experience of teaching becomes a warmer, emotionally enriched pursuit. But there is a pedagogical reward as well: we become more effective in leading the discussion process.

Of course forging an alliance with students has its costs as well as benefits. Learning about them requires an investment of scarce resources—time, emotional energy, and research ingenuity. The more we learn about the complexities of discussion participants, the more daunting the pedagogical tasks may seem. A colleague once asked, "Can one ever learn enough about a student?" Certainly, there are limits. But what are they? In a formal, but friendly relationship, what is appropriate information? And learning about students can be intimidating, too, for the more we understand the many worlds in which they live, the more we appreciate the gulf between those worlds and ours.

Despite these costs, I have found that the rewards prevail. Knowledge of students enables us to meet the first obligation of all instructors—at the very least to avoid injuring those whom we seek to help. I recall, to my chagrin, asking a student to comment on a one-page statement I had distributed a few minutes earlier in class. He blushed and declined. After class he explained his frustration: he was dyslexic. And I recall the story of a secondary-school science instructor who began his methods class early in the semester by calling on the boy who sat directly in front of him in the first row. The instructor did not know that the boy, although fascinated by science, was shy and clumsy in public speaking. The student stammered some sort of answer, and the instructor handled the ensuing dialogue equally badly. That boy—a Boston Brahmin now ninety years old—still recounts the incident with fresh pain and anger in his voice. Its ultimate impact was a poor orientation in course substance and subsequent avoidance of science in college and career—despite an early, passionate interest in the subject. How easily we can damage students' confidence, scar their spirits!

Many of the techniques of our craft carry some dangers. Role playing, for example, requires us to be particularly sensitive to students' backgrounds. I would not lightly assign a student a role that might give personal offense—ask a devout Mormon to pretend to be the sales manager of a liquor firm, or a member of a minority group to play the role of a bigoted manufacturing executive. It is easy to mistake labels for people, unless we know our students as individuals. One young woman recalled that most of her college instructors had used her as "our Korean source" because of her name, appearance, and birthplace. In fact, the daughter of a diplomat, she knew little of Seoul, and much about Paris and Madrid.

Knowing students can also help us humanize the all-too-often cold and formal setting of a classroom in which students, as we know from experience, sometimes feel like necessary nuisances. The Nobel laureate Robert Solow has embroidered on Arthur Guiternian's definition of education—a student sitting on one end of a log and a great teacher on the other—by noting that some professors appear to be sitting on their students and talking to the log. How true! Students appreciate our taking an interest in them, and as a result, the whole class has more fun. And when we sense the students' good feelings, our own efforts seem more positive to us. "This is a first-rate group," we say. "the class is really rolling

this year." We telegraph our buoyant mood with our step and posture as we enter the classroom. Our energy level is high as we lead the discussion. And communication improves. We hear the message in students' comments with greater appreciation when we understand something of their background and current interests. And the teacher-student dynamic improves, too. As we learn about students, they are encouraged to learn about us. And learning brings appreciation.

Our knowledge of students helps us meet them "where they are." And that is where learning begins. No matter what the curriculum or course plan may assume, students occupy unique intellectual and emotional spaces, and the discussion teacher is well advised to seek out their locations. What sort of a learner is Tim? Does he know when and how to get help, and how to test its appropriateness? Is he frightened or excited by the unknown? Does he cut corners in defending his points of view? Is he self-aware? Does he know his own blind spots and "hot buttons"? How does he work with classmates? Is he willing to have his ideas tested rigorously, to explore a classmate's argument, even though it contradicts a strongly held conviction of his own? How does he view peer "error," as a chance to demonstrate personal superiority or an opportunity to help a classmate learn? Does he have the leadership skills to contribute to the educational objectives of the day? Does he frame questions that catch the current "drift" and extend its range? Does he truly listen? Can he accumulate and integrate prior comments and construct a unified whole? Wasn't it T. S. Eliot who said that hell is where nothing connects? Does Tim see the connections?

As discussion teachers, we need to see our students on life's wider screen. What academic and work experiences do they bring to the discussion classroom? Have they tutored in secondary school, sold encyclopedias in poor neighborhoods, worked as systems analysts, done research for a state regulatory agency, or managed an overseas branch of a corporation? In what other worlds do they live? What current interests, whether social, political, or recreational, consume them?

Such knowledge can help us in our minute-by-minute leadership of a discussion. If Carol is at her best when given time to reflect on an issue, I would not "cold call" her. If Sam's father is dying, or if Hal is in the final week of producing the second-year class play, perhaps they should not open the discussion. If Ida has managed a day care center and the topic of the day is child care in the workplace, how should I bring her into the dialogue—as an expert, an advocate, a challenger, or a backup resource? What will do her, as well as the class, the most good?

Meeting students where they are encourages us to ask ourselves where we are. What are our wider worlds, current interests? How do they affect our leadership of the group? Our own circumstances can have an enormous, inadvertent impact on what we do in class. In planning the course, for example, we may tend to teach first what we ourselves learned last. We often want to give priority to our discovery of the moment, because we find it fresh and exciting. But this may not help our students. They may need to learn first what we also learned first, because it tends to be basic.

Knowing where we and our students are, intellectually and emotionally, can help us with the ever-present problem of how to choose among several students with raised hands and anxious expressions. Almost inevitably, it is a mistake to be guided by the democratic instinct to favor the person whose hand has been raised the longest. Most likely, that student's comment will be "out of phase" because it will address whatever points were in play when the student first raised his or her hand.

Often inexperienced instructors assume it is desirable to always recognize the participant whose background experience best matches the point under discussion; it is, however, but one

factor to be considered. If the class is discussing federal revenue policy and Arlene is an experienced tax accountant, should one call on her? The simple fact of her experience might lead to a boring or intimidating barrage of information. Given a choice between a participant with a specialized background and one skilled in making cogent comments and relating then to the flow of discussion, I would choose the latter. Or I might call on the student who could best profit from tackling the problem under examination and working with the specific comments just made. At points where the flow of discussion has become sufficiently turbulent (or turbid) to warrant summary, the instructor might do well to recognize a participant with a sophisticated command of intellectual synthesis and a talent for clear expression.

Since knowing our students in depth can confer such palpable benefits, why is it not the norm? I have mentioned some of the costs, but there is also a perceptual barrier to be overcome. All too often we see only what we want to see or what we are accustomed to seeing. Marcel Proust wrote of the simple act of looking at someone we know:

> We pack the physical outline of the creature we see with all the ideas we have already formed about him, and in the complete picture of him which we compose in our minds those ideas have certainly the principal place. In the end they come to fill out so completely the curve of his cheeks, to follow so exactly the line of his nose, they blend so harmoniously in the sound of his voice that these seem to be no more than a transparent envelope, so that each time we see the face or hear the voice, it is our own ideas of him which we recognize and to which we listen.[2]

As Proust suggests, the difference between "our own ideas of him" and a student's ideas about himself can be substantial. We need to ask ourselves how to narrow the gap by obtaining appropriate and useful information.

Let's take a look at my former student "Bob Smith." Like all students, he was a complex of past happenings, present circumstances, and future aspirations, a melange of roles and responsibilities. The richness of this complexity emerged as I began to understand him in the round. According to the registrar's sheet, he was "Robert W. Smith, 27, graduate of Wainsworth College, candidate for the MBA degree with a major in entrepreneurial management." That was just the tip of the iceberg.

There was Bob Smith, spouse, who lived with his wife and two young children in a mixed industrial-residential area of Boston. Bob belonged to several community service clubs and headed a program for physically disadvantaged inner-city children. And there was the former Lt. Robert W. Smith, U.S. Infantry, veteran of two years' duty in Vietnam. Wounded in combat, Lt. Smith had been awarded the Silver Star for bravery. And there was R. Wainsworth Smith, a graduate of the college his great-grandfather had founded, who left school with average grades and a record noting a two-week suspension from classes for having participated in a student protest. And there was Rob Smith, the youngest child in his family, with two older brothers in political and professional careers. There was also Bobbie Smith, son of two academic parents, both active in the Society of Friends.

Bob's background—prominent family, social concerns, military experience—made itself felt in the classroom. It conditioned his choice of issues and levels of involvement in the discussion at large, as well as in relationship with peers, students outside the class, and the instructor. Faulkner's *Requiem for a Nun* puts the point well: "The past is never dead. It's not even past."[3] Students bring their pasts to the classroom, as well as their hopes for the future. We teachers need to understand both dimensions in order to teach them well in the present.

But where, and how, can we obtain the intelligence needed to turn each student from a cipher to an ally in the learning process? Just around the campus—the classroom, our offices, the local coffee shop or hangout—there is a rich lode of information to be mined. The student newspaper and various campus social functions also offer ample opportunity for teachers to get an informal sense of what's going on as well as specific information—who made the dean's list, who was awarded a prize. Coming to class quite early during the first weeks of a semester can prove rewarding. Students who arrive at about the same time as you do—early birds—usually have a song to sing: a personal concern or request for help or understanding. These pleas may not be verbalized at the first meeting, but they are generally communicated soon after that. I have found them inevitably of major significance to working with the individual, and sometimes to working with the whole group. But the discussion class itself is the richest source of all, for it allows us to take continual readings of our students' academic accomplishments, their skill in helping to guide the discussion, and their involvement in specific topics.

The office is but a more intimate classroom, the most appropriate setting for individualized instruction. When students initiate appointments, we can usually assume that the topic they raise is important to them. Often the items on their agendas are problems of some sort, and chats about their difficulties with course materials can move on to requests for the instructor's thoughts on career planning or more personal matters. In this regard, we teachers need to be wary of moving too far into areas that are not merely personal, but private. There's an enormous difference between knowing that Hans is an avid stamp collector and knowing the details of his current romantic life. We are guides, not professional counselors. Nonetheless, when professionally handled, personal conversations can provide rich opportunities for insight and, in turn, feed the educational process.

A colleague observed that a group of students is like a pack of cards face-down. To read those cards most accurately, to gain maximum useful personal data, we need to formalize our informational search a bit. I have found it useful to ask students, on a voluntary basis, for personal statements that provide information in three areas. Initially, I inquire about the student's view of the Course, asking questions such as: "What is your preparation for this course? How do you see it relating to past and upcoming studies? Which of the topics in the syllabus hold the most—or least—interest for you? In what areas do you feel most confident, and where might you appreciate special assistance? By what measures and in what ways will you evaluate the worth of this course? How might I make the ritual of academic grading personally useful for you?

Second, I seek to learn about participants' backgrounds. I ask the students to describe, in whatever detail they consider appropriate, two or three particularly meaningful incidents from their academic or professional experience and to explain why they chose these episodes. I ask: What did you learn? What questions do these experiences pose for you now? The "critical incidents" sections of student information statements have proven extremely useful. Almost inevitably they provide a clue to understanding the "real" person, as well as leads to help link his or her experience to classroom dialogue.

Third, I inquire about the future. What are your academic plans for the remainder of the degree program? What are your plans for a job search? What are your career and life goals at this point? Students' answers to such questions often illuminate their motivations.

Experimenting with personal information statements is not complicated. A few administrative suggestions, however, may be in order. I explain the purpose of the statements in class by proposing that students help me so that I may help them. I stress that their cooperation is completely voluntary and that all the information they provide will be held in confidence. I encourage them to modify my questions in any way that seems appropriate to them—and many do this with great creativity. I conclude by asking if there are any physical challenges-sight or hearing problems, for example—with which I might help them cope in this course. I keep the number of questions to a minimum and give no due date for completed statements. Nor do I pressure students who choose not to provide information.

Forging a primary alliance with students means investing intellect, time, energy, and emotion in discovering who they are, where they are, and how they may best find their way to the material. Such efforts help the instructor become a true teacher.

Like the bedrock of partnership and community, alliance with students is both a lofty goal and a matter of everyday practice. All of these converge in the fourth, most practical-minded premise: that discussion teachers must develop skill in managing both the content and the process of the discussion.

Dual Instructional Competency

Discussion teachers must not only (like lecturers) have mastered the content of their courses, but must be equally adept in process. The *what* of teaching (concepts and facts) is no more crucial than the *who* (knowledge of students) and *how.* By mastering the how of teaching the instructor unites the other two aspects and influences the moment-to-moment flow of events. These distinctions, of course, are integral parts of an organic gestalt; they run together and overlap like freshly applied watercolors.

Taken as a whole, mastery of process and content grant what I call dual competency, the central element in effective discussion leadership. But how does one begin to develop this complex mastery? Concentrating on the most fundamental level, I shall offer suggestions about teaching preparation as grounding for the advice presented in much of the rest of this volume. What better foundation for dual competency than dual preparation? The instructor who takes time to think not only about the material, but also about how to "play it" with a particular group students, will enjoy a double advantage of confidence and competence.

Preparation can never completely eliminate anxiety. After all, one is attempting to foresee the unforeseeable. Discussions are group improvisations; how can one possibly know in advance what students will want to say? Although I have no simple answers, I can offer the following well-tested method based on my own experience with case discussions in Business Policy courses. My preparation begins on familiar turf, with a careful review of content, but it also includes assessment of students' and the group's capacity to work in concert, and speculation about teaching tactics to promote effective collaboration. Taken as a whole, this exercise can give an instructor a running start toward dual instructional competency.

First, I evaluate the academic progress of the class as a whole. How well does this group understand basic course concepts and their applications to practice? Where has this class developed mastery; where is it still struggling? What specific topics have been covered? Which remain, and where and how might these materials best be introduced? I make certain that I am in command of the case to be discussed, and I assess it as a learning instrument. What are its strengths, its limitations? Does it include material with the potential to offend? Where is it likely to excite and intrigue? And I try to predict what the students' attitude toward it might be and how well they are likely to prepare it.

Second, I assess the class as a learning group. How does the participants' skill at working together measure up against the challenge of the case? What is their mood—are they having fun or are they glum? What is happening in the wider academic scene that might affect tomorrow's discussions?

Third, I try to estimate each student's current circumstances, his or her academic strengths and weaknesses as well as abilities to contribute to the discussion process. Who might learn most from the upcoming discussion? Will the case be of special interest to students with particular backgrounds or career interests? Will it offer quiet students a useful entry point into the class discussion? Who might find the case intimidating? Which students might be good "coaches" for their peers with difficulties? Which students are likely to take leadership roles in the anticipated dialogues, and who will probably remain on the sidelines?

Fourth, I consider my own mood. How do I feel about this material? Is this a fun section of the course or an academic chore? Are there some sour apples in the group? Where might my personal biases and prejudices affect my leadership of the discussion? All these considerations— as well as family and personal concerns—influence a teacher's behavior in the classroom.

Fifth, I think about the mode, pace, and flow of the upcoming class. Is it to be a drill in applying analytic techniques to the problem defined in the case of the day, or an open-ended search for stimulating and creative solutions to a broader range of problems? What is an appropriate pact—do I want the dialogue to move briskly, cover a large number of topics, and include the maximum possible number of student contributions? Or do I want to probe a limited number of issues in depth-with fewer students speaking at greater length? In terms of flow, do I want the group to build a single construct of the issues involved, by accretion, or would I hope for a more competitive series of arguments and rebuttals presented by individual students in defense of their positions?

Sixth, I work out a rough-cut process plan for the upcoming discussion. What leadership choices might help the group deal most effectively with this material? How should class time be divided between discussions of analysis and action? How should the chalkboard be used—what would I hope to see there at the beginning and end of the class? How active a role do I want to play—should I intervene often or only when changes in direction seem necessary?

Seventh, and last, I think about possible openings and endings for the class. Should I begin with a comment on the previous session and announce my expectations for this one? Should I open with a narrowly focused question, or a broad one? Whom should I invite to speak? What might the student's response be, and how might the whole group, in turn, react? I give similar attention to the end of the discussion. Should I, for example, offer a prepared general wrap-up, let one evolve extemporaneously, or end the discussion without a summary? What mindbenders might I give the students when they leave class? What suggestions, if any, for the next class meeting?

Systematically previewing both content and the major process dimensions—the group dynamic, student and ambitions, instructor's interests and biases, and the interplay among material, discussion mode, and larger course concepts—can help an instructor anticipate, at least in a general sense, the paths a class might want to explore. At the minimum, such planning can prevent a few errors (and terrors) and build the confidence and clear-headedness necessary to seeing and seizing teaching opportunities when they arise. Most teachers who work through this, or a similar, protocol several times feel that it sensitizes them to the complexities of discussion teaching. At its best, this preparation can help us harness the learning power generated by the fusion of process and content.

Conclusion

The territory of discussion teaching has never been well mapped. This chapter's four basic premises and accompanying suggestions for practice are but one instructor's sketch. I still find it richly rewarding to explore this world of wonders, and I hope that teachers who practice other modes of instruction might undertake similar explorations. All of us share a splendid vocation with limitless potential. My observations about one type of pedagogy should, therefore, be placed within the context of a promise that I consider even more basic: there is magnificence in all teaching. In any form—tutorial, laboratories, and lectures—our efforts bring bountiful rewards. We enjoy the privilege of life-long learning, a constant link to youth, growth, search, and the world of ideas, and the knowledge that our work has fundamental worth to others. The potential of our daily routines to create impressive results—some of the moment, the most intriguing of the future, makes our work a service of ever-unfolding fulfillment. We are part of something great.

Notes

1. Hugh Prather, *Notes to Myself* (Moab, UT: Real People Press, 1970), unpaged.

2. Marcel Proust, *Remembrance of Things Past,* tr. C. K. Scott Moncrieff (New York: Random House, 1935), I, 15.

3. William Faulkner, *Requiem for a Nun* (New York: Random House, 1951), p. 92. Gavin Stevens is speaking to Temple Drake.

Making Coherence Concrete

Taco Bell, Inc. (1983–1994): Using the Case with Education Administrators

Overview

This teaching plan was developed as a guide for using the Taco Bell case with leaders and managers of public school districts to explore the value of strategy and organizational coherence when building a high performing organization.

The case chronicles a decade of transformation and growth at Taco Bell achieved by strategic and organizational design changes led by CEO John Martin. After creating an explicit strategy, Martin deliberately aligned all business operations to the strategy in an effort to meet product quality and financial targets. Following the first phase of changes under Martin's leadership, his administration refined the strategy and took more steps towards organizational coherence by building a results-oriented culture in which employees understood Taco Bell's core strategy and felt empowered to experiment to produce better results.

With this teaching plan, case participants will discuss the merits and challenges of achieving organizational coherence in support of a strategy to improve performance.

Case Summary[1]

The Taco Bell, Inc. case details the actions of John Martin, newly named CEO, as he leads the company through a decade of incremental and radical changes. By the end of the case, total system sales within Taco Bell, a Mexican-style fast-food restaurant chain and a division of Pepsico, had grown from $700 million in 1983 to $3.9 billion in 1994, and the company managed over 10,000 eat-in restaurants and a wide variety of other retail sites around the world. In addition, a new line of Taco Bell products were being sold in supermarkets, convenience stores and other retail outlets. But despite the firm's success, the Taco Bell case is much more than just the story of its leader's actions. It is really a story about the thousands of employees within Taco Bell who make decisions and take actions in a very different way. It is the actions of these employees that create true change.

Positioning

This case may be used with a variety of audiences to illustrate issues of strategy, coherence, and organizational change. Because it is a broad case that opens up a number of issues, it is ideal for introducing a module on strategy and coherence. This teaching note is designed specifically to give K–12 education administrators an opportunity to discuss how to achieve high performance by creating the conditions for success throughout the organization.

Learning Objectives

- **Clear strategy linked to results.** An organization's strategy should be clear about what business it's in, be focused on solving current performance challenges, and describe how employees will produce results.

- **Organizational coherence.** The design of the organization (its structures, systems, resources, stakeholder relationships and culture) must create the conditions in which people can execute the strategy successfully. In other words, the organization should support rather than constrain high performance.

- **Culture change.** Structure/systems/resources change the way people must behave → this can lead to belief changes (culture). Asking people to change beliefs without changing the conditions around them will likely not be effective. Sustainability of results comes when people throughout the organization are thinking and acting in different ways than they were before.

- **Role of headquarters.** In a highly decentralized management structure, the role of headquarters remains important, but must change from compliance and control to capacity-building and support. A main function of headquarters is to create conditions under which all, not just some, units can produce expected results.

Discussion Questions

1. Identify and evaluate the managerial changes instituted at Taco Bell during each of the following periods:

1983–1989: The "Mexican fast food" strategy
1989–1991: The "feeding people" strategy
1991–1994: The "convenience food" strategy
Why was it necessary for the strategy to evolve three times in ten years? In each period, analyze the degree to which the systems, structures, capacity, and culture of Taco Bell were coherent with its strategy. Do the choices that CEO John Martin made during each period of change make sense to you? Why or why not?

2. Is Taco Bell positioned to reach its new goals at the end of the case? What advice would you have given John Martin in 1994?

3. Which of the general ideas about strategy and organizational coherence in the Taco Bell case relate to improvement efforts in public school districts? Which ideas do not relate? Why?

Teaching Plan and Analysis

This 75-minute teaching plan is based on an executive education course designed for PELP participants. The teaching plan can be modified to suit an 80-minute or 90-minute session.

Summary

I. **Introduction.** (5 minutes)

II. **Taco Bell in 1983.** In this segment, participants will discuss the state of Taco Bell when Martin arrives as CEO. The instructor may begin by saying, "What does a day in the life of a local Taco Bell look like in 1983? If you visited a store at random with John Martin, what would you see?" The instructor should push participants to link each observation with implications for performance. (10 minutes)

III. **First wave of changes between 1983–1989.** This segment is aimed at evaluating the initial changes Martin made during his tenure. The instructor may begin the discussion by saying, "What changes did Martin make from 1983 to 1989? Why were they important? What purpose did each serve? What's your overall evaluation of the effort?" While the participants evaluate the changes, the instructor should also point to the results and the pace of change. (20 minutes)

IV. **Next phase—Why a need for change?** During this portion of the discussion, participants will discuss why Taco Bell needed to change again following the first wave of changes and they will evaluate the additional changes made by Martin. The instructor may start the discussion by saying, "Why was there a need for change in 1989?" After participants reveal the lack of coherence between the organizational design and the strategy, the instructor may shift the discussion to an evaluation of the changes made to achieve coherence. (20 minutes)

V. **Links to public education.** This segment allows participants to draw parallels between challenges faced by Taco Bell and school districts. To transition to this discussion, the instructor may say, "How do the challenges faced by Martin compare to those facing public school leaders? How might some of Martin's actions be applied to public school systems?" The instructor should push the participants to think about how they can learn from the actions Martin took when faced with similar challenges. (10 minutes)

VI. **Wrap-up big ideas.** In closing, the instructor may review the big ideas outlined in the "Learning Objectives" section, drawing on specific student comments from the discussion. (10 minutes)

Introduction (5 minutes)

The instructor may begin the session by saying, "Taco Bell allows us to examine a key lever available to leaders, the design of the organization. We're going to discuss the first two phases

of change in Taco Bell and assess the coherence between the strategy and the organization. I've written each phase on the board to help us keep the time frames and the relevant strategy straight."

The instructor can post the following chart in advance of class as a device to keep the discussion grounded in specific phases of change in the ten year horizon of the case. Because the time-frame in the case is so long, participants often blur the evidence in the case across the various phases of the change process—the instructor should be diligent about keeping the class focused when discussing each phase, since Martin's organizational design choices are specific to the strategy in each phase. The chart is a concrete way to push students to offer evidence for their arguments that fall within the relevant time span.

Phase of change	Revenue	Units	Strategy
1983–89	700 million	1500	Mexican Fast Food
1989–91	1.66 billion	3000	Feeding People
1991–94	4.6 billion	10,000	Convenience food

Taco Bell in 1983 (10 minutes)

In this segment, participants will explore the state of Taco Bell when Martin started in 1983. The instructor may begin by asking the following questions: "What does a day in the life of a local Taco Bell look like in 1983? If you visited a store at random with John Martin, what would you see?

As participants share their observations, the instructor should push them to link each observation to specific implications for performance. In the past, participant responses included the following observations (not an exhaustive list):

• All food prepared onsite in an assembly line and food quality varied depending on who was cooking on any given shift.

- The restaurant lacked the appropriate technology to facilitate recording orders or purchasing raw materials which resulted in customer fulfillment errors and shortages of key ingredients. Customers also stood in long lines during peak hours because of the restaurant's inability to track customer demand.

- Headquarters "policed" restaurant managers through district manager roles thereby fostering a culture of compliance with little focus on coaching or developing restaurant managers.

- Customer experience and performance highly depended upon the skill level of restaurant managers and workers since the complex food ordering and preparation system was done onsite. High turnover of employees coupled with low employee salaries made it even more difficult for restaurants to maintain the skills needed to provide a consistent level of service during any given shift.

- No drive-thru windows made it difficult for Taco Bells to compete with other similar fast food chains when customers wanted the option of ordering from a car.

Overall, key performance challenges that should surface from the discussion include (1) variable quality at scale, (2) a culture of compliance, and (3) inconsistency across units.

First wave of changes between 1983–1989 (20 minutes)

In this section, participants will have the opportunity to analyze and evaluate the early changes made to the organization by Martin. The instructor may transition to this segment by saying, "What were the most important changes Martin made from 1983 to 1989? What purpose did each serve? What's your overall evaluation of the efforts?"

Participants usually highlight incremental changes such as the physical modernization of the restaurants, technological updates, menu expansion, restaurant expansion and improvements in employee training. Implemented over a six-year period, these changes significantly improved the organization's operations and allowed Taco Bell to adopt some successful characteristics of other fast food competitors. The pace of change was slow and steady and enabled Taco Bell to expand by 1200 units.

After participants discuss the changes made, the instructor may shift the discussion to an evaluation of the organization's efforts. Participants may point to financial successes, such as the doubling of sales and the 76% increase in earnings. However, it is also important to note that following competitors actions, like introducing new menu items to attract new customers, sometimes negatively affected costs, efficiency and customer service, suggesting that the organization needed better direction.

Next phase—Why a need for change? (20 minutes)

In this segment, participants will evaluate the changes made between 1989 and 1991. To transition into this portion, the instructor may begin by saying, "Why was there a need for change in 1989?"

While implementing the first wave of changes, Martin realized that the business needed more focus and subsequently developed a strategy focused on customer value based on fast food customer research. In contrast to the first phase of changes, Martin believed that in order to "feed people," preserve food quality and lower pricing, the organization would have to radically transform quickly to compete as a major player. At this point, the role of headquarters began to shift from a role that enforced corporate policies and procedures to a role that set the strategic direction of all Taco Bell restaurants. Prior to this point in the case, there appears to be a lack of clarity around the overall corporate strategy about how Taco Bell restaurants should produce results.

Participants should point out that the organizational design at the time did not support

Martin's new strategy of "feeding people" high quality food at low prices. Creating a shared understanding of fact as the definition of quality was a critical step. It is important for participants to understand that the overall goal was to manage all Taco Bells at scale so that coherence between the organization's strategy and organizational design was evident at each Taco Bell restaurant. Management should be able to walk into a Taco Bell anywhere in the country and see the strategy in action.

Next, the instructor may shift the discussion to evaluating the changes made during this phase by saying, "Let's evaluate the changes made."

The instructor should use the PELP Coherence Framework elements to organize participant responses on the board:

Resources: In the first steps towards alignment of organizational design to the new strategy, headquarters implemented K-Minus to move the food preparation kitchen from local restaurants to headquarters. This shift in resources improved product quality consistency, reduced restaurant labor and real estate costs, and freed up more space in Taco Bell restaurants for customers to eat-in. Another key development in resources was the shift in emphasis from policing to professional development and coaching for restaurant general managers and district managers. Leadership understood that managers needed to acquire new knowledge and skills to execute the overall strategy and improve performance.

Structure: Martin's administration redefined roles for restaurant and district level managers. The new role for restaurant managers gave them more responsibility and accountability for store results. District managers' oversight increased from 6 restaurants to 20 restaurants and their role emphasis shifted from policing to coaching and development. Also, corporate headquarters took on the strategic function to enable local restaurants to achieve coherence with the overall strategy—this included developing and clearly articulating the overarching strategy, and shifting its own role from compliance to support.

Systems: The redesign of the food assembly process at the restaurant level through the SOS (Speed of Service) program increased peak hour transactions by 54% and reduced customer waiting times by 71%. TACO (Total Automation of Company Operations) provided managers with timely data designed to help manage performance results at a given restaurant. It also improved communication and efficiency across departments. To ensure that company standards were met at restaurants in the absence of district policing roles, leadership also implemented standard control mechanisms, such as the toll-free customer comment number, the mystery shopper program, and the surprise marketing surveys. In addition, the introduction of a competitive compensation system allowed Taco Bell to attract better skilled workers and provided financial incentives to improve restaurant performance.

Culture: After creating the conditions under which employees had to behave differently to achieve strategic goals, Martin shifted the strategic direction of the organization once again (from feeding people to convenience) and took further steps to build a culture of ownership focused on achieving results. He gave many more employees more responsibility and decision-making along with access to data and managerial information through TACO II and POAs (Points of Access). He also encouraged learning and innovation by building an intellectual network and a futuristic model restaurant.

As participants discuss the key changes made between 1989–1994, the instructor should make sure that participants map each change back to the appropriate strategy and its implications for performance. The instructor may also want to ask participants to compare this phase to the initial phase of changes. Participants may point out that the pace of the second wave was fast and directive in contrast to the slow pace of the first wave. They may also note that the results were much more dramatic in that Taco Bell tripled profits and tripled the number of convenience food units over three years.

Links to public education (10 minutes)

In this section, participants can describe the links between challenges faced by Martin and those faced by urban school leaders. The instructor may begin the discussion by saying, "How do the challenges faced by Martin compare to those facing public school leaders? How might some of Martin's actions be applied to public school systems?"

Some sample responses include:

• **Lack of a clear strategy.** Just as Taco Bell initially lacked a clear strategy that focused on producing results, many school districts have yet to define and/or execute a strategy to improve performance and produce student outcomes. Like Taco Bell, school districts could benefit from the development of a clear strategy and the redesign of the organization to support the execution of the strategy.

• **Lack of accountability.** Across many school districts, employees are not held accountable for student outcomes due to a variety of historical and contextual reasons. Just as Taco Bell pushed more authority and accountability down to those who were closest to the customer, school districts are finding ways to give principals and teachers more decision-making power tied to the accountability for student achievement.

• **Role of district as enforcer, not supporter.** Contributing to a culture of compliance, many school district central offices are set up to operate as enforcers of policies and procedures, often creating an antagonistic relationship with principals and teachers. If district administrators shift their conception of the role of the central office to one of support and capacity building for schools, perhaps they may be better able to ensure that all schools, not just some schools, are able to succeed.

• **Technologically behind in use of data to inform decision-making.** The out-of-date systems described when Martin first arrived at Taco Bell mirrors many of the data infrastructure systems of large urban public school districts today. It is critical that district administrators develop the technology infrastructure to support principals and teachers in the use of performance data to improve instruction.

• **Coherence difficult to achieve.** Like Taco Bell, school districts manage many different units which makes it difficult to fully align the whole organization to an overall strategy. School administrators may learn from Martin's deliberate actions to achieve coherence improve performance by linking the organization's systems, structure, resources, and culture to the organizational strategy.

Wrap-up big ideas (10 minutes)

Review the big ideas outlined in the "Learning Objectives" section, drawing on specific student comments from the discussion. It is also important for the instructor to acknowledge that while there are many transferable lessons from Taco Bell, there are also plenty of differences between a fast food company and public school districts. Strategy and organizational coherence were critical to the success of Taco Bell during the time span of the case, but at the end of the day, the restaurant chain merely sells tacos and burritos. The public value created by school districts is much more important. Nevertheless, school districts *are* organizations, and the principles of strategy and coherence are at least as important for education enterprises as they are for fast food restaurants. After all, the stakes for producing high-performance are much higher.

Notes

1. This case synopsis was taken from "Taco Bell, Inc. (1983–1994)" teaching note, HBS Case No. 399–096, Boston: Harvard Business School Publishing, 1999.

Bristol City Schools (BCS)

Overview

This case describes efforts to manage the Bristol City Schools (BCS) for high performance. It is one of a series of cases developed by the Public Education Leadership Project at Harvard University to describe for other school leaders, executives, and graduate students the challenges and realities of leading and sustaining large-scale improvement in a public school district.

The case follows BCS's progress in improving the quality of instruction through a professional development pilot program. Additionally, the case exposes issues within BCS's recruitment process and its performance evaluation system as an entry point for participants to consider the concept of organizational *coherence*. This refers to the dynamic process by which leaders manage all of the elements of the organization (e.g., culture, resources, systems, structures, and stakeholders) to support effective strategy execution. To introduce students to the concept of organizational coherence in a public education setting, the instructor should assign the "Note on the PELP Coherence Framework," PEL–010, as a prereading.

Case Summary

Jean Campbell has been superintendent of Bristol City Schools (BCS) since July 2001. Upon her arrival, Campbell was charged by the BCS Board of Education to focus on improving student achievement. Under her leadership, student test scores rose steadily, and the gap in achievement between white and minority students began to narrow. Campbell also established a comprehensive professional development program to improve the quality of instruction at BCS.

However, the 40-school rollout of the professional development program revealed several notable capacity challenges. While teachers are fully participating in the professional development program, area superintendents are not, as they are experiencing numerous time constraints. Overburdened by administrative duties, area superintendents have difficulty following their walk-through schedules and undergoing individualized training. In addition, teachers dislike walk-throughs, and many BCS staff members, including area superintendents, have resigned over the past year. BCS is also experiencing inefficiencies in its recruitment and performance-evaluation systems.

This note was prepared by Lecturer Stacey Childress and Research Associate Tiffany K. Cheng.

These issues have caused Campbell and her leadership team to question whether their vision of improving instructional quality is truly affecting daily practices and attitudes throughout the organization.

Positioning

This case could be used in a wide variety of settings and with different audiences, ranging from experienced school leaders to graduate students in business, management, or education courses. It was written to be used in the Public Education Leadership Project at Harvard University's executive education program for teams of school district leaders. This case intends to offer readers an opportunity to discuss the relationship between organizational coherence and effective strategy execution as follows.

Learning Objectives

This case is designed to demonstrate the challenges created by a lack of coherence between a strategy and an organization's design. The situation in which Campbell and her team find themselves offers an opportunity to explore these challenges in a realistic setting. The learning objectives for the case are as follows:

- **Develop participants' analysis skills.** Students will learn to identify and articulate an organization's strategy for improving performance, as well as the underlying theory guiding its development and execution.

- **Deepen understanding of PELP Coherence Framework.** Students will learn to apply the conceptual framework through a discussion of how a district's elements (its structures, systems, resources, stakeholders, and culture) can be brought into coherence with a district-wide improvement strategy.

- **Demonstrate how to build a coherent organization.** This case provides participants with an opportunity to understand the forces and factors that enable or impede coherence.

- **Practice action planning.** When developing a strategy to improve educational outcomes for students in a school district, leaders must determine what supports are necessary to enable operational success and how to implement those supports effectively across the entire organization.

Assignment

Before class, participants should read "Bristol City Schools (BCS)," PEL-001, and consider the questions below; the "Note on the PELP Coherence Framework," PEL-010, should also be assigned if it has not been read previously.

Discussion Questions

1. What is Campbell's strategy? Is there an underlying theory of action about how to improve student outcomes that is driving the strategy?

2. What is your diagnosis of the degree to which the systems and culture at BCS are coherent with the strategy?

3. What advice would you give Campbell?

Teaching Plan and Analysis

This 90-minute teaching plan is based on the collective experience of a number of instructors who have used this case with hundreds of school district leadership teams and graduate students.

Summary

I. **Introduction.** (5 minutes)

II. **Diagnosis.** "What is Campbell's strategy? Is there a theory of action driving this strategy?" (10 minutes)

III. **Diagnosis and evaluation.** "Why are people 'confused'? What are the major problems you see in the district? Why are they there?" (25 minutes)

IV. **Recommendations and action planning.** Discuss action steps that would help Campbell's strategy gain leverage in the district. "What would you do if you were in Campbell's shoes? How should Campbell address the persistent problems? Are there areas that Campbell should take up as priorities?" (25 minutes)

V. **Understanding the PELP Framework.** (20 minutes)

VI. **Conclusion.** (5 minutes)

Introduction (5 minutes)

The instructor can begin the class by outlining the purpose of the case in the context of the course or module. One sample opening follows:

Today, we are going to discuss the Bristol City Schools (BCS) case and attempt to uncover underlying organizational misalignments that are hindering the leadership team's efforts to improve teacher quality. In fact, Superintendent Jean Campbell expresses that she does not understand what the "confusion"[1] within the district is all about. She would say that her vision has been clearly articulated over the last few years. In other words, the superintendent is "confused" by the "confusion."

In a couple of minutes I'm going to ask two of you to write a letter to Campbell. Let me give the instructions to everyone. Then, I'll designate a couple of you as letter writers. Imagine that you are a colleague from a nearby district. Sometimes, it is helpful for someone from outside our organization to share their impressions with us. So, imagine yourself in that role. Write a letter to Jean and offer two or three reasons you see as an outsider why people might be confused. Avoid giving her recommendations about how to fix those things in the letter—focus specifically on what you think are the sources of confusion, and offer to talk further about how she might address them.

The instructor should call on two partici-

pants to each craft a "Dear Jean" letter. The letter writers can complete the assignments during the first 10 minutes of the class discussion about Campbell's strategy and theory of action. When the strategy and theory-of-action conversation has run its course, the instructor should call on the letter writers as a way to kick off the diagnosis of the organizational challenges facing Campbell.

Diagnosis (10 minutes)

Instructors can open up this discussion pasture by asking students to identify BCS's strategy and theory of action: "What is Campbell's strategy? Is there a theory of action driving this strategy? We should be able to see the strategy in action." In the past, participants have identified the theory of action and corresponding strategy as follows:

Theory: If we invest in teacher knowledge and skills, then instruction and student achievement will improve.

Strategy:

• Monthly professional development for teachers, principals, and area superintendents

• Walk-throughs with principals and area superintendents to assess implementation of curriculum and pedagogical strategies taught in PD sessions

• Professional development in summer content sessions

• New standardized curriculum

• Professional development for principals focused on coaching teachers and conducting walk-throughs

• Redesigning the area superintendent role to emphasize instructional improvement

Diagnosis and evaluation (25 minutes)

After the initial diagnosis, participants should connect the intended strategy to its actual outcomes. The instructor can ask two participants to share their letters to begin the diagnosis, capturing the big ideas from the letters as they are read aloud. After the letters are read, the instructor can ask others to join the diagnosis by asking, "What are other major problems you see at BCS? Why are they there?" This is an opportunity for students to identify and evaluate Campbell's actions.

Culture: Instructors should ask participants to describe the existing culture in BCS: "What adjectives or words would you use to characterize BCS's culture?" Participants may point out that BCS's culture does not seem deliberately shaped by the district's leadership. While the district continues to place professional development at the top of its priority list, major disagreements between two of Campbell's assistant superintendents over the conduct of teacher evaluation and supervision reveal deeper conflicts in the values, norms, and basic assumptions held by BCS leaders. There is evidence that the implementation of Campbell's professional development plan has heightened issues of trust throughout the entire organization. Moreover, departments within BCS's central office operate in isolation with few embedded practices of collaboration. These are just a few observations of BCS's culture, which is critically at odds and incoherent with Campbell's improvement strategy.

Systems: Another commonly identified issue is the ambiguous purpose of the walk-throughs. While the walk-throughs are not intended to be evaluative, there is one example of an observer's making what was interpreted as an evaluative comment to a teacher during a walk-through in the case. Naturally, teachers do not trust the district's assertions against walk-throughs as evaluations and view the process with disdain. Adding to the confusion about walk-throughs is an evaluation process that includes classroom visits, often conducted by the same people who are conducting the non-evaluative walk-throughs. The evaluation process is executed inconsistently, depending on the principal or other evaluators.

The district's recruitment process is another area of difficulty for BCS. Despite attempts to streamline the hiring process, there are considerable inefficiencies preventing the district from recruiting a cadre of talented teachers. Some individual schools scramble to fill vacancies in July, long after nearby districts and private schools have completed their recruitment of available candidates. Also, it is unclear if all principals know how to access the online application system that coordinates the intake of resumes.

At the central office, there is increasing tension between the instructional and human resource departments because of a lack of coordination in processes and procedures. The conflict has persisted in the face of additional changes that aim to improve student outcomes. Much of the communication between these leaders seems driven not by collective responsibility for achieving district goals. Rather, blame-shifting and defensive behaviors are reinforced as cultural norms.

Structure: Participants will likely point to the poorly designed area superintendent role. With all the additional responsibilities of instructional review and professional development facing area superintendents, it is not surprising that they are overwhelmed. Common sense dictates that they will first do the things they have to do (compliance issues), then the things they know how to do best (old ways of doing business), and lastly the new work (walk-throughs, new relationship with principals, etc.). This leads to variability in performance among the area superintendents and certain burnout.

Resources: Decreases in public funds have forced budget cuts in BCS. Campbell chose to retain the budgeted allocation for the professional development plan but decreased administrative and support expenditures. She also instituted hiring and wage freezes. These decisions have greatly affected BCS's capacity to execute the strategy of improving instruction through professional development with fidelity. Without key resources, Campbell's program to improve instruction has created several challenges. First, principals have not been trained in the new curricula. How can they assess curriculum implementation? Second, instead of focusing on important instructional leadership activities, monthly principal conferences have devolved into "griping sessions." It is clear that resource constraints have compromised the original intentions of the improvement strategy.

Recommendations and action planning
(25 minutes)

Having identified the various sources impeding organizational coherence, participants should be directed to work in small groups for 10 minutes. Instructors can help frame the development of action plans by asking students, "What would you do if you were in Campbell's shoes? We've identified many of the problems at BCS. How should Campbell address these? What should Campbell take up as her top three priorities, and what should she do?"

After the time in pairs, instructors should facilitate a sharing of action plans for the next 10 minutes. The instructor should push participants to describe concrete steps they would take if they were Campbell. Several key points that have surfaced in past sessions include the following:

- **Stress the role of culture.** Campbell must redesign the organization to produce desired behaviors. As it is, BCS is producing (albeit accidentally) exactly the kind of behavior it is designed to produce: confusion, distrust, isolation, skepticism, and burnout.

- **Emphasize systems over structures.** The district's focus on changing structures within central office has done little to address dys-

functional systems that are causing the majority of issues. In order for a school district to enact a strategy successfully, systems and resources should be the initial levers of change. Then, the entire organization can be brought into coherence once the strategy begins to produce desired outcomes.

- **Redistribute administrative responsibilities to lessen area superintendents' load.** Area superintendents must be released from noninstructional activities if they are expected to manage the walk-through systems more effectively and consistently. Since walk-throughs are the place to look for evidence of the professional development program, these processes should take priority.

Understanding the PELP Framework
(20 minutes)

In this section, instructors should introduce the PELP Framework and refer to the note that was assigned as required reading. Emphasis should be placed on the strategy, or set of actions, that exists to provide capacity and support to the instructional core. The organizational elements (culture, structure, systems, resources, and stakeholders) of a district must work together to enhance the work of teachers and students in classrooms in order to improve educational outcomes and achieve performance goals.

The instructional core consists of three interdependent components:

1. Teacher knowledge and skills
2. Students' engagement in learning
3. Rigorous academic content

Together, they represent the critical functions guiding teaching and learning in classrooms. Thus, a strategy must address all three components, but it is likely that one will be the point of entry for the work.

The instructor can use examples from the

case and the discussion to illuminate the components of the framework.

Conclusion (5 minutes)

At the close of the session, instructors should emphasize the ways in which leaders change a school district's existing culture. In order to create and reinforce a new culture and vision, leaders must manage the systems, structures, resource-allocation methods, and relationships with stakeholders by modeling the behaviors they wish to encourage. BCS must continue to refine its systems, as well as other organizational elements, in order to achieve its goal to improve educational outcomes for all students.

Notes

1. See "Bristol City Schools," PEL–001, p. 6.

Pursuing Educational Equity at San Francisco Unified School District

Overview

This case focuses on efforts to raise student achievement in the San Francisco Unified School District (SFUSD) during 2001–2004. It is one of a series of cases developed by the Public Education Leadership Project at Harvard University to illustrate for school leaders, district administrators, and graduate students the complexities of leading and sustaining large-scale organizational improvement in an urban public school district.

"Pursuing Educational Equity at San Francisco Unified School District," PEL-005, was written as a "fan" case, one that lays out many issues for participants and instructors to discuss. It provides readers with an opportunity to evaluate SFUSD's "Excellence for All" strategy and its implementation. "Excellence for All" aimed to close the performance gap between racial groups in the district, and the case explores a variety of systems and structures that the district redesigned to align with the strategy. The case focuses on a new resource allocation system as a concrete entry point into a discussion about the

district's efforts to mesh its strategy, culture, systems, structures, resources, and stakeholders.

A key concept in the case is achieving and sustaining organizational *coherence*. This refers to the dynamic process by which leaders manage all of the elements of the organization (e.g., culture, resources, systems, structures, and stakeholders) to support effective strategy execution. To introduce students to the concept of organizational coherence in a public education setting, the instructor should assign the "Note on the PELP Coherence Framework," PEL-010, as a pre-reading.

Case Summary

Set in 2004, the case begins with Superintendent Arlene Ackerman contemplating whether the implementation of a new resource allocation system is effectively aligned with SFUSD's overall strategy to achieve educational equity. Readers understand that the district serves a diverse student body; however, like many of their urban district counterparts, SFUSD's African-American and Latino student populations persis-

---

This note was prepared by Lecturer Stacey Childress and Research Associate Tiffany K. Cheng.

tently score in the bottom two quartiles on state tests. The case proceeds with a description of the history, governance, and political landscape of SFUSD.

After describing the origins and rationale of the "Excellence for All" strategy, the case follows SFUSD leadership's implementation efforts around these actions:

1. Give parents a choice about where their children attend school.

2. Create classrooms that reflect the diversity of the entire student population and in which teachers have high expectations for all learners.

3. Decentralize decisions about instructional programs and their corresponding resources in exchange for increased accountability and results.

In the next section, the case describes the effects of these actions on various components of the district's organization. The participant has an opportunity to incorporate the PELP coherence framework to understand the ways in which the various organizational elements support the district's overall improvement strategy.

The case then includes a specific description of the weighted student formula (WSF) method of resource allocation, its design and implementation, as well as its interdependence with other systems and structures, the organization's shifting culture of accountability, and its relationships with various stakeholder groups.

Finally, the case concludes with Ackerman contemplating the challenges of building organizational capacity for stronger execution of "Excellence for All" at the school level. She explicitly remarks that the WSF system is not a silver bullet for achieving educational equity—that in fact, a more complex solution underpinned by organizational coherence is needed for successful implementation at all levels.

Positioning

This case could be used in a wide variety of settings and with different audiences, ranging from experienced school leaders to graduate students in education, business, or management courses. As a fan case, it can be taught at the beginning or end of a course or module about achieving organizational coherence in an urban public school district.

Learning Objectives

By design, this case provides an in-depth view of SFUSD's progress in implementing a district reform strategy. The WSF story can be used as an entry point for teaching lessons about an institution's capacity to develop and sustain strategic coherence in a complex organization. Potential learning objectives include:

- **Developing an improvement strategy that is grounded in a theory of action borne out of a deep understanding of a performance problem.** Students are able to delve into the nature of the student performance challenge in San Francisco and hypothesize about its root causes. From this analysis, they can evaluate the degree to which the "Excellence for All" strategy is grounded in a theory of causality about how to address root causes, not just symptoms.

- **Strategic coherence.** This case provides an opportunity to apply the conceptual framework through a discussion of how a district's elements (its structures, systems, resources, stakeholders, and culture) can be brought into coherence with a district-wide improvement strategy.

- **Organizational change.** Students will be able to define what it means to have an organizational strategy that improves instructional outcomes and the extent to which the strategy influences and supports changes to educators' daily practices and expectations.

- **Opportunity for analytical skill building.** By focusing specifically on a set of integrated systems designed to support a strategy, students can practice diagnosing and analyzing the various needs and existing capacities within an organization to determine an effective course of action.

Assignment

In preparing "Pursuing Educational Equity at San Francisco Unified School District," PEL-005, students should consider the questions below; the "Note on the PELP Coherence Framework," PEL-010, should also be assigned if it has not been read previously.

Discussion Questions

1. How would you articulate SFUSD's strategy to improve student outcomes?

2. What activities must SFUSD be good at in order to execute this strategy across the district? At the central office? At schools?

3. What criteria seem to drive the reallocation of decision-making authority? What are the organizational implications of moving from a mostly centralized control to one where individual schools are allocated responsibilities for creating budgets? Please use Exhibit 6 in your analysis.

4. How are the weighted student formula and the academic planning process linked? How do they work? Be prepared to explain each in detail in class.

5. What are the biggest barriers to the effectiveness of the weighted student formula and site-based budgeting system? What advice would you give to Ackerman and her team for addressing these barriers?

Teaching Plan and Analysis

This 80-minute teaching plan is based on an executive education course designed for urban public school leadership teams. The teaching plan can be modified to suit a 75-minute or 90-minute session.

Summary

I. **Introduction.** (5 minutes)

II. **Diagnosis.** During this portion of the discussion, participants work to identify the persistent challenges in SFUSD. Instructors may begin by asking, "When Ackerman arrives in summer 2000, what's the nature of the performance problem she faces?" (5 minutes)

III. **Analysis of SFUSD's strategy.** "What strategy does SFUSD develop to respond to the problem? What's the theory that underpins this strategy? Does this approach make sense to you?" (15 minutes)

IV. **Analysis of SFUSD's coherence and ability to execute.** "What does the district need to be good at in order to implement the strategy well? Are they good at these things?" This discussion should include a concrete focus on the WSF system but actually be used to focus on the dynamism and interdependencies of all of the organizational elements at play in supporting the "Excellence for All" strategy. In addition to asking participants to explain the WSF system in practice, instructors should probe participants further by asking questions such as, "How does the academic planning process interact with the WSF? How do both fit the existing culture? How important is the principal evaluation system in relation to the WSF, planning process, and culture?" Instructors may also lead participants into a discussion about the coherence of structures and systems to the WSF. (40 minutes)

V. **Reflections.** This discussion focuses on the strategy's effectiveness. Instructors should probe participants by asking students to assess whether the implementation of "Excellence for All" is working to address the student performance challenges. If the data has not been raised, instructors can direct participants to Exhibit 2. (10 minutes)

VI. **Closing.** In the final minutes of class, instructors can emphasize the key concept of organizational coherence, along with the major concepts explored during the case discussion. (5 minutes)

Introduction (5 minutes)

The instructor can begin class by outlining the purpose of the case in the context of the course. One sample opening follows:

Managing a large, urban public school district for high performance is complex, intense, and difficult. Leaders must not only develop an effective strategy but must also evaluate the degree to which the organization's culture, systems, structures, resources, stakeholders, and environment support and strengthen the implementation of the strategy. Today, we are going to explore the ways in which the San Francisco Unified School District grappled with these issues. As we analyze each of the district's actions, consider whether they collectively support the articulated strategy. Let's get started.

Diagnosis (5 minutes)

The class begins with a diagnosis of the context and set of problems Superintendent Arlene Ackerman inherits as an incoming superintendent. As mentioned above, the instructor can open the conversation by asking, "When Ackerman arrives in the summer of 2000, what is the nature of the performance problem she faces?" Through discussion, participants should identify the following issues, which can be captured on the right side board (see board plan in Exhibit 2).

Overall, the purpose of this initial diagnosis is to uncover the salient performance gap between racial groups in San Francisco and set the stage for students to understand the connection between instructional programming and outcomes.

Student responses will likely include the following:

• **Educational equity/achievement gap.** African-American and Latino children perform much lower than their white and Chinese counterparts on performance measures in the district. In fact, the problem is getting worse. The performance gap widens in the higher grades. Schools do not address the educational needs of their different learner populations (e.g., students with disabilities, English-language learners, socioeconomic status, etc.). Moreover, a report from the consent decree advisory committee has shown that some schools use a "dumbed-down" curriculum for African-American and Latino students. A task force has interpreted some data as evidence of low expectations from educators about students from specific racial/cultural groups.

• **Decisions about instruction and resources reside with a central office that is out of touch with the diverse needs of schools.** The district historically operated in a compliance mode in relation to the consent decree and made little progress in meeting the requirements for student performance targets. District leadership had so far been focused on top-down mandates for school improvement and held the purse strings for all resources, allocating staff headcounts to schools instead of money.

• **Schools navigate the central bureaucracy based on their relationships with individuals at headquarters.** This generally means that school leaders who are already "in the know" are more likely to garner the sufficient resources and support for their schools, while those that are not tend to miss out on opportunities to strengthen their resource base. The district has evidence the former are in high-performing schools and the latter in struggling schools.

Analysis of SFUSD's strategy (15 minutes)

In this analysis, participants should identify key components and corresponding results of SFUSD's strategy plan. Instructors may open this discussion by asking, "What is the theory of action driving SFUSD's strategy?" This question will likely evoke the following responses:

- Adults closest to the students will make good decisions if they have the right tools and support systems. (This includes parents, teachers, and principals.)
- Allocating different funding amounts for different learners will lead to more equitable outcomes.

Once the theory of action is determined, the instructor will want to help participants determine whether SFUSD's strategy plan, "Excellence for All," reflects the theory. She may ask, "What strategy does SFUSD develop to respond to the problem? How well does the strategy seem informed by the theory? What is the supporting evidence for your analysis?" The instructor should note participant responses on the left side board and refer back to the initial diagnosis discussion points. In the past, students have discussed the following key elements:

- WSF makes the strategy real by linking funding allocations to a school's academic planning process in order to encourage more focused activities that ultimately improve student achievement.
- The district provides school choice to parents who can select school programs that best meet their child's learning needs. By engaging more parents in the schooling process, other stakeholders (e.g., teachers, principals, school site councils [SSCs]) will be better supported to create an instructional program that achieves equitable outcomes.

- The district empowers the actors closest to children (e.g., teachers, principals, parents) by moving decisions for determining instructional programs and corresponding funding amounts from the central office to individual schools. Simultaneously, the district holds principals and schools accountable for improving student performance results by instituting a principal evaluation system.
- Since school performance and academic programs are made transparent to the community through school-selection fairs, some schools will be chosen more often and others less. In theory, underselected schools will either improve through competition or become financially unsustainable because of low enrollment. This would then allow SFUSD to close underperforming, underselected schools.

Analysis of SFUSD's coherence and ability to execute (40 minutes)

After the discussion of SFUSD's district improvement plan, instructors should focus on the strategy implementation process. By using the PELP coherence framework, students may identify multiple components (e.g., structure, resources, systems, culture, stakeholders, and environment) that contribute to their assessment. Instructors should ask, "What does the district need to be good at in order to implement the strategy well? Are they good at these things?" Record responses under the appropriate framework category, recognizing that some actions could easily fit under more than one category and that almost all will impact multiple categories. Probe participants to consider whether they believe the action under discussion coheres with the district's overall improvement theory of action and strategy.

Some potential responses include the following (the sequence is not important):

Culture: Here, the instructor can ask students to analyze SFUSD's decision to transfer power over budget decisions from the central office to individual schools: "What are the cultural implications of moving from a mostly centralized control to one where individual schools are allocated responsibilities for creating budgets?" Instructors may wish to direct attention to Exhibit 6. Previous participants identified the following issues:

- **Accountability.** Shifting decision-making power from the central office to individual schools for instructional programs, staffing, and other budget-related issues is a clear delineation of expectation for performance improvement. Both assistant superintendents for instructional support and operations (ISOs) and principals are accountable for student performance and undergo evaluation processes to identify ways to improve strategy execution.

- **School as the locus of decision-making.** The empowerment of SSCs changes behavior at schools. The connection between the WSF system and academic planning makes student needs the focus of conversations about resources. Moreover, community members become actively involved in making decisions about school programming for their students.

Structure: It can be useful to focus on the change in the locus of decision-making power as a key to understanding the structural change to decentralization from centralization: "What criteria seemed to drive the allocation of decision rights?" The central office redefined its role in order to support schools and principals. It took on important functions with the implementation of new systems and processes (e.g., creating performance targets for individual schools, school placement, enrollment forecasts, holding principals accountable, etc.). There is a clear separation of roles—the central office and school now held different responsibilities for resource allocation/budget creation. This suggests that there is recognition of skill differentials between the central office and school leadership. At the school level, SSCs become critical members of

the decision-making body. They are empowered to better support school programming that improves student achievement.

Systems: Participants will likely identify several processes and procedures that SFUSD leadership built in order to support the management strategy. To support the goals of creating diverse classrooms and giving parents choice over which school their children would attend, SFUSD hired WestEd to build a new educational placement system to assign students to schools. The system used a diversity index, which used six nonrace factors in describing students (e.g., socioeconomic status, academic achievement status, mother's educational background, language-proficiency status, home language, and academic performance rank of the sending school). SFUSD also developed a data-planning model, which provided SSCs, teachers, and school principals with data specific to current performance levels and student performance gaps that existed at the school level and a process for adjusting instructional programs and practices to respond to the data. The WSF system in its entirety (i.e., base funding, foundation amount, weights, loss/gain limit, and allocation pools) distributed resources to individual schools based on a myriad of characteristics that focus on students. The principal evaluation process instilled a great deal of accountability—principals were required to create management/leadership plans to meet academic targets and the priorities as outlined by the school's academic plan. In addition, principals were evaluated on how well they managed the SSCs. Principals were also responsible for how closely they aligned resources to academic programs. In all, school performance data served as the central component of the evaluation process. While some participants are eager to discuss how these additional decision-making responsibilities empower principals, some may question whether valuable time is taken away from a principal's instructional leadership activities.

Resources: In this section, instructors may wish to ask participants, "What beliefs about student learning are necessary in order to promote the WSF system as a viable approach to resource allocation?" The ensuing discussion might touch on the validity of the weights themselves (e.g., in accordance with the consent decree, it does not use race as a factor and instead bases weights on social factors; does it cover the educational needs of students, is the loss/gain limit sustainable over time?). Sometimes, students will challenge the construction of the formula itself. Instructors can pursue this further by asking, "What could make it stronger?"

In addition to the WSF, the district rethought a number of other resources to support the strategy. Assistant superintendents for ISOs were responsible for providing ongoing professional development to principals but also gave technical advice to assist principals with the WSF implementation. Also, principals and SSCs received training from the central office on the WSF system, budgeting process, and software. Under the STAR Schools program, low-performing schools received additional resources from the central office in the form of additional school personnel, instructional resources, and district support. One outstanding question regarding their ability to implement with excellence is the degree to which the district has invested (or not) in helping principals better understand how to use their newly granted autonomy to make sound instructional and resource decisions.

Stakeholders: Another stakeholder group to consider is the role of the teacher's union. The case mentions that the teacher's union has shifted from a "collaborative" to "cooperative" stance toward district leadership. Moreover, there is a question as to whether the teacher-salary formula for staffing ratios actually translates into a systemic placement of less experienced teachers in lower-performing schools. Finally, SFUSD institutes SSCs as an indication that parents and community members are crucial partners to improving school outcomes. However, participants may recall that in practice, "heavily weighted" parents rarely serve on SSCs, disabusing the notion that choice and the WSF system alone will increase these forms of traditional parental engagement. Those who do serve seem to exhibit a skills and knowledge gap with respect to conversing with educators about effective instructional strategies.

Environment: Like other urban cities, San Francisco has continued to experience a tremendous decrease in student enrollment numbers, impacting the funding levels. While expenses have increased steadily, revenues have not kept pace. The consent decree is also a strong environmental force that requires concerted action on the part of the district in meeting student performance goals. Whereas previous attempts to implement district improvement strategies ignored or viewed the consent decree as a barrier, Ackerman explicitly uses the consent decree as a lever to strengthen the "Excellence for All" strategy. The school district's board of education also reflects the changing political environment in SFUSD. It is noted in the case that from 2000 to 2004, "the 'board' shifted from nearly unanimous support for Ackerman's proposals, to a 4–3 split in favor of most of the resolutions proposed by the superintendent and district staff."

Some thoughts on "Has the district created a market in which its schools compete with one another for students and therefore money?": Occasionally, students will observe that Ackerman was actually trying to create effects that mimic a market by instituting parental choice, the WSF, and principal autonomy simultaneously. This is especially likely if the case is being used in a graduate school setting with MBA students.

Should this issue arise, instructors may find it helpful to offer (or elicit from students) a formal definition of a "market." (A market economy is an economy that allocates resources through the decentralized decisions of many firms and households as they interact in markets for goods and services.)

In SFUSD, there are elements of choice, information, transparency, and value exchange. If parents can choose to place students in any school, if transparent performance information is readily available to parents about all schools, if the money follows the student, and if there are serious consequences if enough "customers" do not choose a particular school, making it financially unviable, then it is very much like a market. In the past, some students have suggested that the leadership team's goal of creating a market served to keep administrators honest about accountability. That is, lower-performing schools become economically unviable because of low enrollment numbers, giving the district an easy way to close underperforming schools. It can be useful to push students who tend to think of this new organizational construct as a market to evaluate the dynamics that might inhibit it from truly working as a market. For instance, will community sentiment allow the district to close schools that suffer under these rules? Is it likely that some schools might improve their performance but still lose enrollment for factors outside their control (neighborhood safety, etc.)? Is student performance likely to be the overriding variable for all parents when they choose their child's school? What would be the consequences in the "market" if parents chose a convenient location or a safe environment as being more important than or equally as important as student achievement?

Reflections (10 minutes)

If a discussion around the data has not explicitly come up, instructors may direct students to look at Exhibit 2 and ask, "Is the strategy working to address the racial inequities in student performance?" Participants should focus on the percent changes by ethnic groups and decide whether the data reveals an effective strategy. What recommendations might you make to accelerate the progress?

Closing (5 minutes)

Instructors can close by emphasizing that the components of the "Excellence for All" strategy served as just one way to raise academic performance expectations for all students and simultaneously achieve educational equity. While the strategy seemed to be producing positive gains, the organizational coherence that the leadership attempted to create in support of the strategy was just as important as the content of the strategy.

Finding and Supporting Personnel

Southwest Airlines: Using Human Resources for Competitive Advantage (A)—Using the Case with Education Administrators

Overview

This case describes human capital management at Southwest Airlines and its role in creating a high-performing organization. The case is particularly helpful for participants from the public sector or a highly regulated private sector industry, which often faces significant labor constraints. This teaching note was developed to aid instructors in teaching the case to leaders and managers in public education. It reflects the collective experience of several instructors who have used the case with central office- and school-level leaders, charter management organization executives, and graduate students.

"Southwest Airlines: Using Human Resources for Competitive Advantage (A)," HR-1A, depicts the power of aligning strategy and organizational elements (e.g., structures, systems, culture, resources, and stakeholders) in order to drive high performance. Participants will have an opportunity to analyze the company's strategy and diagnose the key success factors, particularly the company's human resources

practices and culture. The PELP Coherence Framework will be introduced to help students with the organizational diagnosis and to explore the organizational interdependencies required to drive effective strategy execution.[1] Specific norms, values, and tactics will be explored. Students should leave this class with a deeper understanding of how to manage human resources and culture as levers for executing strategy and producing results.

Case Summary

The case is set in 1994 with Southwest Airlines leading the airline industry on several performance metrics, including profit, aircraft utilization, market share, and customer and employee satisfaction. Southwest's competitive advantage stems from its clear strategy—providing low-cost fares and offering point-to-point service to underserved markets—and, the company believes, its people. However, the company faces looming threats: United and Continental have each just announced plans to also launch low-

---

This note was prepared by Lecturer Stacey Childress and Research Associate Caroline King.

cost, point-to-point travel to directly compete with Southwest. Case protagonist Ann Rhoades, vice president of Southwest's People Department, wrestles with two concerns: (1) ensuring that Southwest is effectively supporting and leveraging its people and (2) maintaining people as an advantage against competitors.

First, the case provides an overview of Southwest's history, strategy, and its sources of competitive advantage. The company's strategy is to offer low-cost fares and point-to-point service to underserved markets near metropolitan areas. In this sense, Southwest originally envisioned cars and other forms of surface transportation as its main competitors rather than other airlines. The company's competitive advantage stems from its strategy, people, operations, and culture and the coherent integration of these elements. Sources of competitive advantage include: cost structure, employee productivity, aircraft utilization, customer service, leadership, and a culture of fun and celebrations. Southwest particularly emphasizes the importance of its people. Preserving the Southwest culture despite tremendous growth is so important to the company that it created a 65-person culture committee from all regions and levels in order to "preserve and enhance the Southwest spirit."

The case then describes the "People Department," as the human resources function was renamed five years prior out of concern that the old human resources group acted more like a "police department." Rhoades heads up the division of approximately 100 people, which in turn serves 18,000 employees, known as the department's "customers." Rhoades requires all People Department employees to have had line experience, and the department's mission statement reflects its core functions: recruiting, training, serving the workforce, and preserving the Southwest spirit.

These functions are each described in more detail. The company invests a lot of time and resources in recruiting to ensure that it hires people who embody the Southwest culture and val-

ues; customers and current employees participate in the hiring process. Training emphasizes customer service and the mission and values of the company; the format is often team-based and experiential. Southwest's workforce is 89% unionized, but the company has avoided the acrimonious labor disputes and walkouts experienced by competitors. Contributing factors include: few work rules in labor contracts, profit-sharing for all employees after one year of service, and compensation equity. The workforce is relatively young—the average age is 34—and at 4-½%, turnover is half the industry standard. The People Department intentionally guards and promotes the Southwest spirit through a number of policies and activities, such as frequent celebrations, thanking each other, a catastrophe fund to support in-need employees, building trust by sharing information, and fostering mutual respect between managers and line workers.

Finally, the case outlines competitive threats facing Southwest, namely announcements by United and Continental to launch short-haul, low-fare flights as a separate business line. These two new "airlines-within-an-airlines"—United's Shuttle and Continental Lite—would bring direct competition to Southwest markets.

The case closes with Rhoades wondering how to sustain Southwest's competitive advantage by effectively managing and supporting its people.

Positioning

This case can be used in a wide variety of settings and with different audiences, ranging from experienced school leaders to graduate students in education, business, or management courses. The case outlines strategy, organizational coherence, human resources, and culture issues.

Learning Objectives

Potential learning objectives include:

- **Understanding and application of organizational coherence.** This case provides an opportunity to apply the PELP Coherence Framework in the analysis of Southwest. A clear strategy and a coherent organizational design (structures, systems, culture, resources, and stakeholders) that support the implementation of that strategy are key success factors for Southwest.

- **Illustrate human resources and culture as managerial levers for driving high performance.** This case illustrates the degree to which employees and the norms, values, and behaviors that comprise their working environment contribute to organizational performance. Students will explore the ways in which Southwest actively manages its human resources system and culture.

- **Inspiration via example.** The public education sector is fraught with frustration around labor issues. Many district and school leaders feel helpless in their ability to change often adversarial union relationships and inflexible labor contracts, often touted as key barriers to improving student performance. Operating in a highly regulated industry, Southwest provides a compelling counterexample by demonstrating that effective management of human resources and culture is a leadership and management function, and that it is possible to effectively manage even in an industry in which the other prominent players are plagued by labor-management difficulties.

Assignment

In preparing "Southwest Airlines: Using Human Resources for Competitive Advantage (A)," HR-1A, students should read the case and consider the questions below. The PELP Coherence Framework should also be assigned if it has not been read previously.

Discussion Questions

1. What is Southwest's strategy? How would it answer the question, "What business are we in?" Why has it been successful for so long? Can its success be replicated by a competitor?
2. Why or why not?
3. Analyze Southwest's human capital management system. How does this system link to the execution of its strategy?
4. How would you describe the culture of the organization?
5. What could cause Southwest to fail?

Teaching Plan and Analysis

Summary

I. **Introduction.** (5 minutes)

II. **Strategy.** Participants will be asked to articulate Southwest's strategy. This opening conversation lays the groundwork for teasing out how Southwest's strategy, operations—particularly the human resources function—and culture reinforce one another to help drive high performance. Instructors can open by asking," What is Southwest's strategy? How does it do business?" (15 minutes)

III. **Organizational diagnosis.** This second discussion topic is aimed at developing participants' organizational diagnosis skills. The PELP Coherence Framework can be introduced or resurfaced to help participants identify and describe the key organizational elements: culture, systems, resources, stakeholders, and structures. Instructors can begin by asking, "What makes Southwest so successful?" (30 minutes)

IV. **Strategic human resource management and culture.** The third portion of the discussion focuses specifically on the company's human resources practices and culture, which will have been identified as key success factors in the previous discussion. The purpose of this conversation is to enable participants to see the deliberate coherence among the organizational elements that support effective strategy execution at Southwest, as well as to see human resources and culture as functions that have to be actively managed. Instructors should probe participants by asking, "Could one of Southwest's competitors copy what it is doing?" (25 minutes)

V. **Reflections for public education and the importance of coherence.** In closing instructors can ask participants, "What lessons can public educators learn from Southwest?" The purpose of this discussion is to help participants draw parallels between Southwest and school systems and reflect on the possibilities for more actively managing human resources and culture, two functions which, in public education, tend to either be overlooked or the status quo accepted. The instructor can wrap up this discussion by emphasizing how effective strategy execution—in any sector—depends upon building a coherent and integrated organization. (15 minutes)

Introduction (5 minutes)

The instructor can open the discussion by asking participants to hold off on drawing parallels between Southwest and public school systems until the end of the class. This ensures that participants "stay in the case" for as long as possible, which enables them to more fully explore Southwest's strategy and operating practices.

Instructors can begin drawing participants into the Southwest discussion by asking, "Has anyone here flown Southwest? What was your experience? Would you fly Southwest again?" Given the airline's history and coverage, it is very likely a few people will have flown Southwest and can comment on their experiences. Participants are likely to note the low-cost fare, no frills but fun service, employees' friendliness, and on-time departures and arrivals. These descriptors help position the ensuing discussions about strategy and the company's practices and culture.

Strategy (15 minutes)

This discussion pasture focuses on articulating Southwest's strategy. Instructors can begin by asking," What is Southwest's strategy? How does it do business?" Participants are likely to mention the following:

- Cost structure: low-cost fares; savings on maintenance by using one type of plane.

- Point-to-point service (no hubs) to underserved markets.

- No frills (e.g., first class, meals, frequent flyer lounges).

- Clear target market.

- High-employee productivity driven by using one type of plane; high investment in recruitment and training; culture of teamwork; no assigned seating.

- Less congested airports improve turnaround time and aircraft utilization.

- Excellent customer service.

- Simplicity: simple fare structure and frequent flyer program based on number of trips flown, not miles.

To help participants understand that strategy drives what *not* to do as much as what to do, participants may ask, "What won't Southwest do?" Potential responses include introducing longer flight routes or first-class service, flying to major airports, and raising fares.

Organizational diagnosis (30 minutes)

This part of the discussion is aimed at developing participants' organizational diagnosis skills. Instructors can capture on a chalkboard, white board, or chart paper the substance of the discussion using the PELP Coherence Framework elements: strategy, culture, systems, resources, stakeholders, and structures.

Instructors can begin by asking, "Currently Southwest boasts over 30 consecutive years of profit, a record unrivaled in the U.S. airline industry. What makes Southwest so successful?" Likely responses are noted by framework categories below.

Strategy: Adjectives for Southwest's strategy are likely to include: focused, clearly communicated, simple, and consistent over time. Participants may mention that the company's strategy appears to provide management discipline by guiding what the company chooses to do and chooses not to do. In order to explore the connection between widespread understanding of the strategy and effective implementation, a probing question might be, "How well do you think all employees understand the company's strategy? Is it something tightly held by CEO Herb Kelleher and senior leaders only? Do you think flight attendants, pilots, and others could communicate the strategy and their roles in executing it?"

Culture: Participants are likely to describe Southwest's culture as friendly, fun, egalitarian, and collaborative. Many are struck by the frequent use of the word "family" to communicate the culture. Inculcating new employees with the culture begins with the company's hiring practices, which involve current employees and customers. Participants may recall hearing the stories of job applicants, such as the Hawaiian shirt–wearing recruits or the woman who submitted her resume on the icing of a large sheet cake—all of whom were hired by Southwest.

Building and preserving culture is actively managed by the company through training, the culture committee and the employees themselves. Parties are prevalent. Each region receives a party budget for employees and their families, chili cookoffs and other contests are frequent, and senior managers attend rolling regional parties each year. The case describes several examples of employees pitching in to help one another or a customer, such as the pilot loading bags or the catastrophe fund for employees in need. Leadership behavior is also critical. The CEO and headquarters staff reinforce the culture

they desire throughout the organization through their own behaviors.

Systems: Participants are likely to comment on Southwest's customer-friendly systems (i.e., reservations and ticketing, seating, frequent flyer program) and efficient operating systems (i.e., plane turnaround process and time, hours in the air, etc.), which both support high customer satisfaction and employee productivity. Encourage participants to save in-depth diagnosis of human resource systems, such as hiring, compensation, and training, for the next part of the discussion, which is designed to allow for a closer look at human resources. As students mention these aspects of Southwest's human resources systems, the instructor can say, "Terrific, let's come back to that in a few minutes and explore it more deeply. What other systems support Southwest's strategy?"

Resources: Kelleher, Rhoades, and others at Southwest recognize their employees as the company's key assets and sources of competitive advantage. As Kelleher writes in his "declaration of war" memo, "Southwest's essential difference is not machines and 'things.' Our essential difference is minds, hearts, spirits, and souls." Nevertheless, Southwest effectively leverages its physical resources. For example, by using one type of plane, Southwest cuts down on maintenance and training costs, resulting in faster turnaround times and lower costs.

Stakeholders: Employees are Southwest's #1 stakeholder. The U.S. airline industry is highly unionized; indeed, 89% of Southwest's employees are represented by nine different labor unions. Participants are likely to mention that unlike its competitors, Southwest maintains relatively collaborative relationships with its unions. A newspaper article mentions that Kelleher "has somehow managed to get employees to identify personally with this company."[2] This sense of affiliation is achieved by various means: the strong Southwest culture, profit-sharing, fair compensation, and allowing employees to bid for shift and work hours. The results are impressive. At 4-½%, turnover is less than half of other major U.S. airlines, and the company only had one six-day walkout, back in the 1980s.

Customers are very important, but from the company's perspective, come second to employees. The company expects its employees to take care of customers, but also expects customers to behave reasonably towards its employees. The company prides itself on providing excellent and friendly customer service. Customers feel like Southwest employees will go out of their way to please them. The People Department ensures all job applicants are treated well because those who do not receive jobs are also potential customers.

Structures: While structures are not described in great detail, participants may infer from Kelleher's accessibility and employee autonomy that Southwest is a relatively flat, nonhierarchical organization. Employees on the front lines are empowered to make decisions about operations and customer service, knowing that the corporate leaders will back them up.

Although roles and responsibilities are clearly defined, it is also the case that employees demonstrate flexibility and the willingness to "pitch in" and do tasks outside of their stated responsibilities, such as the pilots seen loading bags. This flexibility and sense of teamwork are built into the expectations about the flexibility of role definitions, and reinforce the Southwest culture of "whatever it takes."

As the company has grown and employees become more geographically dispersed, preserving the Southwest spirit and "sense of family" could become a bigger challenge. Southwest instituted a novel structure to address this—the 65-person culture committee representing different regions and functions. The committee is charged with "preserv[ing] and enhanc[ing] the Southwest spirit."

Transition: The identification of the com-

ponents of the separate organizational elements should be used to transition into the next part of the discussion. Participants should come to realize that while each piece of the Southwest model is important, its real power is that all of the pieces are interdependent, coherent with one another, and support strategy execution.

Strategic human resource management and culture (25 minutes)

The third discussion topic focuses specifically on the company's human resources practices and culture, which will have been identified as key success factors in the previous discussion. The purpose of this conversation is to enable participants to understand the deliberate coherence among the organizational elements that support effective strategy execution at Southwest and to see human resources and culture as functions that have to be actively managed.

Participants probably mentioned various practices of the company's human resource system and described the culture earlier in the discussion. The instructor should now probe each component and have students make the connections between all of the culture, the human resources practices and their fit with the strategy.

Human resources: The company changed the name of its human resources group to the "People Department" five years prior, and under Rhoades' leadership, embodies the Southwest spirit. In hiring, the company uses group interviews and involves current employees and customers to ensure "fit" with Southwest's culture, norms, and values. Hiring is extremely selective—in 1993, of 98,000 applicants, 16,000 were interviewed, and only 2,700 hired. Southwest prides itself on hiring and firing based on how the employees' attitudes reflect the airlines's spirit.

Training is cross-functional, largely experiential, emphasizes customer service, and cascades from senior management to line employees. The company believes this is so important that it creates and delivers all of its own training rather than outsourcing it. Some follow-on training is done in intact work teams. The training is as much about job-specific skills as it is about inculcating new and existing employees with Southwest's culture.

In terms of compensation, starting base pay is relatively modest, but accelerates after a few years of service. This reinforces the sense of family and longevity in the workforce. All employees can participate in profit-sharing after one year with Southwest—the frontline employees also become owners through stock purchase programs. The wages of senior executives are kept modest relative to other airlines in order to preserve a sense of fairness with line employees. In addition to financial rewards, the company gives frequent public awards to employees who exhibit behaviors that the company values in its culture.

Culture: This conversation builds on the description of culture given earlier in class. The culture is purposeful, and it is grounded in high expectations for performance. The case notes a high degree of peer accountability ("employees don't put up with a lot of complaining"). The culture isn't fun and celebratory for the sake of those things, but because the company believes those aspects of the culture drive performance.

The concept of coherence: Participants should come to an awareness that all of Southwest's structures, systems, resources, and stakeholder relationships reinforce the company's strong culture, and together these organizational elements enable the execution of the strategy. This is the concept of organizational coherence.

One approach the instructor can use to help participants discover this important concept is to ask, "Could one of Southwest's competitors copy what they are doing?" Participants are likely to respond that it would be very difficult for the Shuttle or Continental Lite to replicate Southwest's human resources practices and culture given United's and Continental's histories of poor labor relations, distrust between line em-

ployees and managers, and lower productivity. These airlines also have a set of existing systems and structures that may not support the new strategy and may be difficult to change.

The point of this conversation is to enable participants to see that the Shuttle and Continental Lite are picking and choosing elements of the Southwest strategy (e.g., low-cost fares, point-to-point service) but that to be successful, all elements of the organization need to be coherently implemented and managed. It was not clear at the time the case was written whether United and Continental would attempt to make their culture and human resources practices more coherent with their new strategies. However, it appears as though they did not because both efforts have underperformed: Continental Lite folded two years after it was launched, and the United Shuttle in California has never met the corporate expectations for performance.

Southwest's human resources practices and culture stand out as key drivers of the airline's success and both are actively managed. While the coherence that Southwest has achieved is not rocket science—any airline or organization can do it—it does take disciplined management and leadership.

Reflections for public education and the importance of coherence (15 minutes)

The purpose of this discussion is to help participants draw parallels between Southwest and school systems and reflect on the possibilities for more actively managing human resources and culture, two functions which, in public education, tend to either be overlooked or accepted as status quo.

In closing, instructors can ask participants, "What lessons can public educators learn from Southwest?" Potential responses include:

• Devise a clear strategy to produce results. Strategy should be based on a deep understanding of the factors and actions that contribute to organizational performance.

- Implement the strategy over a period of time with excellence and consistency, which is at least as important as the content of the strategy.

- All parts of the organization must support the strategy (concept of coherence).

- Actively manage and invest in building culture. Culture is not simply about parties and happy employees; it is also about high expectations and results.

- Prioritize the human resources function (recruitment, training, retention) and change mindset from compliance and control to support and capacity-building.

- Use the human resources functions to build and strengthen organizational culture, norms, and values.

- Treat employees as internal customers; provide excellent customer service.

- Openly share information; foster non-hierarchical and open relationships.

The instructor can conclude this discussion by emphasizing how the Southwest example illustrates that effective strategy execution depends upon building a coherent and integrated organization.

Notes

1. See Stacey Childress, Richard Elmore, Allen Grossman, and Caroline King, "Note on the PELP Coherence Framework," No. PEL–010, Boston: Harvard Business School Publishing, 2006.

2. Kenneth Labich, "Is Herb Kelleher America's Best CEO?" *Fortune,* May 2, 1994.

Reinventing Human Resources at the School District of Philadelphia

Overview

The "Reinventing Human Resources at the School District of Philadelphia" case illustrates the challenges of effective human capital management in a dynamic urban public school district setting. It is one of a series of cases developed by the HGSE/HBS Public Education Leadership Project to describe for other school leaders, executives and graduate students the challenges and realities of leading and sustaining large-scale organizational change in an urban public school district.

The case examines the School District of Philadelphia (the District)'s efforts in 2005 to execute a human capital management strategy that will support increased student performance. Through the eyes of new Senior Vice President for Human Resources Tomás Hanna, the case highlights the challenges of leading change in a traditionally "transactional" department of a large public bureaucracy. The case provides an opportunity for students to analyze the role of the human resources function and leadership in supporting organizational strategy, evaluate

Hanna's efforts to date, and diagnose Hanna's key internal and external challenges going forward.

A key concept in the case is achieving and sustaining *coherence,* which as articulated by PELP, refers to the dynamic process by which leaders manage all of the elements of the organization (e.g., culture, resources, systems, structures, and stakeholders) to support effective strategy execution. To introduce students to the concept of managerial coherence in a public education setting, the instructor may wish to assign the "Note on the PELP Coherence Framework," PEL–010, as a pre-reading.

Case Summary

The case begins with Tomás Hanna reflecting on his first 90 days as the District's Senior Vice President for Human Resources (HR). Hanna, the former coordinator of a blue ribbon task force focused on improving recruitment and retention (the Campaign for Human Capital), feels positive about the changes underway. During his brief tenure, the department is moving quickly to implement a new hiring process (site based

This note was prepared by Professor David A. Thomas and Research Associate Caroline King.

selection), previously hostile relationships with collective bargaining units are improving, and Hanna has recruited a talented senior team. Hanna also acknowledges formidable challenges, including capacity constraints, organizational marginalization, and internal resistance to change. The introduction sets up Hanna's two overarching leadership challenges: (1) moving from an external change agent to internal senior manager, and (2) transforming the work and strategic positioning of a traditionally "transactional" HR department within a 27,000 employee organization.

As background, the case describes the historical, political, and demographic changes that have shaped the District into a predominantly minority and low-income large urban school district under the state's control by 2005. A brief summary of the District's reforms and performance under CEO Paul Vallas from 2002–2005 is also outlined. For additional background on the District, the instructor may wish to read "Finding a CEO for the School District of Philadelphia: Searching for a Savior?," HBS Case No. 803–72. More broadly, the New Teacher Project's 2003 report *Missed Opportunities: How We Keep High-Quality Teachers Out of Urban Schools* provides a general overview of the state of human resources departments in public education.

Next, the case characterizes the HR department prior to Hanna's arrival. CEO Paul Vallas argued that the HR function had not evolved beyond the "assumptions of the old economy," and as a result, the district was not effectively competing to recruit and retain the most talented teachers and principals. Indeed, the school year often opened with numerous unfilled vacancies and 50% of teachers left the District within three years. Principals, teachers and central office staff remarked on an "appalling lack of customer service" from HR staff. Hence, the opening quote from Vallas stating "We've got to put the human back in human resources." The

relationship between HR staff and the local teachers' union had deteriorated to the point where union President Ted Kirsch described it as "highly contentious and lacking any semblance of trust, respect, and dialogue." A former senior HR manager commented that HR was internally "viewed as the people who processed new employees" and as a result, HR staff was "not invited to the table when District leadership made strategic decisions." Lacking information technology and other comprehensive systems and processes, HR conducted many transactions manually and inefficiently.

Efforts to reform HR had been attempted before. Prior to Hanna, Vallas had brought in two new HR directors to "shake things up," without success. Meanwhile, a number of initiatives were designed to "workaround" the deficiencies of HR, such as the Campaign for Human Capital (the Campaign) and the transfer of benefits from HR to the finance office in late 2002. The Campaign is particularly notable, as it focused on strengthening teacher recruitment and retention in the District and was managed by Hanna. Under Hanna's direction, the Campaign initiated efforts in HR to more strategically recruit new teachers to Philadelphia, design retention incentives, and develop principal leadership. The Campaign also identified the district's centralized hiring practices as a major obstacle to improving new teacher recruitment and retention. More broadly, the Campaign exposed the depth of the problems within HR and the implications for the District's strategy. School Reform Commissioner and Campaign co-chair Sandra Dungee Glenn remarked, "The Campaign demonstrated that the District's ability to improve student achievement hinged upon a attracting, developing, and retaining a highly-qualified workforce, but it also exposed the brokenness of the HR department. We realized we didn't have the leadership or capacity in HR to drive a human capital management strategy."

Coming on the heels of the Campaign, the District negotiated a new contract with the Philadelphia Federation of Teachers (PFT). Signed on October 14, 2004, the contract ushered in a fundamental change to the District's hiring processes. Historically, new teacher hiring was tightly controlled by the central office (HR), and teacher transfers were governed by seniority provisions. Under the new 2004–2008 contract, principals gained the authority to hire 50% of teaching positions through site-based selection. Having won this important concession, Vallas looked for new HR leadership to implement site-based selection and reform HR more broadly, ultimately choosing Hanna.

The case then shifts to Hanna's first 90 days, during which Hanna focused on five main areas: (1) building a new team, (2) implementing site-based selection, (3) institutionalizing the Campaign's recommendations, (4) engaging external actors, and (5) enacting a customer service-oriented culture. For each area, the case summarizes Hanna's actions to date, as well as presents perspectives on the challenges and opportunities from multiple stakeholders. This section should facilitate ample student diagnosis of Hanna's incipient leadership and key managerial challenges.

Finally, the case ends with Hanna outlining his long term goals for HR. Ultimately, Hanna intends to reposition HR within the District from the "headache that needs to be fixed to a strategic partner." To do so, Hanna acknowledges that he must move out of day-to-day operations. Indeed, while supportive of Hanna's efforts to date, COO Natalye Paquin highlights the challenges Hanna faces as he transitions from responsibility for executing one project (the Campaign) to managing HR: "It takes a much different skill set to conduct the symphony orchestra versus tune and play all of the instruments yourself." Concurrently, numerous concerns weigh on Hanna, such as implementing a performance evaluation system, complying with federal regulations to have a fully certified teaching staff by 2006, and ensuring that the best teachers are serving the most academically at-risk students.

Learning Objectives

- **The human resources function.** This case gives students an opportunity to analyze the human resources function and organizational role. Attracting, retaining, developing, and supporting a high-quality workforce are critical to effective strategy execution. The strategic positioning of HR is particularly salient in organizations dependent on the knowledge and skills of frontline workers, such as public schools or the service industry.

- **Leadership.** The case illustrates the importance of effective HR leadership and management. By analyzing Hanna's leadership style and efforts to date, students can explore the capabilities required to effectively lead and manage organizational change within an internal department, across organizational divisions, and in collaboration with external stakeholders.

- **Systemic coherence.** Students are also introduced to the concept of managing for coherence within public education. Given that multiple forces strive to push school districts out of alignment (e.g. collective bargaining units, governing boards, federal and state regulations, etc.), skilled and disciplined leadership is required to create and sustain the organizational coherence necessary for effective strategy execution.

Positioning

This case could be used in a wide variety of settings and with different audiences, ranging from experienced school leaders to graduate students in education, business, or management courses. It can be used at the beginning of a course or module to lay out issues of human capital management, effective strategy execution, leadership development and managing change.

Assignment

In preparing "Reinventing Human Resources at the School District of Philadelphia," PEL-026, students should consider the questions below; the "Note on the PELP Coherence Framework," PEL-010 should also be assigned if it has not been read previously.

Discussion Questions

1. What explains the problems that existed in the School District of Philadelphia's department of human resources (HR) prior to January 2005?

2. What is Tomás Hanna's vision for HR?

3. Evaluate the actions that Tomás Hanna has taken to date.

4. What should Hanna do to address the core challenges that remain?

Teaching Plan and Analysis

This 80-minute teaching plan is based on an executive education course designed for PELP participants. If this case is taught in a human capital management module alongside the Memphis and Boston cases, this plan can be modified to 90-minutes by extending the closing to 15 minutes in order to allow for comparative analysis.

Summary

I. **HR Role and Function.** (20 minutes)

II. **Analysis of HR executive.** (10 minutes)

III. **Diagnosis of Hanna's strategic tasks.** (5 minutes)

IV. **Evaluation of Hanna's effectiveness.** (20 minutes)

V. **Recommendations.** (10 minutes)

VI. **Debate: Can HR be saved or should it be outsourced?** (10 minutes)

VII. **Closing.** (5 minutes, or 15 minutes if used as a module wrap)

HR role and function (20 minutes)

The class should begin with an evaluation of the current state of the HR department in the School District of Philadelphia. This discussion is intended to help students analyze the HR function and strategic positioning within a school district.

Suggested question: Going back to December 2004, how would you describe the HR function in the School District of Philadelphia?

Participants are likely to mention the HR department's "appalling" lack of customer service as experienced by teachers, principals, internal departments, and other stakeholders. Another important observation is the marginalization of HR within the District. The HR director did not report directly to the CEO. HR staff was "viewed as the people who process new employees" and consequently, not at the table when strategic decisions were made. In Vallas's opinion, the department "operated under the assumptions of the old economy," waiting for personnel to come to the District rather than taking a proactive, competitive approach to recruiting and retaining the most talented teachers and principals. The department's acrimonious relationship with the teachers' union and inefficient/outdated systems and processes are also notable.

Suggested follow-up question: What impact does the state of HR have on the District?

Participants are likely to mention the numerous unfilled vacancies and alarming teacher attrition rates. Fifty percent of new teachers leave the District within three years. Senior district leaders, principals, and teachers are highly dissatisfied and feel that HR is a hindrance rather than a support.

Next, push the class to draw connections between their description of HR and the results they have mentioned.

Suggested question: How do you put these characteristics and results together? For example, appalling customer service and the high attrition of new teachers. Why blame HR? Teachers do not quit HR, they quit schools.

Participants should identify the following implications:

- Not recruiting and hiring the best candidates

- HR leadership is unclear of purpose/role within District (ask "as if" question below)

- Monitoring contract compliance—"keeper of the keys"

- "Us" versus "Them" mentality (e.g. HR versus senior leadership, HR versus schools)

- Employment agency (reactive) versus being a strategic partner (proactive)

- Inefficient systems and processes cause redundancies and hinder more strategic recruitment

The key theme to explore with students during this discussion is a diagnosis of how the HR department perceived its role within the District prior to Hanna's leadership. You may consider asking students to ask the "as if" question: HR leaders were behaving "as if" their role was. . . ?

Building on this discussion, ask students to describe what the desired role of HR should be.

Students should identify HR's core business in the school district as recruiting the best teachers and retaining them. Participants are likely to suggest that since HR acts as the "face of the District" to potential and current employees and other stakeholders, that HR should provide exemplary customer service.

If students are educational practitioners, en-rolled in an education school, or fairly familiar with the sector, it is helpful to broaden the HR discussion beyond Philadelphia. Students without prior experience in urban public school districts may have a difficult time engaging in this discussion.

Suggested question: Consider the state of HR departments across urban school systems. On a scale of 1–4, how typical or atypical is Philadelphia's HR department (e.g., leadership, challenges, systems, culture, role perception? Ask students to vote using a show of hands.

How typical is HR in Philadelphia?			
1	2	3	4
Not at all typical			Very typical

Students will most likely vote 3 or 4, and the instructor can conclude that Philadelphia's HR department and challenges are not atypical.

Again for a seasoned audience, ask participants to consider the impact of broader societal changes on the role of HR over time.

Suggested question: Have the demands on HR changed over the past 20 years? What has changed in the environment that may have turned a previously high-functioning HR department into a dysfunctional department?

Participants are likely to identify the wide-sweeping demographic changes experienced by urban districts, which have shifted from serving middle-or upper-class and white students to enrolling largely low-income and minority students. As a result, districts require a more diverse workforce and employees that are committed to serving a challenging student population who may not have supports at home, such as parent involvement and resources that supplement in-school learning. Concurrently, economic and cultural changes have created more professional opportunities for women, and younger teachers are less likely to make a career out of teaching.

HR departments find themselves forced to compete with other employers for talented young people, and with the opportunity and challenge of attracting mid-career professionals through alternative routes. The trend of multiple career changes also implies that retention will be an ongoing challenge.

Additionally, participants are likely to note that the federal and state governments have increased accountability for student performance. Under the No Child Left Behind Act of 2001, all 50 states have adopted standards, mandatory assessments, and performance-based sanctions and rewards. School and district performance is measured by the proficiency rates of students on the state assessments and progress made towards ensuring 100% proficiency for all students by 2014. As a result, district and school leaders and individual teachers are under considerable pressure to improve student achievement—a particularly daunting task in a district such as Philadelphia in which only one-third of students met state standards.

The slowing of the national economy from 2000–2005, combined with declining local resources, has also created serious budget constraints on urban districts. Consequently, districts are under pressure to use their resources as efficiently as possible. Given that salaries and benefits typically constitute 85% of a district's budget, HR departments are under intense scrutiny by superintendents and school boards.

Analysis of HR executive (10 minutes)

Having established the desired role for HR, transition into a discussion of the ideal characteristics of an HR director. It is recommended to start generally, and then move into an analysis of the choice of Tomás Hanna to lead HR in Philadelphia.

Suggested question: Considering the current demands on HR and its' desired role within the district, who do you put in charge? What characteristics would you want in an HR director?

Participants are likely to identify the following attributes:

- Depth of HR knowledge

- Mindset: customer-service and results oriented

- Knowledge of customers (e.g., teachers, schools, students, district leaders, etc.) and their needs

- Team building skills; collaborative

- Effective at execution

- Vision for HR aligned with district leadership's vision

- Committed to building the organization—recruiting, supporting, and retaining high-quality workforce

Suggested follow-up comment and question: Hiring the "right" person is a critical management challenge in any organization. Given these characteristics, does the choice of Tomás Hanna to lead HR in Philadelphia make sense to you?

Participants are likely to give Hanna high marks for his demonstrated leadership and execution skills evidenced by the success of the Campaign for Human Capital. Hanna's history in the District as a teacher, principal, and administrator could be mentioned as evidence that Hanna understands the needs of HR's customers and operating environment. Hanna's ability to hire a new, and seemingly capable, senior HR team illustrates that he can identify and acquire talent. Participants may also cite Hanna's ambition and desire to assume increasing responsibility at the senior management level as positive attributes.

On the other hand, participants may be concerned about Hanna's ability to execute in his role as the director of HR. Hanna's effectiveness as the Campaign's project manager does not necessarily demonstrate that he has the sophisticated managerial skills needed to drive improvement in the 100 person HR department. Some participants may also take issue with Hanna's own job turnover, as he held four different jobs in 12 years.

Diagnosis of Hanna's strategic tasks (5 minutes)

Segue into an analysis of Hanna's strategic tasks; an evaluation of his performance to date, and diagnosis of the skills, culture and capabilities required within the HR department to deliver on the strategic tasks.

Suggested question: What are Hanna's most important strategic tasks?

Participants should identify the following tasks:

1. Become strategic partner to district leadership

2. Implement site-based selection

3. Deliver exemplary customer service and satisfaction to all employees (potential, new, current)

4. Build credibility and culture of HR

Evaluation of Hanna's effectiveness (20 minutes)

Set up a vote on Hanna's performance: On a scale of 1–6, how would you rate Hanna's effectiveness to date?

Hanna's efforts to date

1	2	3	4	5	6
Poor					Excellent

Explore students' vote. Suggested questions: How well is Hanna doing so far on delivering on these four strategic tasks? What has he done effectively? What has he done less effectively?

Hanna's efforts to date
- (+) Hired new team and is helping to develop their skills and relationships
- (+) Working across organizational boundaries (key to gaining strategic position, and changing culture in HR)
- (+) Pulls people together (cross-functional training, cross departments, external stakeholders)
- (+) Building relationships and modeling new culture within HR (open door policy, empowering staff, courted PFT)
- (−) Doing too much himself, too mired in the details
- (−) HR strategy incomplete: not at the school level
- (−) Site-based selection tracking and other information systems are inadequate
- (−) Weak site-based selection training for principals

Students are likely to judge Hanna's performance relative to their experience within the public education sector. Students from within the sector are likely to give Hanna high marks (e.g., between 4 and 5). It is difficult to predict how students from outside the sector will rate Hanna's performance, although MBA students and participants with little familiarity with public sector bureaucracies are likely to assign a lower rating.

Recommendations (10 minutes)

Next, engage students in a discussion of their recommendations for Hanna.

Suggested questions: It is April 2005, what should Hanna do next? What advice would you give him? Looking ahead, what should be his key priorities—in other words, what are the key things that will undermine the District's strategy to improve student achievement if they are not done?

Participants are likely to stress the importance of successfully implementing site-based selection. For Hanna, site-based selection is a "make or break" task in terms of earning the confidence of senior leadership and external stakeholders. Students may suggest that Hanna create a deeper sense of urgency among his staff to ensure successful implementation.

Second, participants may encourage Hanna to seek a direct reporting relationship to the CEO in order to signal the strategic importance of the HR function. While Hanna has a close relationship with the CEO, some students may question if this informal relationship is enough to ensure that HR has a seat "at the table" when senior leaders are making strategic decisions. Participants may also argue that a direct reporting relationship would facilitate Hanna's efforts to build bridges to other internal departments and send an important message about the strategic importance of the HR function to the HR staff that Hanna inherited.

Participants are also likely to recommend that Hanna and his team continue to build upon the Campaign's efforts to improve teacher recruitment and retention. Specific suggestions may include strengthening principal leadership development programs, addressing poor working conditions in hard-to-staff schools, and implementing non-monetary incentives.

In order to improve the efficiency of HR operations, participants may also recommend that Hanna implement technology upgrades and streamline existing processes. Finally, participants are likely to encourage Hanna to quickly hire a deputy director to take over the management of day-to-day HR operations.

Debate: Can HR be saved or should it be outsourced? (10 minutes)

Before closing, facilitate a debate over the rationale for school districts to "revamp" HR departments versus outsourcing the HR function. Expect a provocative debate, particularly among educational practitioners who are generally resistant to outsourcing this core function.

Suggested question: In 2005, can these antiquated HR departments be successfully reformed? Why are school districts still trying to save HR? Why not outsource recruitment, hiring, and placement like many high-performing for-profit companies?

Closing (5 minute)

Given that this case surfaces a number of important concepts related to human capital management, the instructor may wish to end class by summarizing a few main ideas:

1. Creating and sustaining coherence is a precursor to achieving high-performance for any organization. In a public school district, every department must understand its role in supporting the strategy to accelerate student achievement and senior leadership must ensure that the work of the departments is managed coherently such that everyone is marching in the same direction. A fundamental challenge for district HR departments is moving them from being tactical processors of people and paperwork to being a "strategic partner" that meets the district's human capital needs by recruiting, retaining, and developing the people who deliver high-quality instruction to students. Overcoming this challenge requires first HR leaders to understand that the human capital management function is essential to effective strategy execution. HR leaders must also address the changing dynamics of the district's external and internal environments in order to meet the needs of HR's key customers—senior leadership, principals, and teachers.

2. How do we think about the staffing the HR director role? Managers often have to choose between someone who is an expert on the HR function versus someone who knows the "work" of the organization (e.g.,

teaching and learning in the Philadelphia case). Each approach has strategic implications for the organization. An HR expert may know the function, but has to "buy" strategic relationships within the organization. On the other hand, someone who knows the "work" has to either develop the requisite HR skills or "buy" additional talent.

3. The Philadelphia case depicts the challenges inherent to managing a change process. How does a manager take an internal department from where it is (tactical and ineffective) to where it needs to be (strategic and high-performing)? As Hanna's efforts to date illustrate, this process includes setting a vision, building a coalition for change, creating a sense of urgency, and using "small wins" to gain credibility and momentum for large-scale change.

Staffing the Boston Public Schools

Overview

This case was developed by the HGSE/HBS Public Education Leadership Project to provide a multi-dimensional picture of teacher staffing practices (both hiring and school assignment) in the Boston Public Schools during 2004–2005. It is one of a series of cases created to describe for school leaders, executives and graduate students the challenges and realities of leading and sustaining large-scale organizational change in an urban public school district.

The case, "Staffing the Boston Public Schools," PELP No. 024, provides background on the district's policy, regulatory and bargaining context. It outlines how the district's strategy for improving student performance from 1995–2005 introduced new demands for effectively staffing schools. By describing the annual staffing process, the requirements of the collective bargaining agreement, ongoing HR reorganization, and the experience of one principal of an underperforming elementary school, the case illustrates the many interdependent factors that affect the outcome. It also illuminates the challenges faced by district officials, union leaders, principals and teachers as they try to improve both policy and practice. The case gives participants

an opportunity to consider why some schools remain hard to staff, to understand the roles that different parts of the school system play in the current arrangements, and to debate appropriate next steps for Boston.

Case Summary

Set in 2005, the case opens with BPS Superintendent Thomas Payzant wrestling with the ongoing challenge of recruiting and retaining a workforce of teachers who are qualified and committed to do the work necessary to raise student achievement. After reviewing four explanations for the persistent staffing problems in urban school districts, the case goes on to describe the background at BPS in 2005. It outlines the district's ten-year reform strategy "Focus on Children," which included six essentials of whole school improvement and a commitment to sophisticated curricula in math and literacy. It also outlines the policy and regulatory context that BPS leaders faced at this time. The case describes the evolution of collective bargaining agreements, highlighting changes since the mid-1980s. It focuses on the hard-won changes in the 2000 contract, which reduced the role of seniority in transfers, provided more job

This note was prepared by Professor Susan Moore Johnson and Research Associate Jennifer M. Suesse.

security for first-year non-tenured, provisional teachers, and compressed the timeline for transfers and hiring, which would require the district to improve administrative practices in its human resource department (HR). The case then summarizes how the district's HR operations changed 2000–2004, including and the appointment of a new HR director in late 2003.

Following this background, the case focuses on one under-performing, hard-to-staff elementary school: The John Marshall Elementary School in 2004–2005. Accounts by the Marshall's principal, Teresa Harvey-Jackson, illustrate for readers how the recent changes affect the principal's approach to staffing. They also illuminate the challenges to effective staffing that remain, despite the progress made.

The case concludes with a description of ongoing efforts to improve staffing at BPS: first, a reorganization of the HR office; and second, efforts to improve the labor-management relationship between the Boston Teacher's Union and BPS management. At the end of the case, Payzant comments on the challenges he sees in the future.

Positioning

This case could be used in a wide variety of settings and with different audiences, ranging from experienced school and union leaders to graduate students in education, business, or management courses. Written to be used as part of a module on managing human capital, the case was intended to offer readers a chance to explore their own understanding of the root causes of staffing problems in urban public school settings. It could also be used in courses or modules that focus on the role of collective bargaining and unions in public education.

Learning Objectives

By design, this case focuses on the implementation of staffing policies and procedures. It provides a good vehicle for teaching lessons

about leadership, change management, strategy development, systemic alignment, and labor-management relations. Key learning objectives include:

- **To help participants identify and understand the array of factors that shape staffing practices.** Many participants come to the case discussion with knowledge of only one aspect of the staffing process (e.g., budget approval, HR infrastructure, labor-management negotiations, school-site interviews). Typically, they identify a single source of the problem (e.g., seniority-based transfers, delayed budget approval) and believe that the solution rests in fixing that factor (e.g., eliminate seniority, use technology more effectively). This case demonstrates that no single explanation is sufficient to explain the problems of staffing in large, urban districts and, thus, no single change can lead to substantially improved outcomes.

- **To help participants analyze the extent to which the components of the staffing process are aligned.** Hiring and assignment practices involve many parts of the school system, each of which plays a role in determining annually whether the schools are staffed in a timely and sensible way. Each component of this system, from the point where the district forecasts staffing needs to the assignment of particular teachers to schools, must be coordinated. Without thoughtful alignment and faithful implementation, the system operates in haphazard and piecemeal ways, leading to illogical, delayed and often unfortunate outcomes.

- **To help participants see opportunities to act effectively in their role, thus contributing to a coherent approach.** When participants realize that the actions of all individuals involved in staffing play a role in the outcome, they can act with greater understanding and confidence in their sphere. Also, case discussion heightens participants' awareness of the futility of blame and the importance of collaboration—between labor and management, legislators and district officials, the superintendent's office and HR, central office and the schools—in solving this problem.

Assignment

Before discussing this case, students should read "Staffing the Boston Public Schools," PELP No. 024. They should also be prepared to address the following questions:

Discussion Questions

1. What factors and forces currently shape the assignment and hiring process in the BPS?

2. How do the key players in the case (Payzant, Contompasis, Harvey-Jackson, McGann, and Stutman) define the problem that the BPS faces in effectively staffing the schools? What constraints and opportunities does each face?

3. How would you assess the progress that has been made so far?

4. Consider the challenge of ensuring that every hard-to-staff school has a stable teaching staff of well-qualified teachers. What are the components of a comprehensive solution? What specific steps would you recommend to Superintendent Payzant and President Stutman?

Teaching Plan and Analysis

This teaching plan is based on an executive education course designed for the PELP inaugural class of urban public school leadership teams. The teaching plan can be modified to suit a 75-minute or 90-minute session.

Summary

I. **Introduction.** What is the big issue here? Why is this important? (5 minutes)

II. **Situating the case and reviewing the current staffing process.** What are the important facts about Boston and the BPS that are central to understanding the case? How does the current staffing process work? (10 minutes)

III. **Considering and assessing the progress made.** What progress has been made in improving staffing policy and practice since the 1980s? How would you rate that progress? Why? (20 minutes)

IV. **Analyzing the different perspectives of the players.** Take the perspective of X. In this person's view, what would be the most important change to achieve better outcomes? What is the first step? (30 minutes)

V. **Devising a coherent and comprehensive strategy and planning for its implementation.** What are the components of a solution? Who should do what? What should be centralized, what decentralized? (20 minutes)

VI. **Wrap-up.** Summary and further questions for reflection. (5 minutes)

Introduction (5 minutes)

What is the big issue here? Why is this important?

Given the many details in this case, it is essential that participants remain focused on the core issue—how a district can ensure that all schools are staffed with teachers who are well qualified for the subjects they teach and who match the needs of the school where they are assigned. The instructor might provide information about the consequences of ineffective staffing practices (especially low-income students) by assigning "The Real Value of Teachers," Education Trust, Thinking K-16, Winter 2004. This piece includes research findings that establish the central role of the teacher in student learning, the persistence of teacher turnover in hard-to-staff schools, and the high percentage of unqualified teachers working in low-income schools. For this case to be compelling, participants must recognize the high stakes that are involved in these decisions.

Situating the case and reviewing the current staffing process (10 minutes)

What are the facts about Boston and the BPS that are important to understanding the case? How does the current staffing process work?

Although staffing and labor-management issues are similar from district to district, there are no all-purpose solutions. The process of analysis is similar from site to site, but each case is unique. Therefore, in order to understand what happens in this case, participants need to recognize such things as the district's dependence on state and local funding, the role of collective bargaining and the BTU in determining policy, the long tenure of Superintendent Payzant and the investment in his school improvement strategy, and the active involvement of the mayor and community organizations in education.

Participants also need to understand the basics of the current staffing practices, especially the sequence of steps: *probable organization* (including possible staff reductions); *voluntary transfers and possible openings;* excess pools (placing involuntary transfers and teachers returning from leave); *hiring.* Although these are explained within the context of the Marshall School, it's useful to specify them early in the discussion. To save time, the instructor might list these steps in order on the board and ask participants to briefly explain each. If more time is available and participants are centrally concerned with the issue of staffing, it would be productive to focus more discussion on each step of the process.

Considering and assessing the progress made (20 minutes)

What progress has been made in improving staffing policy and practice? How would you rate that progress? Why?

Very often, experienced administrators assume that little progress has been made on this issue, particularly in the labor-management arena. As this case documents, however, im-

provements have been made over time, both at the bargaining table and in practice. As a result of negotiations, seniority plays a far less prominent role in staffing assignments than it once did, the timeline has been compressed substantially to allow earlier job offers, and principals have gained the authority to protect the assignments of first-year teachers. Also, the HR department has reorganized to provide better service to applicants and has begun using technology to track candidates. Although this section of the discussion is brief, it makes the point that participants are entering a situation where changes have been made and where further changes can be made.

Although it is possible to cite progress made, some participants are likely to conclude that there has been little progress of consequence. They may observe that the pace of change has been much too slow or that the union still holds too much power in these decisions. By providing a rating scale and gathering participants' assessments, the instructor signals the expectation that participants will view this differently. I suggest a rating scale of 1 to 5, using 1 to indicate that BPS has achieved "not much that matters," and 5 to show that they are "establishing a system that really works." A quick tally of the scores provides an informative snapshot of the range of views in the class. Asking individuals who have chosen #1, #3, and #5 to explain their positions sets up the discussion for the rest of the class. Sometimes I note the tally of votes on a side board in order for reference later in the discussion.

Analyzing the different perspectives of the players (30 minutes)

Take the perspective of X. In this person's or group's view, what would be the most important change to achieve better outcomes? What is the first step?

One of the most important lessons of this case is the very different perspectives, diagnoses, and priorities of individuals and groups described in the case. Particularly notable are the divergent assessments of the principal and central office administrators. These differences can be highlight by asking the participants to focus on the perspective of one key actor or group, including:

1. Superintendent Payzant and Chief Operating Officer Michael Contompasis
2. HR director Barbara McGann
3. Principal Teresa Harvey-Jackson
4. BTU president Richard Stutman and other union members
5. New and prospective teachers

The instructor divides the class into sections and assigns one role or group to each. Participants then spend 10 minutes in discussion. From this assigned perspective, what would be the most important change to achieve better outcomes? What is the first step? They should be encouraged to base their views and proposals on text from the case.

Discussing different groups' responses to these questions illustrates both the conflicting views of key players and the need for a coherent, integrated approach. Two groups (the union members and the new and prospective teachers) are likely to have more complicated and have competing interests within them. For example, there will be different views among new and veteran union members about the BTU priorities, and newly hired and prospective teachers may have different concerns.

Devising and implementing a coherent and comprehensive strategy (20 minutes)

What are the components of a solution? Who should do what?

Having established the importance of developing an integrated strategy, participants can contribute proposals for change, explaining who should do what and which elements should be centralized and which decentralized. Components of a coherent plan might include:

1. **Working toward earlier budget approval.** This would involve the Superintendent working with state and city officials

2. **Changing the sequence of steps in the staffing process.** For example, placing teachers on involuntary transfer or returning from leave before voluntary transfers or freeing up principals of hard-to-staff schools (where veteran teachers rarely choose to transfer) to post jobs and hire early. These changes would involve informal and formal collaboration between the union and management.

3. **Giving schools more responsibility for defining staffing needs and selecting staff.** This would require changes in the collective bargaining agreement and HR practices as well as a plan to increase the capacity of school site committees and principals to assume greater responsibility.

4. **Improving HR services to prospective teachers.** This would require continuing to expand the use of technology and integrated services in HR.

5. **Improve communications between HR and the schools.** This might include creating new reporting relationships between the schools and HR, which involve the central office administrators who supervise the schools.

6. **Ensuring that principals regularly evaluate teachers and move to dismiss weak ones.** Supervising administrators in the central office would have to hold principals responsible for conducting evaluations. This would also require administrators in HR to provide increased training and legal support for principals who seek to dismiss weak teachers.

Wrap-up (5 minutes)

Further questions

In addition to summarizing the plan that emerges during the prior segment, the instructor might identify further questions that this case raises. Examples include:

1. On the issue of staffing, what is the right balance between school-site autonomy (which advances the interests of individual schools) and centralized control (which advances the interests of the system)?

2. What is the best way for the district to deal with unwanted, tenured teachers?

3. Are entrepreneurial principals part of the answer or part of the problem?

Conclusion

In closing, one can reemphasize the importance of coherence in systematically approaching questions of school and district improvement. In addition, this case offers an opportunity to consider the importance of addressing issues like staffing from multiple directions simultaneously.

Building a High-Performing Organization

NYPD New: Using the Case with Education Administrators

Overview

This teaching plan was developed by the Public Education Leadership Project at Harvard University to introduce the concept of changing an entrenched organizational culture through deliberate, concrete managerial actions that support the organization's performance goals. The teaching plan was developed for school district administrators who manage, or are preparing to manage, a school or groups of schools.

The case, NYPD New, describes the strategy and management processes implemented over a two-year period by newly-appointed New York City Police Commissioner William Bratton and his executive team to combat the city's sky-rocketing crime rate in the mid-1990s. Bratton and his staff worked to create a results-oriented police department from one that previously emphasized and measured effort, even though budgetary limitations and civil service regulations made it difficult to reward achievements of individual officers and units.

This teaching plan allows participants to explore the development of NYPD's rapid culture change and the structures and systems the commissioner and his team implemented to support the new expectations about performance. Participants will also have an opportunity to discuss the balance between giving front-line managers more autonomy in exchange for more accountability for results. The plan spends significant time on a new accountability system that shifted resources and people among police precincts based on the nature of the problem in various neighborhoods and the capacity of the unit to respond effectively.

Case Summary[1]

In January 1996, Commissioner William Bratton of the New York Police Department (NYPD) is confronted with the need to develop an action plan that will help the Department sustain the results that it has achieved in the previous 24 months of his administration, during which the department led the United States in crime reduction. Through the introduction of many of the concepts and techniques practiced by successful managers of for-profit organizations, the

Commissioner has been able to transform NYPD from an efforts-oriented to a results-oriented organization. However, budgetary limitations and civil service regulations make it difficult both to reward the remarkable achievements of NYPD units and to sustain the current pace of change. They also require that the attention of management be shifted to achieving higher productivity, possibly leading to a reduction in the staffing levels for various jobs.

Positioning

This case may be used in a wide variety of settings and across a wide range of audiences to illustrate issues of organizational change, strategy, and accountability. This teaching note is designed specifically to give current or future education administrators an opportunity to discuss how an organization can use concrete managerial actions to change a culture and produce desired outcomes.

Learning Objectives

- **Culture can be changed with deliberate managerial actions.** Bratton spearheaded deliberate managerial actions to support a cultural shift in the police force that moved the organization's focus from efforts to results. By changing a number of systems and structures that were critical to the work of policing, the organization created an environment in which people were required to behave differently, in ways that were coherent with the new strategy. As a result, the beliefs of people in the police department began to change as the organizational design and leadership behavior supported the new culture.

- **Culture is interdependent with systems, structures, resources and stakeholder relationships.** Each must be coherent with the others in order to implement a strategy.

- **Loose/tight managerial control does not have to be an either/or choice.** Precinct

commanders in the case receive significant autonomy, but are asked to be more directly accountable for their unit's results. This sets up a tension between loose and tight approaches to organizational design. Bratton's "loose" managerial control over police precincts was coupled with "tight" systems, like CompStat, to ensure that precincts achieved their goals. The generalizable lesson is that in order to "loosely" manage an organization really well, the organization has to be really "tight" on a few dimensions and design and implement those in a way that supports organizational performance.

Discussion Questions

1. What were the most critical challenges Bratton faced when he took the job at NYPD?

2. What were Bratton's most important decisions and/or actions to address those challenges and achieve results?

3. What were the most important management processes that Bratton established at NYPD? What were they designed to do?

Teaching Plan and Analysis

This 90-minute teaching plan is based on an executive education course designed for PELP participants. The teaching plan can be modified to suit a longer or shorter session.

Summary

I. **Opening/establishing context.** During the introduction, participants will discuss the challenges and issues confronting NYPD when Bratton arrives in 1994. The instructor may begin the discussion by asking, "What challenges did Bratton face when he arrived at NYPD? Why do they exist?" It is important for the instructor to highlight the cultural issues separately in preparation for a later discussion of the culture's evolution under Bratton's leadership. To highlight some positive events that coincided with Bratton's arrival, the instructor may also ask, "What dynamics are working in Bratton's favor when he enters? Why are they important?" (20 minutes)

II. **Theory of action.** In this segment, the participants will have the opportunity to explore Bratton's theory of action to transform the organization. The instructor may begin the discussion by saying, "If the goal is to reduce crime rather than simply responding to crime, what is Bratton's theory of action about how to get from where they are to where they need to be?" The key elements of Bratton's strategy are: a reduction in quality of life crimes leads to a reduction in major crimes; moving from an efforts-based to a results-based organization is critical to success; police department action can have a positive effect on reducing crime. (10 minutes)

III. **Action steps.** During this portion, participants will discuss the action steps Bratton took to transform various components of NYPD's organization. The instructor might begin the discussion by saying, "Describe the new culture necessary at NYPD to accomplish the goal of moving from an efforts-based organization to a results-based organization." As participants point to specific actions taken by Bratton's administration, the instructor may point out what may appear to be a conflict between managerial actions that loosen and tighten control within NYPD's organization. (25 minutes)

IV. **CompStat.** The purpose of this segment is to ensure that participants gain a common understanding of CompStat and recognize the importance that it played in changing the culture and meeting the performance goals for each precinct and the organization as a whole. To open the discussion, the instructor might say, "CompStat was one of the cornerstones of Bratton's changes. Why was it important?" (15 minutes)

V. **Links to public education.** In this segment, participants are encouraged to draw parallels between the issues faced by NYPD and public education. To transition to this discussion segment, the instructor might ask, "How do the problems that Bratton faced compare to those facing public school leaders? How might some of Bratton's actions be applied to public school systems?" The instructor should push participants to think about whether or not the specific actions taken by Bratton's administration could be applied to school districts. (15 minutes)

VI. **Wrap-up big ideas.** To close, the instructor should review the key points outlined in the "Learning Objectives" section, highlighting specific student comments from the discussion. (5 minutes)

Opening/establishing context (20 minutes)
The instructor can begin class with the question: "What challenges did Bratton face when he arrived at NYPD? Why do they exist?"

This will give students an opportunity to discuss contextual problems related to the crime rate and public's perception of crime and NYPD, as well as internal problems he faces in the organization's culture, structure, systems, etc. Participants may highlight the NYPD's fragmented bureaucracy, the outdated guns and vests used by the police force, the 1960s research on poverty, racism, and crime, the excessive focus on completing paperwork, and the frequent use of overtime to perform basic duties (i.e. testifying, work hours that are disconnected from preventing crime, ex. = car thefts). Participants may also describe the culture in 1994 as one low in trust with a lot of finger-pointing in addition to being hierarchical, macho, and protectionist. The instructor should capture cultural issues separately so that students can specifically address the differences between the starting culture and the evolving culture during Bratton's tenure later in the discussion. (Time: ~ 15 minutes)

Then, the instructor may shift the discussion with the following questions: "What dynamics are working in Bratton's favor when he enters? Why are they important?"

This discussion should bring out the new Mayor's focus on crime; the increased funding from the crime bill; the intrinsic motivation of many police officers to protect and serve; the internal pride in the force, etc. Bratton's mayoral support combined with increased funding to combat crime suggests that Bratton is well supported by key stakeholders and with financial resources to transform the organization. (Time: ~5 minutes)

Theory of action (10 minutes)

In this segment, students will explore Bratton's theory of action about how to transform the organization to achieve desired results. The instructor may begin by asking the following question: "If the goal is to reduce crime rather than simply responding to crime, what is Bratton's theory of action about how to get from where they are to where they need to be?"

The important points are: a reduction in quality of life crimes leads to a reduction in major crimes (broken window theory); police department action can have a positive effect on reducing crime (rather than simply responding to crime); therefore, moving from an efforts-based to a results-based organization is critical to success.; Each of these elements of the theory of action were important beliefs that the organization had to adopt in order to implement the set of actions (the strategy) that Bratton developed. (Time: ~10 minutes)

Action steps (25 minutes)

To transition from discussing Bratton's theory of action to his action steps, the instructor can ask students to examine the culture needed to support the new organization taking into account the previously discussed cultural issues. The instructor may open the discussion by saying, "We did a nice job describing the existing culture when Bratton arrived—how would you describe the new culture necessary at NYPD to accomplish the goal of moving from an efforts-based organization to a results-based organization."

Participant responses may include but are not limited to the following: better communication, autonomy, clear purpose, customer focus, ownership of the problem, transparency, openness, and/or increased trust. After several comments about the desired culture, the instructor can mention that we often think of culture as something soft and mysterious that is difficult to affect through specific actions. In terms of the coherence framework, even though culture is one of several elements, all of the elements are interactive. Concrete managerial actions in elements such as structure, resources, systems, and stakeholders can help people begin to act in different ways, which is a big part of changing their beliefs and over time, the whole organizational culture.

Now students can revisit the challenges outlined earlier to discuss the action steps Bratton took to transform the organization. It is important in this section to emphasize that precinct commanders are given more autonomy in problem solving, resource allocation, decision making, etc., than they had under the previous regime, when most important decisions were centralized. This sets up a dissonance when the students explore CompStat more deeply because of the centralized monitoring and increased accountability the precinct commanders now have for results. The new organizational culture/systems on whole seem more "loose," but some things are actually more "tight." The instructor may also point out that the case presents Bratton's leadership behavior as both visible and consistent. The instructor can use the PELP coherence model to outline responses from students on the board. Following are sample responses:

Structure: Early on, Bratton created 12 new teams of NYPD officers to review existing practices and develop recommendations for change. Following up on the recommendations, Bratton's administration eliminated a reporting level between the precinct commanders and the bureau commanders and ultimately gave precinct commanders more managerial autonomy to meet their targets. Also, Bratton merged police work previously done by three separate entities to one organization.

Resources: Bratton improved the quality of guns and vests soon after his arrival. He also invested in new human talent with hopes of creating a more adaptable workforce. Also, Bratton's administration adopted better technology, like cellular phones, to better equip officers to improve performance.

Systems: Weekly tours were instituted and conducted by the Deputy Commissioner to precinct commands. These played a quality control function and made senior leadership more visible to the field staff. Additionally, Bratton's administration modified the compensation system by rewarding high-performing officers with preferred police assignments, letters of recognition, and overtime hours which had become restricted due to budgetary limitations.

To support the shift to a results-based organization, Bratton's administration instituted CompStat along with new performance measures to help precinct commanders meet the organization's desired goals. This was one of the key systems instituted by Bratton's administration to reinforce the shift to a results-based orga-

nization. The instructor should encourage participants to hold their analysis of CompStat until the next section of the discussion, which allow for a deeper conversation about this critical system.

Stakeholders: Bratton won favor from the key stakeholders, cops, early on by pushing for gun and vest upgrades. He earned the reputation that he was a police commissioner that would back officers up by seeking reliable information on claims against officers, like cases in which officers were accused of using excessive force. Also, Bratton kept a positive working relationship with the Mayor and his administration attempted to build better relationships with the community.

CompStat (15 minutes)

This section begins with a ten-minute discussion to ensure that students are on the same page about CompStat and its importance. It also allows students to visualize CompStat in advance of showing a short video that includes a CompStat meeting. The instructor may begin this segment by saying, "CompStat was one of the cornerstones of Bratton's changes. Why was it important?"

Students should describe the elements of the CompStat process—the instructor should push on each one and ask why it was important, and how it related to the overall goals of NYPD. Once the instructor is sure that the class has a common understanding of the system itself, the instructor may ask the class to visualize what it would be like to be in the spotlight at a CompStat meeting: "What do you think it would feel like to be in one of these meetings if you were a precinct commander?"

After hearing a few comments, the instructor may ask, "Take a look at Exhibit 5. What is the first thing that strikes you about it?"

Students will comment on the pictures of leadership, the depth of information, and the rigor of the analysis: How does this relate to the culture they're trying to build? Is this "loose" or "tight"?"

The instructor may ask students to place the total organization on a continuum between loose and tight at the beginning of Bratton's tenure in 94, and then at the end of the case in 96.

The big idea here is that even though some structures and systems that have been implemented are very loose, CompStat is an example of a very "tight" system. An astute student might point out that while the organization is more 'loose' in 96 then in 94, it's not an either/or decision. Some things are more loose, and some things are still tight, but in a way that supports the goals of the organization. The important insight is that if "loose" is going to work to its full potential, a few things might have to be very "tight"—students may or may not get here.

Links to public education (15 minutes)

In this section, students can discuss the links between problems faced by Bratton and those faced by urban school leaders, as well as similarities between actions he took and some of the changes happening in education management currently. The instructor may begin the discussion by saying, "How do the problems that Bratton faced compare to those facing public school leaders? How might some of Bratton's actions be applied to public school systems?"

Educators typically see a host of connections. The goal of this section of the teaching plan is merely to begin unearthing the analogies rather than to analyze them in detail. Some common responses include (not an exhaustive list):

Challenges:

- Conventional wisdom that crime couldn't be reduced because of poverty and other social factors is similar to some arguments that environmental and social factors make it impossible to expect all children to learn at high levels

- The importance of the assumption in Bratton's theory of action that "we can make a difference" usually resonates with some portion of the class

- The insight about the differences between the way people behave in a culture that rewards effort and the way the behave in a culture that rewards results is a powerful analogy for educators

- The feeling by front-line officers that paperwork and covering their tracks was vastly more important that fighting crime reminds many of the frustrations that teachers and principals can have with administrative demands placed on their time

- The inability to share data across precincts and departments in order to improve the practices of officers is familiar to many—not necessarily because of explicit policies, but more often because of technology and process constraints

- Precinct commanders with no real control of their resources remind many participants of the day to day life of principals

Bratton's Managerial Choices:

- Giving the precinct commanders real autonomy, and moving the focus of the entire organization to the work that was taking place on the front-lines is analogous to much of the school-based improvement work happening in public schools today

- Participants draw the analogy between the "drop-ins" and instructional walkthroughs or school reviews that are now happening in many states and districts

- The focus on using relevant and timely data to make decisions about how to improve the important work of the organization is familiar to people, though they usually express that

NYPD seems farther along than their own district or school

- Adding new resources such as guns, technology, and uniforms is often cited as a practice that is going on for schools and classrooms, particularly in the realm of data and technology.

Wrap-up (5 minutes)

Review the big ideas outlined in the "Learning Objectives" section, drawing on specific student comments from the discussion.

Notes

1. This case synopsis was taken from "NYPD New" teaching note, HBS Case No. 5–900–021, Boston: Harvard Business School Publishing, 2000.

Learning to Manage with Data in Duval County Public Schools: Lake Shore Middle School (A)

Overview

The Learning to Manage with Data in Duval County Public Schools (DCPS): Lake Shore Middle School (A) case illustrates efforts to increase student achievement through data-driven decision-making at both the district and school site levels. The case belongs to a larger case series developed by the HGSE/HBS Public Education Leadership Project to describe for school leaders, executives and graduate students the challenges and realities of leading and sustaining large-scale organizational change in an urban public school district.

The Duval County case is timely as public school districts nationwide struggle to raise student achievement in an environment of increasingly high-stakes accountability created by the federal No Child Left Behind Act of 2001 and rigorous state standards. Concurrently, many school systems find themselves awash with performance data but lack all the needed managerial and technical expertise to use data as strategically as they should for informing efforts to improve teaching and learning in the classroom.

The case underscores that having a great deal of data is not a "silver bullet" for increasing student achievement. Data must be timely and provide the right information for teachers and administrators. Building a performance measurement and management (PMM) system is not an end, but an important means for informing how to adjust and differentiate instructional approaches so that every child can achieve at high levels. Therefore, a PMM must be carefully designed and continuously improved to provide the usable information required. As the case analysis and discussion reveal, discovering how to manage effectively with data—identifying what works and what doesn't to improve teaching and learning—daunting challenge for district and school leaders.

Case Summary

The case describes how DCPS utilizes data at the central office to measure district-wide performance towards strategic goals during retired U.S. Air Force Major General John C. Fryer, Jr.'s first six years as superintendent (1998–2004). Approximately 130,000 students attended the district's 166 schools in SY04,[1] making DCPS

This note was prepared by professors Allen Grossman and James P. Honan and Research Associate Caroline King.

the sixth largest school system in Florida. DCPS, under Fryer's leadership, designed and implemented a sophisticated performance measurement and management system based on the hypothesis that data-driven decision making would lead to improved educational outcomes for all students. The district's performance measurement and management system includes a Mission Control Room (48 indicators of organizational performance), the Research Data Affects Change (RESDAC) reports, the Academic Interpretation and Data Evaluation (AIDE) data system, a performance evaluation system for principals, and school and classroom observation tools.

The case also depicts first-year principal Iranetta Wright's efforts to improve student performance at Lake Shore Middle School in SY04. When Wright arrives at Lake Shore in the summer before SY04, 70% of the students perform below grade level in math and reading on the Florida Comprehensive Achievement Test (FCAT). Wright and her leadership team analyze student achievement data to drive managerial decisions in four areas: strategic planning, organizing to support students and teachers, monitoring performance, and measuring results. Despite the district's PMM system and Wright's leadership, student achievement actually declines at Lake Shore in SY04. The case ends with a description of the school's major challenges for improving achievement in SY05.

Positioning

This case can be used in a wide variety of settings and with different audiences, ranging from experienced school leaders to graduate students in education, business, or management courses. The case highlights issues of strategy, leadership and performance measurement and management.

Learning Objectives

Potential learning objectives include:

1. Concepts:

(a) *Relationship between the availability of data, effective management with data, and improved student achievement:* The case provides a vehicle for exploring the processes required to effectively select and use the burgeoning amount of achievement data collected by public school districts with the goal of improving educational outcomes for all students. The case underscores that making data available is a necessary, but insufficient, first step in achieving high-performance in a public school district and that teachers and administrators need the right data in a timely fashion for it to be effectively used.

(b) *Measurement systems' alignment function:* Carefully designed and implemented PMM systems are effective in helping a school district create coherence among its strategy, goals, organizational programs, and outcomes. District and school leaders must also build the capacity, culture, structures, and processes required to sustain the virtuous cycle of organizational learning and improvement. Further, leaders must manage these organizational elements, as well as relationships with stakeholders, to be coherent with one another and the district's improvement strategy. The Public Education Leadership Project (PELP) Coherence Framework will be introduced to help teach these concepts (See Exhibit 1).[2]

(c) *Measurement systems' implementation process:* Strong leadership and staff buy-in are crucial for creating and sustaining effective PMM systems. District leaders must also consider challenges related to scale as they try to implement PMM across a large number of schools with varying capacity in terms of principal leadership and instructional staff. They must also insure that the strategy for using the data from the system is as carefully planed and implemented the system itself.

(d) *Measurement systems' standards:* With the exception of standardized test scores required by the No Child Left Behind Act of 2001 (NCLB) and state accountability mandates, there are few accepted, sets of standards for measuring organizational performance and student achievement in the public education sector.

2. Skills:

(a) *Understand the complexities of effectively managing* with data to improve educational outcomes

(b) *Analyze the elements of a PMM system,* how they fit together, and implications for strategic and organizational coherence.

(c) *Identify and analyze the organizational elements* (e.g., structures, systems, resources, culture and stakeholders) and understand how they complement or conflict with each other in the use of data to manage performance.

3. Attitudes:

(a) *"Data are your friend":* Given that a major push for data is by external actors and is coupled with high-stakes outcomes, many school leaders and staff perceive data being used as an "I gotcha" rather than a vehicle for learning and continuous improvement. Developing a "data are your friend" attitude continues to represents a significant challenge to shifting the culture in public education.

(b) *Organizational and team learning:* Data can help stimulate discussions among teachers, principals, and district managers, but for student performance to improve, these conversations need to the development of a plan and successful implementation of the plan that leads to improved instruction and student outcomes.

Assignment

In preparing "Learning to Manage with Data in Duval County Public Schools," students should read the case (PEL-008) and answer the ques-

tions below. The "Note on the PELP Coherence Framework," PEL-010, should also be assigned if it has not been read previously.

Discussion Questions

1. How would you assess the effectiveness of DCPS' performance measurement and management system?

2. What are the challenges and opportunities for managing with data at the building level?

3. What advice would you offer to Iranetta Wright in terms of how she should use data to manage for higher performance at Lake Shore next year?

4. What recommendations would you give John Fryer—how should DCPS support Iranetta Wright's efforts and would you suggest any modifications to the district's data system?

Teaching Plan and Analysis

This 80-minute teaching plan is based on is an executive education course designed for the PELP inaugural cohort of urban public school leadership teams. The teaching plan is designed for an 80-minute session.

Summary

   I. Introduction. The role of performance measurement and management. (10 minutes)

  II. DCPS strategy and theory of action. (10 minutes)

 III. Diagnostic analysis. The DCPS data system. (28 minutes)

  IV. Role play. (10 minutes)

   V. Action planning. What should Iranetta Wright do next? (20 minutes)

  VI. Closing. (2 minutes)

Introduction (10 minutes)

Historically, the public education sector has not viewed data as a resource for organizational learning. At the turn of the 21st century, how-ever, NCLB and state accountability mandates began requiring school districts to collect and report multiple streams of data (e.g. disaggregated student achievement data, teacher qualifications, etc.) and rewarding or sanctioning individual schools based on performance. As a consequence, many school districts are making substantial investments of time and money into designing and implementing PMM systems.

The instructor should begin class by helping participants articulate the functions of performance measurement and management system in the public education context. The goal of the discussion is to draw out the managerial role district and school leaders must play in sustaining organizational learning and improvement.

A suggested opening follows:

There is often a perception that the public education sector does not have enough data on student achievement and organizational performance. In fact, there is frequently a lot of data, particularly in the wake of the No Child Left Behind Act of 2001. Every school system is now required to track and report achievement data and every district has a data system of some sort and Duval's may be one of the most advanced. The real issues at hand are what data are most useful and how districts use their data system to inform their strategy and instructional practices to achieve higher educational outcomes? What do we mean by "data-driven decision-making" and how does a district do it? Let's step back for a moment and ask, "What does John Fryer want to achieve with the district's performance measurement and management system?"

Building on participants' comments, the students should rather quickly identify that the primary purposes are to:

• measure the performance of students, teachers, principals, and the district

• continuously inform, evaluate, and improve the district's strategy and instructional approaches

• create a common language and focus for everyone in the district

• build a culture of performance

The instructor might then ask, "So, what are the big managerial challenges facing DCPS?":

While data helps measure, it does not tell you what to do to improve student achievement. Discovering how to manage effectively with data—learning from experience over time what works and what doesn't to improve teaching and learning under what conditions—is the more daunting challenge borne by district and school leaders.

DCPS strategy and theory of action (10 minutes)

The case analysis may begin by discussing the district's theory of action and strategy. A *theory of action* represents an organization's collective belief about the causal relationships between certain actions and desired outcomes.[3] The articulation of a theory of action in the public education sector takes the following form: If the district does X, then achievement will improve for every student. For example: The district will increase student achievement for every student by improving teacher practice.

Key questions posed are: What is the implicit theory of action in the DCPS strategy about how to improve educational outcomes for every student? What is Fryer's theory of action for how to improve organizational learning and performance?

Possible responses include:

• If standards of student performance are rigorous and clear, providing schools with student achievement data will enable principals and teachers to diagnose students' individual strengths and weaknesses and differentiate instruction so every student achieves at high levels

• Organizationally, data-driven decision-making, if well implemented, should help create a strong internal culture of high-performance, learning, and accountability.

• As long as a school's culture supports teachers in efforts to continuously improve curricula and instructional practices, making student achievement results transparent can promote healthy competition and the sharing of best practices among teachers (see Exhibit 2 for a sample board plan).

Having described the theory of action, the instructor can facilitate a discussion of the district's strategy. In the public education context, *strategy* is defined as the broad set of coherent actions the people in the district will take to meet the objective of improving student performance.[4] For example: The district will increase student achievement for every student by improving teacher practice through focused professional development for teachers, principals, and all instructional staff.

Suggested questions include: What is John Fryer's strategy to improve student achievement? What are critical elements of that strategy? Participants are likely to make the following comments:

- The district's five-year strategic plan comprised of Fryer's "High Five" priorities: (1) Academic achievement, (2) Safety and discipline, (3) High performance management, (4) Learning communities, and (5) Accountability. Through the five year goals and performance metrics for each of the "High Five," the strategy promotes coherence among the district's work, resources, and expectations.

- Accountability for results is a key driver for performance. The adoption of performance and content standards further strengthens the alignment between teacher practice and expectations for student achievement.

- To rigorously implement standards-based instruction, Fryer realizes that schools need accurate and timely data to monitor the performance of teachers and students and adjust instructional approaches in order to meet the needs of individual students. In this strategy, principals assume new responsibilities as "instructional leaders." Math and literacy coaches support principals and teachers with the implementation of standards and data-driven

decision-making and the required coaching to change the teacher's behavior in the classroom.

Diagnostic analysis (28 minutes)

The conversation can now shift to discussing the relationship between the district's strategy and the PMM system. Participants move from theory to practice by gaining an understanding of the complexity and challenge of constructing and managing an effective system. The data system in DCPS is more sophisticated than in most large urban public school districts, and it is important that the instructor not comment on its merits. This neutral positioning encourages students to challenge each other and the system's effectiveness.

As DCPS Chief of Staff Nancy Snyder remarked during a case interview, "We're data rich but strategy poor." District and school leaders must learn how to sustain a virtuous cycle of learning and inquiry which comprises: (1) identifying and analyzing the indicators deemed most relevant for improving teaching and learning, (2) using the data to inform managerial and instructional decisions, (3) evaluating and modifying results, (4) sharing and integrating new knowledge, and (5) adjusting the indicators as necessary. This creates a continuous learning process in which managers constantly adapt and improve the data collected and its usage based on experience over time.

Participants could be asked to rate the district's PMM system by assigning a letter grade A through F. This provides a snapshot of the class's perspectives and can encourage a lively discussion particularly if the instructor call on the extreme positions first to show the polarity of opinions. Participants with varying viewpoints should give their rationale for the letter grade they awarded. The instructor can briefly summarize participants' responses and record them on the board.

This exercise should help promote a more nuanced discussion of the pros and cons of the district's PMM system. The instructor can pose an explicit question such as: If you were a teacher, what would you see as the strengths and weaknesses of the DCPS performance measurement and management system? If you were a principal? Superintendent or senior district manager? (see Exhibit 2 for a sample board plan). The instructor should push participants to be as specific as possible in their answers and may ask a follow up question such as: How or why is this element of the system beneficial? or How or why is this a problem?

The purpose of this conversation is not for participants to drill down into the merits of specific elements of the AIDE reports or other tools, as this could consume too much time and the major educational objectives could be lost in the details. Rather, the purpose is to help participants think managerially—*How does this data help me meet all students' needs? How should it or could it?* By asking participants to identify with various users of the PMM system, the discussion should help them realize that these users have different, perhaps even conflicting, needs.

Possible areas of discussion might include the following:

Positive Elements of the PMM System:

- **AIDE easily identifies the lowest performing students.** Enables students to be scheduled into specific classes and receive targeted instructional interventions

- **School and classroom observation rubrics are aligned with the district's strategy.** Helps promote standards-based instruction.

- **AIDE reports are user-friendly, color-coded and accessed at the school site.** Helps promote a culture shift and elevate staff's skill sets to analyze and use data.

- **AIDE reports are aligned with state and federal accountability requirements.** Saves district and school leaders time, simplifies reporting requirements.

- **MAP management tool.** Saves principals and school leadership teams time by focusing them on specific indicators and describing specific ways to use information.

- **DCPS data warehouse enables district to access longitudinal student data at any time, create reports in any format, and aggregate or disaggregate data as needed.** Enables school and district personnel to identify performance gaps by school, teacher, and student and target interventions accordingly.

Drawbacks to the PMM System:

- **No information on what to do for students once gaps are identified.** Data in a vacuum is not helpful, need to link data to managerial and instructional strategies.

- **Insufficient benchmarks and assessments.** Achievement data not timely, principals and teachers unsure of how to adjust instructional approaches on a daily basis.

- **Challenge to communicate data to parents and students in a clear and accessible fashion.** This makes it more difficult to convince them that students should participate in after-school or other programs.

- **Only two years' worth of achievement data.** Need more longitudinal data to see how student's strengths and weaknesses were addressed over time and learn which instructional strategies were most effective.

- **System is highly dependent on principals.** Problematic because all principals won't have the capacity to analyze data or know how to make effective, data-driven decisions.

- **Teachers not consulted about types of data that would be useful to them, and they have the most knowledge about what works and what doesn't work for specific students.** Teachers may have a better idea of what data they need to evaluate their own instructional approaches. Teachers may also lack buy-in to school changes if they have limited input in deciding what data is relevant.

- **Lack of confidence in practice exams that were developed in house and predicted low scores on the state test.**

It is likely that participants will mention the state and federal NCLB accountability metrics. In the interest of time, it is important to underscore how the external environment inevitably influences, but should not be the only determinant of, the internal PMM system. The instructor should discourage a lengthy debate. While participants familiar with external metrics may raise legitimate concerns their validity (i.e. standardized test scores, NCLB adequate yearly progress targets, etc.), this line of discussion could easily redirect the conversation from the managerial analysis at the heart of the case.

Role play (10 minutes)

Following the previous discussion, the instructor may introduce a role play of the possible conversation between Wright and her Regional Superintendent Mary Brown that is set up in the introduction and closing of the case. Having the role play in this part of the session provides additional energy to the discussion and personalizes the tension of the case. Participants have an opportunity to experience Wright's feelings at the end of her first-year at Lake Shore—her disappointment at seeing her school's scores go down compounded by having to justify her managerial decisions to her supervisor, not to mention convincing Brown of her efficacy as a principal.

Select one participant to be Region III Superintendent Mary Brown and one participant to be Iranetta Wright. Ask the two participants to role play Brown calling a meeting with Wright to discuss Lake Shore's 2004 FCAT results, her annual performance evaluation, and goals for SY05. The instructor may wish to invite other participants to briefly discuss how

they might have handled the conversation differently. (The instructor may allude to this role play at the beginning of class and actually identify the participants to role play. This simulates the reality of Wright and Brown who each had time to prepare. It may also contribute to better discussion.)

Action planning (20 minutes)

This discussion includes much more than can be discussed in the allotted time. The instructor should choose which areas are most important based on the placement of the case in a curriculum and the primary focus and experience of participants.

Participants will propose their recommendations for Lake Shore Middle School and the district. It is useful to suggest that many organizational elements must be managed effectively to achieve high-performance in school districts. As the case underscores, a PMM system alone is insufficient, but must be accompanied by a supportive culture, resources, structures, and systems, as well as be responsive to various stakeholders. The Public Education Leadership Project (PELP) Coherence Framework can be introduced to help participants consider all of the organizational elements that need to be managed in a coherent fashion to support data-driven decision making. However, it is important not to spend classroom time actually teaching the Framework. A suggested teaching plan follows.

First, elicit participants' recommendations for improving performance measurement and management district-wide, and specifically, at Lake Shore with the following questions: What are your recommendations to the district for enhancing the use of data to improve student performance? If you were Wright, what would you do next year to improve students' performance and what role would data play in your strategy?

Participants' recommendations should be as specific as possible and might include:

Recommendations for Fryer:

- Develop ability to correlate achievement results with curricular, instructional, and managerial practices so that district (and schools) can share effective strategies and build a body of knowledge about how to interpret data and use it to drive improvement

- Ensure system is improved yearly based on experience using the data, and streamlined if necessary, so that district and school leaders are focusing on fewer indicators deemed to be most relevant for improving student achievement

- Integrate more frequent benchmark and assessment data into AIDE

Recommendations for Wright:

- Create system and processes for teachers to share what works and what doesn't (Lesson plans, instructional strategies, assessments)

- Establish feedback loops—mandatory follow-up meeting for every classroom observation

- Have coaches and teachers design more frequent assessments by department

The instructor can briefly introduce the notion of managing for coherence and the Framework's five categories (resources, culture, systems, structure, and stakeholders). Participants' will see that their previous responses fall into the systems category. As time permits, the instructor can use the following questions to address the four remaining categories and organize participants' responses accordingly. The instructor can begin eliciting recommendations for Wright and Lake Shore.

Culture: What norms, values and behaviors are required to support PMM at Lake Shore?

- Insure that data is not perceived as mostly for accountability but for learning

- Incentives and rewards for collaboration among teachers

- Elicit teachers' feedback about their challenges last year and recommendations for SY05

- Teachers visit other teachers' classrooms

- Mentors for first-year teachers

Structures: What communication networks, roles and responsibilities should be developed at Lake Shore?

- Mandatory monthly department meetings

- Evaluate roles and responsibilities of grade-level house administrators—strengthen accountability

Resources: How should Wright utilize and develop the school's human, financial, and non-financial (e.g. time) resources?

- More time for teachers to analyze student work together and evaluate instructional strategies

- Leadership training for coaches and administrators

- Induction program for new teachers

- Ongoing and individualized professional development for all teachers

Stakeholders: How should Wright strengthen support among parents, teachers, and school advisory council?

- Monthly newsletter to parents

- Parent information meetings and materials about after-school programs and other safety nets for at-risk students

The next part of the discussion may elicit participants' recommendations for how the district can strengthen its performance measurement and management system, data-driven decision making in schools, and improved educational outcomes. Suggested questions to pose include: What should the district's role be? If you were Regional Superintendent Mary Brown or Superintendent John Fryer, what steps would you take to support Iranetta Wright and her staff to improve student achievement at Lake

Shore and other low-performing schools in SY05?

Specific framework questions and possible responses follow:

Culture: What norms, values and behaviors are required to support PMM in the district?

- Incentives for administrators and teachers to serve in low-performing schools

- Incentives for collaboration across schools

Structures: what communication networks, roles and responsibilities should be developed?

- Networking and mentoring programs for teachers, principals, and coaches

Resources: How should DCPS develop and utilize its human, financial, and non-financial (e.g. time, information technology) resources?

- Induction program for new teachers

- Early release time for teachers to meet together

- Additional math and/or literacy coach for schools with FCAT decline

Stakeholders: How should the district build support among parents, teachers, the board, school advisory councils, and the broader community?

- Bring in business alliance members to help principals think through strategy, school management, public relations

- Establish monthly working group with teachers, principals, union, and coaches to evaluate effectiveness of AIDE, identify challenges, issue recommendations

- Strengthen board leadership and ownership of DCPS performance

Closing (2 minutes)

The closing allows participants to leave class with some generalizable lessons about the challenges of managing with data for higher performance. A suggested closing follows:

The easy answer for a naysayer would be that

data are not critical for improving the performance of schools and students. An alternative response would recognize organizational learning and improvement as a complex, difficult, non-linear, and long-term process. Maybe Wright doesn't have the right data, or maybe she hasn't figured out how to use the data effectively. I think we would all agree that informed progress is better than uninformed progress. This is the first time many public school leaders are trying to manage with data.

Learning how to improve organizational performance is a journey, not a destination. District and school leaders must learn how to sustain a virtuous cycle of learning and inquiry which comprises: (1) identifying and analyzing the indicators deemed most relevant for improving teaching and learning, (2) using the data to inform managerial and instructional decisions, (3) evaluating and modifying processes, (4) sharing and integrating new knowledge, and (5) adjusting the indicators as necessary. This creates a continuous learning process in which managers constantly adapt and improve the data collected and its usage based on experience over time.

Notes

1. SY is a PELP convention that denotes "school year." For example, SY04 refers to the 2003–2004 school year.

2. See "Note on the PELP Coherence Framework," PEL-010, Boston: Harvard Business School Publishing.

3. For a more in-depth discussion of theory of action and strategy, see the "Note on Strategy in Public Education" by Stacey Childress, PEL–011.

4. Childress, PEL–011.

Using Data to Improve Instruction at the Mason School

Overview

As the demands for accountability in public education grow, school officials face increasing pressure to improve student performance on standardized tests. Often, district administrators approach the challenge of raising test scores by exerting pressure downward in the system and imposing sanctions on schools that fail or offering rewards to those that succeed. Such approaches are rooted in the belief that teachers already know what they should do to improve instruction—they simply need to try harder. Although sheer effort can initially yield positive results, it is seldom sufficient to sustain growth.

When teachers have easy access to current and relevant information about their students' performance, they are able to diagnose their needs and better adapt the focus and pace of their teaching. Similarly, when a team of teachers at a school has ready access to detailed assessment results, it can make informed curriculum decisions, ensuring that it will cover all essential topics, and it can monitor the progress of all students.

However, most school districts are unprepared to support this type of data analysis. Standards-based assessment is a reasonably new enterprise. Districts may lack the technical tools and expertise needed to ensure access to timely assessment data by teachers and school-level leaders. Complicating matters further is the propensity of different departments within the central office to work at cross purposes, issuing contradictory directives or providing incompatible information. In their attempts to acquire a better summary of their schools' performance relative to state or federal expectations, district officials typically neglect their teachers' needs for formative assessments that help guide instruction. School districts must increase their capacity to provide, interpret, and utilize data in support of high-quality teaching and learning among adults and students alike.

"Using Data to Improve Instruction at the Mason School," PEL-047, focuses on the Boston Public Schools' approaches to analyzing and providing access to assessment data. This case, developed for the Public Education Leadership Project at Harvard University, describes for other school leaders, executives and graduate students

This note was prepared by Professor Susan Moore Johnson and Research Associate Tiffany K. Cheng.

the challenges and realities of leading and sustaining large-scale organizational change in an urban public school district. The Mason Elementary School is used to illustrate how teachers can use data systematically to improve instruction and the performance of all students.

A key concept in the case is achieving and sustaining organizational *coherence*. This refers to the dynamic process by which leaders manage all of the elements of the organization (e.g., culture, resources, systems, structures, and stakeholders) to support effective strategy execution. To introduce students to the concept of organizational coherence in a public education setting, the instructor should assign the "Note on the PELP Coherence Framework," PEL-010, as a prereading.

Case Summary

In this case, Principal Janet Owens is asked by her deputy superintendent to prepare for a possible meeting with the incoming superintendent. Owens, the principal at the Samuel Mason Elementary School (hereinafter referred to as "the Mason"), prepares to explain her school's successes in raising student performance levels for all students. The case opens with a history of accountability in the Boston Public Schools (BPS), from the market-based system of Controlled Choice that was introduced during desegregation to the standards-based accountability that was implemented under NCLB (the No Child Left Behind Act). For more than 40 years, the district has faced the challenge of serving all students, and recently it has focused on reducing the variability of performance among schools and between student sub-groups. A short history of former superintendent Payzant's tenure is provided to help the reader understand Payzant's reliance on data and professional development to improve instruction and student performance. The mission and work of BPS' primary partner,

the Boston Plan for Excellence (BPE) is also noted in this opening section.

The case then outlines the various tools developed by the district to assist principals, teachers, and schools in improving instruction. Early tools for tracking assessment data were cumbersome and time-consuming. Finally, BPS and the BPE created two tools that seemed to better support teachers' work with data: MyBPS Assessment and FAST-R. However, the central office is left without access to MyBPS Assessment, making it impossible for teachers to closely compare performance of classrooms and schools on the state's assessments. There is also some lack of alignment and coherence among departments of the central office as they prepare to provide teachers with additional assessment tools.

The remaining part of the case documents the Mason's sustained improvements in student performance and offers the reader a more detailed view of the school's leaders, processes, supports, resources, and culture that work together to enable high-quality teaching and learning. The case ends with the thoughts of Owens as well as other district administrators and outside partners regarding the new superintendent's possible priorities and demands as he plans a districtwide improvement strategy.

Positioning

Overall, this case could be used in a wide variety of settings and with different audiences, ranging from experienced school leaders to graduate students in education, business, or management courses. It was written to be used in the PELP executive education program for school leaders. The Mason case intends to offer readers a chance to integrate theories of organizational alignment and change in the public school setting through the story of a local school's efforts to improve student outcomes.

Learning Objectives

By design, this case offers participants the opportunity to consider different uses of assessment data within a school district. It asks students to compare the needs that schools and district offices have for information and illustrates how a school can be organized to ensure that teachers use data effectively as individuals and as a group. Potential learning objectives include:

- **Recognize different types of assessments.** Participants will learn to distinguish between the district's summative assessment needs—information about performance across schools—and the teachers' needs for both summative and formative assessments—which provide "live" feedback about their instructional effectiveness. Districts and schools have different data needs, both of which must be met.

- **Explore technology challenges and choices.** By reviewing the sequence of approaches considered and used by BPS, students can begin to grasp the complex tools and skills needed to build and maintain a responsive and informative data system.

- **Understand the need for alignment among departments.** While the district's office of research and evaluation generally maintains responsibility for assessments, initiatives and programs must be systematically linked to administrators in other departments with responsibility for curriculum, student services, and technology. When these departments fail to collaborate on a strategy's design and implementation, teachers and principals will not have the tools they need to improve instruction.

- **Identify school-based needs.** In addition to having access to technology tools through the district, effective analysis and use of data at the school level requires additional supports: an expert who understands the links between data analysis and instruction, a principal who helps the staff maintain its focus, and sufficient resources and flexibility to ensure that teachers can work together.

- **Develop an understanding of a school culture where data is used effectively.** One of the key levers for school improvement is the development and active management of organizational culture. This case highlights a principal's deliberate efforts to understand and provide what her teachers need while also holding high expectations for them to use data in deciding what and how to teach. Schools where teachers work interdependently in using data to improve instruction develop strong norms that support critical reflection on instructional practice.

Assignment

Before class, participants should read "Using Data to Improve Instruction at the Mason School," PEL-047, and should consider the questions below. The "Note on the PELP Coherence Framework," PEL-010, should also be assigned if it has not been read previously.

Discussion Questions

1. How would you evaluate the effectiveness of BPS' central office so far in developing an informative and responsive system for data analysis?

2. What are the key elements of the Mason's success? Which of these can be transported to other schools? Which are more difficult to develop?

3. What are the components of an assessment system that is aligned with the needs of individual schools and the priorities of the district?

4. What advice would you give the new superintendent?

Teaching Plan

This 80-minute teaching plan is based on an executive education course designed for PELP participants. The teaching plan can be modified to suit a 75-minute or 90-minute session depending on the purpose and schedule of the course.

Summary

I. **Introduction.** (5 minutes)

II. **Central office evaluation.** (20 minutes)

III. **The elements of the Mason's success.** (20 minutes)

IV. **A model assessment system for the district.** (15 minutes)

V. **Recommendations: Advising the new superintendent.** (20 minutes)

VI. **Closing.** (5 minutes)

Introduction (5 minutes)

The instructor might draw upon material from the Overview above to frame the case discussion. One sample opening follows:

Using assessments for accountability is only the most recent step in the BPS' long pursuit of equity. However, simply testing students provides no assurance that they will be taught better. Rather, improved instruction depends on teachers having and effectively using detailed data about their students' performance. Although school-based approaches to data analysis are especially promising because they allow the principal and teachers to track students' progress from grade to grade, schools must rely on the district to provide timely access to the assessments and results that they need. By examining the experience of the Mason School within the context of the Boston Public Schools' effort, we can better understand the working relationship between the school and the district. Let's get started.

Central office evaluation (20 minutes)

The discussion can begin with an evaluation of the central office's success in building an effective system for data analysis. Instructors should ask participants to evaluate the district on a scale of 1 (lowest) to 4 (highest). Once the instructor tabulates the scores on the board, students will see the range of responses and the general score for the district. The instructor should ask students who assigned a score of 4 to explain their rationale. The instructor can begin to make two lists: one that summarizes the responses of those who graded the district with scores of 4 or 3, the second that summarizes the responses of those who gave scores of 1 or 2. In filling out these lists, it works best to begin with the extremes (4 and 1) and then to add any remaining reasons from those who scored the district with 3 or 2. This helps to highlight distinctions between what worked and what did not work. Note that students may interpret and assess different aspects of the same point differently. For example, one student may praise the district for creating MyBPS Assessment because it meets teachers' needs, while another may criticize the same decision because it limited district administrators' access to detailed school-based data. In this case, MyBPS Assessment should be included in both lists.

Typical responses to the question, "How would you evaluate the effectiveness of BPS' central office so far in developing an informative and responsive system for data analysis?" include:

Positives (4 and 3):

- Recognizing teachers' needs for data

- Building new systems when old approaches proved inadequate

- Moving from paper-based to computer-based systems

- Engaging skilled partners outside the district

- Encouraging school-based teams to attend the HGSE course

- Making MyBPS Assessment easily accessible to each teacher

- Providing professional development to support principals and teachers

- Having the pilot school option to provide autonomies in scheduling, staffing, budget, governance, and curriculum

Negatives (2 and 1):

- Lack of clear and consistent responsibility for developing an assessment system

- Lack of alignment and cooperation among departments of central office

- Neglect of underperforming schools

- Slow pace of change

- Favoring successful schools in providing coaches and professional development

- Creating MyBPS Assessment without providing access to central office administrators for detailed school-based data

- Failure to develop a formative assessment that teachers can readily use

- A failure to scale up from exemplary schools

Given that all items on these lists cannot be discussed in detail, the instructor should guide the students to focus on those that are most important. Since the factors that supported success at the Mason will be discussed in the subsequent section, they may be put on hold for now, while the class focuses more at the district level. A key decision that was made at the district level—that MyBPS Assessment should be constructed using the existing MyBPS platform—had far-reaching implications for management. If there are both teachers and district administrators participating in the discussion, a debate may emerge about the wisdom of this decision. Those considering it from the district's perspective are likely to argue that central office administrators surrendered crucial access to data that they might have used to compare schools, grade levels within schools,

and classrooms. Those who discuss this case from the perspective of the classroom are likely to say that this decision shields the teacher from unwarranted intrusion by district officials who are more intent on top-down control than bottom-up learning.

In this discussion and the segments that follow, a distinction will emerge between "summative" assessments, which provide information across groups of students reporting on their level of mastery, and "formative" assessments, which are diagnostic in nature and yield information about areas of strength and weakness for individuals or groups. In this case, there are few true formative assessments—FastR—although schools and teachers seek to use data drawn from parts of the MCAS (a summative assessment) to inform their teaching.

The elements of the Mason's success (20 minutes)

Participants will likely agree that the Mason's teachers and principal have developed effective systems for analyzing data and using it to inform instruction. This discussion is designed to help students recognize the many elements that enabled this school to make such progress. Participants should be asked, "What are the key elements that enabled the Mason's improvement and success?" Likely responses include:

- Access to the district's support and resources (MyBPS, FastR, coaches, training)

- A principal who relies on teacher leaders, while also holding teachers accountable for data usage and results

- A teacher leader (Hilary Shea, the Data Queen) who is knowledgeable about using data and is committed to helping teachers develop skills in data analysis

- Pilot school status, which gives the Mason autonomy in

Staffing: Positions can be created, split, or eliminated in response to the school's needs.

Budget: The school can allocate its lump sum of resources as it chooses to support its program.

Curriculum and assessment: The Mason can choose whether to use the BPS curriculum and (with the exception of MCAS) the district's assessments.

Schedule: A daily schedule that includes six Preparation and Development periods each week, making possible a weekly 90-minute block of Common Planning Time.

- The Boston Teacher Residency (BTR) Program, which provides the school with a corps of full-time teaching interns at no additional expense

- Experience with the Literacy Collaborative, which accustomed teachers to collecting and analyzing data

- Having every teacher licensed in regular and special education so that the school can function efficiently as a full-inclusion school

- A strong teaching staff (most served initially as interns before being hired), most of whom are teacher leaders with specific responsibilities and some extra pay

- Routine review of every student's performance, including a safety-net approach to providing supplementary instruction to individual students who need it

The instructor should probe participants further in their analysis by asking such questions as, "Which of these elements seem easy to replicate at other schools? Which of them require additional resources or higher levels of organizational capacity?" Students should be encouraged to think of practices the district could support or create that would promote high performance at other schools.

A model assessment system for the district (15 minutes)

In this segment of the class, we ask students to step back and define the components of a model assessment system for a large urban school district. Students are not expected to stay within the realities of Boston, but to look more broadly at what is needed and what might work. They should be encouraged to take into account the needs of the district and the needs of the schools. Students, working in dyads or triads, should spend 5–7 minutes comparing and discussing their lists prepared in response to discussion question #3 (see list of questions starting on p. 3).

Their lists may contain:

- A user-friendly tool that enables the following to occur:
- District officials to review data by school and by grade
- Principals and school-based data coaches to examine data for all classes and individuals
- Individual teachers to examine data for individual students and to compare class data with other classes within the school and with other schools
- Formative assessments for all subjects and grades, including an extensive data bank that is available to individual teachers
- A cross-functional central office team, composed of members from various departments, that is charged with designing and coordinating the district's approach to supporting data analysis
- Flexibility in staffing, budget, curriculum, and assessment, and scheduling for schools that achieve some basic level of achievement
- Funded positions for school-based coaches in data analysis
- A system of professional development that includes both workshops and computer-based modules

- Structured opportunities for school-to-school visits by teams of teachers and principals
- External partners with special expertise in technology, training, and organizational development to assist the district and the schools

Recommendations: Advising the new superintendent (20 minutes)

The final substantive section of this class returns to the original question of the case—how to advise the new superintendent. The instructor can build this discussion from the list of model components from the prior segment, posing this question: "Given this list, what would you recommend as next steps for the incoming superintendent? Where should he start?"

This discussion will reintroduce the realities of BPS. Instructors should ask the students to make a set of recommendations about how to move ahead on this agenda. If time permits, two or three students could play the role of consultants advising Rivera, the new superintendent, who is played by the instructor. "Rivera" presses the students to explain their priorities and strategies. Students may be inclined to advise the superintendent to unilaterally make several major changes at once—e.g., grant autonomy in staffing to all schools; fund positions for data coaches in all schools; create an interdepartmental task force within the central office; and an expanded menu of professional development. In response, the instructor may ask the advisors which initiatives will depend on additional resources or collaboration with others, including the union and external partners.

Closing (5 minutes)

During the final minutes of the class, the instructor can summarize some of the priorities and tensions that emerged from the discussion. These might include the need for alignment and coherence in the central office, the importance of technological expertise to ensure that the system is current and user-friendly, and the tension between the needs of the district for oversight and the needs of the school for autonomy to interpret and act on their data.

Compensation Reform at Denver Public Schools

Overview

The case, "Compensation Reform at Denver Public Schools," focuses on how public school leaders in one urban district worked together to design an innovative system for compensating teachers. The plan was meant to align pay with organizational improvement. This case is one in a series developed by the HGSE/HBS Public Education Leadership Project (PELP) to showcase management issues in urban public school districts, in the hopes of describing for other school leaders the challenges and realities of leading and sustaining large-scale organizational change in an urban public school districts.

Specifically, this case describes the evolution of teacher compensation reform at Denver Public Schools (DPS), from its origins as a pay-for-performance (PFP) pilot, jointly sponsored by DPS and the Denver Classroom Teacher's Association (DCTA) from 1999–2003, to the adoption of a new compensation system in March 2004. This new system, called ProComp, was developed by the DPS/DCTA Joint Task Force on Teacher Compensation (JTF) Whereas most school districts use a standardized salary scale, which offers the same pay to all teachers who have the same seniority and academic degrees, under ProComp individual teachers can earn higher pay by increasing their skills and knowledge, contributing to improved student performance, receiving successful performance evaluations, and serving in the most academically challenging schools.

Pay-for-performance is not new to the education sector.[1] However, with recent demand for public accountability and increased use of standardized assessments, many school district leaders, policy-makers, and community members are once again calling for its adoption. This case provides a timely opportunity to consider one recent experiment with compensation reform.

Learning Objectives

This case can be used in a variety of settings. It provides an account of the PFP pilot implementation and the subsequent development of ProComp at DPS. Together, these two narratives provide a vehicle for discussing the use of pay as an incentive in public schools, the strengths and weaknesses of this particular system and the challenges for a school district in initiating and sustaining such a reform. It also offers an oppor-

This note was prepared by professors Allen S. Grossman and Susan Moore Johnson and Research Associate Jennifer M. Suesse.

tunity for participants to discuss the challenge of creating systemic coherence and building institutional capacity for accountability.

The learning objectives for this case are:

1. **Organizational change.** Discuss what allowed DPS, with its multiple stakeholders, to initiate and sustain this reform over time and through multiple changes in district leadership. The class can discuss the process by which this change occurred, analyze which factors enabled change, and consider how an organization can learn from a pilot.

2. **Compensation and incentives.** Understand how all pay systems include incentives that affect performance. Analyze the strengths and weaknesses of ProComp relative to the standardized salary scale. In a context where virtually all pay systems continue to be uniform in structure and deal with inputs rather than outputs, this case introduces the rationale for individualized pay based on teachers' performance and offers the opportunity to consider the use of a compensation system as a lever for organizational improvement.

3. **Systemic coherence and capacity.** Discuss the demands that a new compensation system such as ProComp presents for a district's organization: its structures, systems, capacity and culture. This is an opportunity to apply the PELP coherence model (model included in Exhibit 1) and to consider the processes and managerial capabilities necessary for implementing a pay-for- performance system.

Case Summary

The case begins by providing context and background for evaluating DPS's compensation reform effort, with brief demographic profiles of Denver and DPS, as well as a brief overview of Colorado's reform initiatives. It also provides a summary of the relevant DPS history, culture

and leadership including a brief biography of Superintendent Jerry Wartgow and an outline of DPS-DCTA relations.

A short description of national compensation reform efforts introduces the next section, "Experimenting with Compensation: The PFP Pilot." Then, the case describes how DPS and DCTA worked together to launch the pilot during 1999. Initially a compromise emerging from the bargaining table, the PFP pilot gathered momentum and eventually lasted four years. The case describes how work got started, and what teachers and administrators learned from the process of setting and measuring teacher objectives. It also describes some of the concerns involved with a performance-based compensation plan experiment, including implementation hurdles and required infrastructure. By the pilot's conclusion, 13% of DPS schools participated in the program and the case includes reflections from the many stakeholders on what they learned, as well as a brief summary of the pilot's results.

Finally, the case outlines the transition "From Pilot to ProComp," by describing how DPS launched a joint DPS-DCTA task force to develop ProComp, and then successfully got a majority of DCTA members to vote in favor of implementation. The case concludes with Wartgow and a few School Board leaders musing on future challenges and opportunities of implementing a new compensation system at DPS.

Assignment

Before class, students should read "Compensation Reform at Denver Public Schools," PEL No. 002. This case discussion of compensation reform at Denver Public Schools will focus on the use of teachers' pay as part of a plan for organizational improvement, highlighting topics such as developing institutional capacity for accountability, effecting organizational change, and working to address systemic incoherence. The following four study questions can be assigned to students before class.

Discussion Questions

1. What key factors sustained Denver's compensation reform initiative over 5 years and 5 superintendents?

2. In your estimation, is ProComp an effective incentive system for teachers and for the school district? Why or why not? What actions does it encourage and reward? How does the new system differ from the standardized salary scale? Which approach to pay do you think is better and why?

3. Assuming DPS can raise $25 million from Denver voters, what are the biggest challenges for successful implementation? What advice would you give to the leaders of both the administration and the union for overcoming these challenges?

4. Would you suggest redesigning your district's compensation plan? Why or why not? If yes, is it possible to develop and implement? Why or why not? (*This final question is recommended only if the case is taught to practitioners.*)

Teaching Plan and Analysis

This teaching plan is based on an 80-minute executive education course designed for a class of urban public school leadership teams. The case was written to be used with both executives and graduate students in business, management, or education courses. The teaching plan can be modified to suit a 75-minute or 90-minute session.

Summary

I. **Introduction.** To open the discussion, the instructor may explain the purpose of the case within the context of the course and describe the difficulty in designing good compensation systems in organizations. (5 minutes)

II. **Analysis of ProComp as an incentive system for teachers.** To begin the analysis of ProComp, the instructor may poll participants by saying," I want to ask each of you to step into the shoes of a classroom teacher in Denver. Would you vote in favor or against ProComp?" When participants defend their position, the instructor should push them to highlight the pros and cons of ProComp as an incentive system. Then, the instructor may ask participants to compare the incentives embedded in ProComp versus a standardized salary scale. (25 minutes)

III. **Assessment of ProComp's strengths and weaknesses for DPS.** In this segment, the discussion will focus on the strengths and weaknesses of ProComp with respect to DPS. At this point, the instructor may wish to ask participants to vote on whether DPS should implement ProComp. As participants comment on their position, the instructor may probe further by asking the following questions: "What is the likelihood that this will have an impact on improved student performance and how will that be apparent? What, if any, unintended consequences might arise from ProComp? Is this mostly a rehash of the old system or back door a way to raise teacher's pay? Is it worth the effort? Is this plan too ambitious? Or not ambitious enough?" (20 minutes)

IV. **Analysis of the change process.** During this portion, participants will reflect on the evolution of ProComp and the events that led to its creation. The instructor may begin the discussion by asking, "How did DPS and DCTA reach this point?" The instructor should push participants to focus on the process that enabled the change. Also, the instructor may ask, "What were they trying to accomplish at the very beginning of the pilot? What were the key factors that advanced and sustained this compensation reform initiative?" (20 minutes)

V. **Action planning.** At this point, participants can discuss the actions that stakeholders should take to sustain the change effort. The instructor may use the following questions to begin the dialogue: "If you were Wartgow, Allen, or Jupp, what would you be worried about? What could go wrong? What are the risks of NOT implementing at this stage? How will you know if it's working or how it can be refined? What are the costs if Pro Comp fails?" It is important that participants understand that there needs to be a mechanism in place to continually evaluate and refine the compensation system to keep it aligned with the performance goals of the organization. (15 minutes)

VI. **Update and wrap-up.** In closing, the instructor may review the key learning objectives from the case and provide students with a brief update on the status of ProComp. (5 minutes)

Introduction (5 minutes)

In beginning the class, the instructor can outline the purpose of the case in the context of the course and provide an introduction to the challenges of designing and managing an organization's compensation system. The introduction can be used to set up a vote about whether or not participants, as teachers, would choose to support ProComp. A suggested opening follows:

This case is timely, as conversations are happening around the country regarding the use of incentives in public education. The Denver initiative seems to defy conventional wisdom, which says that it is impossible to replace the standardized pay system used in virtually all public school districts. Over the past century many districts have tried to adopt new pay systems. Performance-based compensation was attempted by 48% of schools in the 1920s and again by 10% of schools in the 1960s, but again and again these reforms failed.[2] Although the final results are not yet in, the Denver initiative won acceptance was sustained over five years and five superintendents.

We'll begin by talking about the incentives embedded in a pay plan and the strengths and weaknesses of this system. Then we'll consider how the change process worked and what will be needed to move ahead with ProComp.

Analysis of ProComp as an incentive system for teachers (25 minutes)

I want to ask each of you to step into the shoes of a classroom teacher in Denver. Would you vote in favor or against ProComp?

By asking participants to respond as teachers might, the initial discussion can focus on the incentives that are embedded in ProComp and standardized pay plans. On the board, tally the responses to the vote. Ask students on each side of the vote, "Why did you vote that way?" It is important that students be reminded that they are voting as an individual teacher would. Also, given the realities of this case, a vote against ProComp is a vote for continuing with the standardized salary scale.

The chart on the next page is a list of reasons that students may offer to explain their votes for or against ProComp. Their responses can be tracked on the board.

As participants offer their reasons, the instructor may probe how the new plan would differ from the standardized salary scale. For example, the student who says that ProComp rewards learning new skills might be asked to explain how this differs from the standardized scale that rewards taking courses and earning degrees. The student may respond that this incentive is more targeted to specific skills that the district identifies. The instructor may also note that the

For ProComp	Against ProComp
• Rewards learning new skills.	• It's too complicated to work.
• Encourages individual initiative and high standards.	• Principals aren't prepared to conduct these evaluations and it is not a good use of their time.
• Incorporates multiple elements.	• Not really that different from what exists already.
• Ensures a base salary so it's not too risky.	• Test scores don't adequately capture what teachers or students are doing.
• Treats teachers with respect; says your work matters.	• Could be used punitively instead of constructively.
• Takes account of student performance.	• Teachers will simply jump through hoops to get more money, but not teach better.
• Gives me credit for teaching well.	• It's not really more fair, since it will reward teachers in some schools at the expense of others.
• Changes how work gets done; encourages individuals to set goals.	• Teachers with the most challenging students will be penalized.
• Evaluation will become more objective and data-driven.	• Performance appraisals don't really change day-to-day performance.
• It's the lesser of two evils.	• Teachers will write objectives that they know they can meet. There will be no rigor.
	• It will undermine collegiality.

longer list of reasons that individuals usually raise against ProComp reveals the challenge of winning approval.

The instructor may choose to provide a brief overview of how incentives in pay systems can have different purposes. A district's approach to distributing pay rewards certain teachers and activities and not others. This can be purposeful or inadvertent. The following can be used on the board or a slide to present some basic distinctions:

Pay as an Attractor → Recruitment and employment of candidates

Pay as a Satisfier → Retention, loyalty, and longevity

Pay as a Motivator → Improved or targeted performance

The students can then discuss the incentives embedded in a standardized salary scale vs.

ProComp. The standardized salary scale is likely to attract candidates who seek certainty about their pay or who can earn more in teaching than in other lines of work. (These may not be the best possible candidates.) It does little to motivate teachers to improve their practice, except to take courses or earn degrees. In contrast, ProComp might attract ambitious candidates and provide the promise of accelerated pay increases. Because ProComp also includes a base salary index, it continues to reward loyalty. The system is primarily designed to encourage more effective teaching, by including additional factors in an individual teacher's pay, such as student outcomes, teaching appraisals, and specific professional skills to be acquired. Throughout this discussion, some participants will argue that this focus on the extrinsic incentive of pay is misguided, since the rewards that motivate teachers are primarily intrinsic, e.g., the satisfaction of watching students succeed. It is worth considering whether (1) this focus on intrinsic rewards simply reveals the kind of people who have been attracted to teaching by the standardized salary scale and (2) whether ProComp would undermine the effectiveness of intrinsic incentives.

If there is time, the students may be asked to discuss whether ProComp meets the basic standards of an effective pay-for-performance system. Researchers have found that such a plan must:

1. Be available to all, rather than only a few

2. Provide a measure of performance that is widely understood to be valid

3. Offer substantial pay differentials so that individuals will bother to invest in the system

4. Provide answers to the following questions from teachers:

   • Why is teacher X being paid more than I am?

   • What can I do to earn higher pay?

Students are likely to agree that the plan is open to everyone. They will probably debate whether the assessments (principals' appraisals, test scores) are valid, in that they do not measure some important student outcomes. When they compare an individual's pay under the old and new systems, they are likely to conclude that the differentials are substantial. Finally, given the detailed specifications of the system, they are likely to agree that the teachers' questions in # 4 can be answered, though perhaps not fully.

If the instructor chooses to spend more time analyzing the components of ProComp, the following questions are worth students' close consideration:

1. What actions does ProComp reward (or punish)?

   • Producing better than average student achievement (penalized for not achieving

minimum on the Colorado Student Assessment Program (CSAP))

   • Receiving good evaluations (penalized for not receiving adequate evaluation)

   • Setting and meting achievement objectives

   • Accruing degrees and Professional Development Units (PDUs)

   • Working in hard-to-staff positions and schools

2. Where are the largest and smallest financial awards in ProComp?

   • Receiving more degrees (9%) and PDUs (2); thus, like the standardized system

   • Student growth (1%); CSAP (3%)

3. How does ProComp compare to the old system?

   • Old system provided longevity pay for teachers ($1263) with > 13 years experience only every 5 years; ProComp enables them to increase earnings every year.

   • Old system offered small increases for new and early-career teachers. Now they can increase earnings at a greater rate, though entry salary remains the same.

   • ProComp gives credit to teachers for attaining more than one master's degree.

Assessment of ProComp's strengths and weaknesses for DPS (20 minutes)

The discussion may then turn from the individual to the system. Depending on the time available, the students may be asked to vote once again on whether they think that ProComp is worth implementing. They would then explain their votes and the instructor may list strengths and weaknesses on the board. This discussion will focus on the system's having the potential for improving student learning and being a good use of resources. It will also require students to consider what it will take to make this system work. As participants begin to list strengths and weaknesses, instructors may choose to probe with some of the following questions:

- What is the likelihood that this will have an impact on improved student performance and how will that be apparent?

- What, if any, unintended consequences might arise from ProComp?

- Is this mostly a rehash of the old system or back door a way to raise teacher's pay?

- This plan is complicated and the benefits may be modest. Is it worth the effort?

- Is this plan too ambitious? Or not ambitious enough?

Strengths/Benefits:

- Phase-in ensures that nobody loses. Therefore, ProComp is politically viable.

- System will attract and retain strong teachers.

- Moves the system to a sharper focus on instruction.

- The Pilot showed that focusing on objectives improved student performance. ProComp will extend that.

- Forces district to be clear about what constitutes adequate progress and to clarify expectations.

- Principals will be given appropriate responsibility as managers.

- Promotes labor-management collaboration.

- Compensates acquisition of knowledge and skills as it happens, instead of in lumps, and connects that learning to work of teaching.

- Change is good.

Weaknesses/Concerns:

- Benefits are not likely to be significant enough to be worth the effort and expense.

- Too complicated to work well.

- District's systems are not adequately aligned to support it.

- May generate unproductive competition among individuals who must work together.

- This is an unproven system.

- Will require extensive investment in principals' professional development.

- ProComp looks shiny and new, but is not really that different from what exists already.

- There are no incentives for principals.

- Students are not assessed for each subject.

- Student assessments and data systems are not yet sophisticated enough to track individual teachers' contributions to student learning.

- Over time, adequate funding will disappear.

- DPS can't afford to fund both old and new systems.

- Teachers are likely to "game" the system rather than improve their teaching.

Analysis of the change process (20 minutes)

It is now opportune to ask the question, "So, how did DPS and DCTA reach this point?" Push the class to reflect on the process that led to this sustained change effort. Ask, "What were they trying to accomplish at the very beginning of the pilot?" "What were the key factors that advanced and sustained this compensation reform initiative?"

Factors That Enabled DPS/DCTA to Advance and Sustain the Effort:

- *Involved multiple stakeholders throughout the process,* including Board members, community organizations, technical assistance providers, foundations, and the press. These groups were able to provide financial, intellectual, and managerial resources without many restrictions, and their involvement helped to maintain the project's visibility, create an avenue for community dialogue, and provide a lever for accountability. Having the Board's support was a critical aspect of maintaining the project's momentum.

- *The political context of accountability* increased educators' readiness to focus this compensation system on outcomes as well as inputs. More frequent and consequential assessments resulting from state and federal laws increased both the legitimacy and the possibility of Denver's having a performance-based pay plan.

- *Pilot structure* protected internal change agents from external pressure and created an "incubator" or "skunkworks" for internal development efforts. This entity became both a formal and informal leadership structure, as well as means for establishing and building trust. Members of the Design Team were able to monitor the morale from both school sites and central office, and the team had a reach into the system—even at the classroom level. One flaw of this system was that principals were left out of the loop. The structure also enabled DCTA and DPS to establish a working partnership that became a vehicle for resolving issues between the two organizations. In retrospect, the Design Team's isolation from the larger system was probably both an advantage and a disadvantage.

- *People*—DCTA assigned some of its best people to work on this effort, and their contributions were noticed. Their capacity for listening helped the pilot to become a linking mechanism and a place for teacher's to give input and feedback, so ideas could emerge from both "top-down" and "bottom-up" sources and changes could occur at both levels. The turnover on both sides, however, was an ongoing challenge.

- *External funding* provided focus, especially since some of that money was intended to supplement individual teachers' paychecks in the form of bonuses. (People pay attention to paychecks). The funding also galvanized some members of the institution to address lack of systemic coherence, and pushed some individuals to identify DPS' lack of a strategy.

- *Creation of OASIS* led to conversation, training, and peer review around objectives that were focused on teachers. It also established the practice of objective setting and tracking student growth, which many regarded as the first step in offering differentiated instruction. OASIS forced the institution to start creating and maintaining the systems necessary to support and reward this practice such as generating and reporting student achievement information in a form accessible to classroom teachers. It also highlighted the limitations of existing student assessments, the lack of agreement upon standards of adequate student progress, the dearth of integrated professional development opportunities, and the need for developing and collecting multiple measures.

Discussion of the change process should also highlight the "warts" of the process, since the case also tells the tale of a very bumpy road. Some key weaknesses include:

- Lack of connection between compensation reform and overarching district strategy

- Lack of plan for implementation. This point is particularly important as the absence of the plan may have been responsible for stoking the position of the opposition at a number of stages of during the process.

- Lack of communication. Often members of the DPS community were not aware of the status of the project or its content. This is even true of teachers who would be most affected by the experiment. One exception to this was the efforts made by the Joint Task Force to maintain a current web site where teachers could pose questions and calculate how ProComp would affect their paycheck.

Action planning (15 minutes)

Performance-based pay plans have collapsed in the past because of bureaucratic bungling, loss of funding, or the failure to adequately explain why some people deserved to be paid more than others. Therefore, the successful launching of ProComp provides no guarantee that it can be sustained. The system must adapt to changes in the composition of the teaching force and the political context. We recommend spending the last segment of this discussion talking about the next steps for Denver leaders. A few discussion questions include:

- If you were Wartgow, Allen, or Jupp, what would you be worried about? What could go wrong?

- What are the risks of NOT implementing at this stage?

- How will you know if it's working or how it can be refined?

- What are the costs if Pro Comp fails?

- Rather than getting into the details of a specific action plan, the purpose of this discussion is to ensure that the class understands that this process is far from over. Even when ProComp, or any new system, is implemented, DPS will need a mechanism to continually evaluate whether or not it is achieving its desired objectives and the ability to modify the system accordingly. In too many cases, compensation and incentive systems are put into place and then left alone, which most often leads to decay.

Update and wrap-up (5 minutes)

In closing, the instructor may review the big ideas from the learning objectives and give participants a brief update on the status of ProComp in DPS. Following is a list of key ProComp updates:

- In November 2005, Denver voters elected to pass the $25 million mill levy to fund ProComp.

Without its passage, ProComp would not exist.

- In January 2006, the new compensation system went into effect for teachers who opted into the system and for all new DPS teachers hired after January 2006. The regular salary schedule will continue to exist until the last teacher in it retires or leaves.

- During the first opt-in period, approximately 30% of Denver teachers joined.

- As of January 2006, approximately 1,200 of DPS's teachers had joined ProComp.

- Nurses have been added to hard the hard to staff position lists and the list of schedules has been expanded.

- DPS set up a Review Panel composed of teachers and administrators to hear pay disputes. The Review Panel has the authority to override a pay denial.

- Only 30% of teachers are affected by a CSAP incentive because it doesn't apply to Grades 1–3, 11, 12 and specialists.

How is the plan different now vs. when the case was written?

- Not much different, although they leave it open to be changed.

- Key additions seem to be the new safeguard Review Panel and more clarity around objectives.

- Lots of field testing of the evaluation system and PDUs.

- ProComp is a 9-year agreement in place from 2004 to 2013. It provides for external evaluation every 3 years. Annual negotiations to improve ProComp will occur from 2007–2013 and be based on evaluations.

- The $25 million levy MUST go to ProComp; a trust agreement between DCTA and DPS assures this.

Finally, when teaching this case to district leaders, we suggest ending class with time for reflection on whether or not ProComp is relevant for them. "If so, how would you modify it to suit your needs?" "If not, what have you learned about your compensation system?"

Notes

1. See Allen Odden, "Incentives, School Organization, and Teacher Compensation," *Rewards and Reforms: Creating Educational Incentives That Work,* ed. Susan H. Fuhrman and Jennifer A. O'Day, San Francisco: Jossey-Bass, 1996, chap. 7. See also Susan Moore Johnson, "Merit Pay for Teachers: A Poor Prescription for Reform," *Harvard Educational Review* 54, no. 2, May 1984, pp. 175–185; Richard J. Murnane and David K. Cohen, "Merit Pay and the Evaluation Problem: Why Most Merit Pay Plans Fail and a Few Survive," *Harvard Educational Review* 56, no. 1, February 1986, pp. 1–17.

2. See Murnane and Cohen, "Merit Pay and the Evaluation Problem."

Exhibit 1
Incentive Slides

Incentives within Organization

- All organizations have incentive systems whether formal or informal. Incentives include:
- Promotions
- Influence
- Decision rights
- Working conditions
- Money
- Recognition
- Incentive strategy is about aligning performance with "the things people value," taking into account all of the richness and complexity of human beings
- Passion and accountability—intrinsic motivation and extrinsic rewards—are complementary features of high performing organizations. (Jack Welch)

Location of Decision Rights

- Centralized—incentive systems aligned around monitoring and control
- Existence of influence activities—lobbying by subordinates
- Decentralized—incentive systems to ensure that those making decisions are accountable for the decisions they make
- Location of specific knowledge not easily transferred
- Intrinsic motivation of employees raised by making decisions

Managing Incentive Systems

- Usually a combination of objective and subjective
- Objective and subjective considerations in constant tension
- Incentive systems cannot just be turned on and let go; they need to be managed
- Generally difficult and messy

Objective Performance Measurement

- Controllability—Difficult to know whether an outcome was the result of controllables (effort, knowledge, skills) or from uncontollables (after school program, parents, luck)
- Alignment—When a job requires multiple tasks, it is typically the case that performance regarding some tasks is easy to measure (e.g., absenteeism, discipline) relative to other tasks (e.g., effective knowledge transfer)
- Interdependency—Value often created by teams of individuals. When given outcome is result of joint performance, difficult to determine individual contributions of any team member

Subjective Performance Evaluation

- Does it include everything an individual does to create value
- Mentoring
- Cooperating
- Leadership
- Accepting unpleasant tasks
- Pleasant to work with and be around
- Requires substantial resources because hard to do well
- Most people dislike evaluating others, especially when performance is weak
- Requires differentiation—claiming and supporting view that some are better performers than others—differentially better and worse than others
- Potential source of conflict
- Result is many evaluators find it easier to give virtually everyone positive evaluations
- Can become politicized—better evaluations to people with whom they worked closely
- Gaming the system—low rankings to people leaving the system

Conclusions

- Relying solely on objective measures—either narrow and misaligned or overly broad and uncontrollable—can have perverse effects
- Organizations fight through the mess and maintain commitment to rigorous subjective evaluation as part of incentive structure
- "Differentiation is hard. Anybody who finds it easy doesn't belong in organization, and anyone who can't do it falls in the same category." —*Jack Welch*

Source: Adapted from Brian J. Hall, HBS No. 904-043 "Incentives Within Organizations."

Managing at Scale in the Long Beach Unified School District

Overview

The purpose of this case, developed for the HGSE/HBS Public Education Leadership Project (PELP), is to examine the managerial mechanisms by which leaders can create and/or materially influence a school district's organizational culture to support continuous improvement of student outcomes. It illustrates that effective management of a district is highly dependent on accountability at all levels based on the utilization of data and a set of integrated processes/procedures that lead to organizational coherence. It shows how the management at the Long Beach Unified School District (LBUSD) created a culture of performance and accountability by using management levers available to them. The case can also be used to show how the effective use of differentiating and integrating mechanisms are powerful forces for managing decentralization at scale.

Case Summary

In this case, a fictitious, newly appointed urban public school superintendent, Holly Evans, visits LBUSD to study its organization and approaches to improving student performance.

The bulk of the case focuses on the culture that supports and drives accountability in the district. Evans participates in a focus group with principals from around the district and from all levels where they all describe the culture of the district as results driven, collaborative, data driven, and focused on children. The principals also discuss the implications of the district's policies of rotating principals across school sites and to the district office and setting goals for each school year. They explain that there is a friendly competition among schools.

Evans then interviews each of the district's assistant superintendents—one for elementary, one for middle, and one for high schools. Each describes her philosophy of management, including hiring, goal setting, and evaluation. Finally, Evans learns about the centralized professional development efforts across the district. The case concludes with questions for her consideration (and those of the participants): "What have I learned? Where should I begin? What will transfer to my district?"

This note was prepared by professors James E. Austin and Allen S. Grossman and Research Associate Jennifer M. Suesse.

Positioning

This case could be used in a wide variety of settings and with different audiences, ranging from experienced school leaders to graduate students in business, management, or education courses. It was written to be used in a series of management cases for an executive education program for teams of school district leaders. This case intends to offer participants an opportunity to consider the role of culture as a tangible and essential organizational element that managers can explicitly create and sustain.

Learning Objectives

- **Develop operational and strategic understanding of managing organizational culture to enhance performance.** Broaden proficiency for identifying, developing, and managing organizational culture by illustrating management levers that can be used to influence culture directly (e.g., language, values, and norms) and indirectly (e.g., accountability systems, reporting structures, etc.). Show how culture can be a powerful mechanism for integrating schools around a district-wide improvement strategy in a fundamentally decentralized system.

- **Demonstrate how coherent organizations can reinforce and are reinforced by organizational culture.** Stimulate reflection: How can I build a strong, productive culture in my district? What levers are available, and how are they managed?

- **Deepen understanding of how one can successfully manage a system containing elements of two opposing management structures.** Managing a decentralized system does not imply a lack of central management but the deliberate creation and sustaining of integrating mechanisms.

- **Analyze integrating and differentiating mechanisms.** Deepen understanding of

PELP coherence framework and the interaction of individual organizational elements through the analysis of one district's strategy for managing a portfolio of schools with varying capacities of leadership, performance, and student demographics. A shared and well-understood culture is the primary integrating mechanism across all schools.

- **Develop appreciation for how an accountability system can be crafted and implemented.** At LBUSD, the expectations are clear that all principals will improve, even those in higher-performing schools. The case highlights how this is not just a "system" but a nuanced, complex management process that must be continuously attended to.

Assignment

Before class, participants should read "Managing at Scale in the Long Beach Unified School District," PEL-041; we recommend that the "Note on the PELP Coherence Framework," PEL-010, also be assigned if it has not been read previously. This case can but need not be taught following "Long Beach Unified School District (A): Change That Leads to Improvement," PEL-006.

Discussion Questions

1. How would you describe the culture at LBUSD?

2. How well does the district achieve accountability at the school and district level?

3. In what ways are the key-results group and professional development important to district performance?

4. What other factors contribute to the district's performance?

Teaching Plan and Analysis

This 80-minute teaching plan is based on an executive education course session for PELP's class of urban public school leadership teams. The teaching plan can be modified to suit a 90-minute or 120-minute session by lengthening the work in dyads.

Summary

I. **Introduction.** (2 minutes)

II. **Culture: The Long Beach Way.** (25 minutes)

III. **Culture as management practice.** (25 minutes)

IV. **In-class working groups focused on analysis of individual school district cultures.** (10 minutes)

V. **Culture reports and embedding mechanisms.** (13 minutes)

VI. **Closing.** (5 minutes)

Introduction (2 minutes)

The instructor can begin class by outlining the purpose of the case in the context of the course in two minutes or less. Overall, this session is designed to highlight an organization's deliberate approach to creating a culture of performance in order to effectively manage schools with differing performance and leadership capacities. Themes of organizational coherence, integration, and differentiation are central throughout the discussion. This case was written to offer participants an opportunity to consider the use of culture as a powerful and critical mechanism for managing a district to high performance. (While the case can be taught without reference to the PELP coherence framework, if the instructor decides to use it she may want to put an overhead of it up in the classroom. If the "Note on the PELP Coherence Framework" is not assigned, then the introduction can easily be modified to eliminate the reference.) One sample opening follows:

In this case, we have the opportunity to discuss the important concepts of organizational coherence, integration, and differentiation. We will consider whether the programs and organizational elements fit together to create a coherent organization that is focused on driving and supporting teaching and learning in the classroom. Behind our analysis lies the original PELP coherence framework. This is a visual representation of the elements necessary for organizational coherence: strategy, stakeholders, systems, structures, resources, and culture. These elements surround the instructional core, which includes the interactions between students and teachers and specific content. The elements of the instructional core interact with one another to create the fundamental activities of a public schools system— teaching and learning.

In our discussion today, we will try to understand how the organizational elements of a school district can work together to facilitate greater learning in the classroom, with a particular focus on organizational culture. We will scrutinize Long Beach's culture as well as probe how their management approaches contribute to organizational coherence. How did the current culture come into being at Long Beach? Is it consistent at all levels? What specifically are the leaders doing to create and sustain this culture? What is the impact of these activities on what happens in the classroom?

Culture: The Long Beach Way (25 minutes)

The discussion should focus on what deliberate actions LBUSD management takes to create and sustain a culture that coheres both to the other organizational elements as well as the district's improvement strategy. It is important for participants to create a common and concrete definition of organizational culture. While the right culture is critical to establishing a coherent and high-performing organization, it is often considered by managers as the fuzzy, amorphous element of an organization. Many leaders, even in business, do not fully appreciate that they can take deliberate actions to shape their organization's culture. There are many definitions of culture, but we chose the following for its relative simplicity:

Culture = pattern of shared values, norms, and basic assumptions that guide behavior[1]

This part of the discussion can be opened with the question: "What is culture?"

Based on LBUSD's definition, which the instructor should capture on a side board, participants should be asked, "What are the key elements that make up 'The Long Beach Way'?" We recommend keeping the discussion focused on describing the LBUSD culture:

- **Kids come first.**

- **All children matter/All can succeed.**

- **All people throughout the system must continuously improve.** In LBUSD, this belief leads to a deep commitment to professional development and continuous improvement in various competency areas. These activities act as the means for investing in and developing educators' knowledge, skill, and commitment. Using professional development to build internal capacity affects the organization's structure, system, and culture. This is a good example of how the organizational elements in the framework must work together to support the strategy.

- **The organization's success is ultimately measured by what happens in the classroom.** Success is viewed as a collaborative achievement. Since values are often defined by the actions one takes when things are not going well, it was particularly significant when the district preserved funding levels for professional development and classroom teachers during budget cuts. The ways in which leadership communicates its values are especially telling when it is allocating pieces of a shrinking pie.

- **Adults have both individual and collective responsibility for student perfor-**

mance. This notion of universal responsibility yields accountability and is created by what leaders do. For example, LBUSD enacts a rotation policy and creates incentives for meeting outcome goals, which in turn affects behavior.

- **Trust between the district and the schools and among the personnel at all levels is critical.** Trust is built by actions, as noted in the previous bullet.

- **Relationships are important.** One clear example would be LBUSD's historically cordial relationship with the union. There is a heavy focus on people, not programs.

- **Essential elements of effective instruction (EEEI) provide a common language for improving instruction.**

- **Interdependence/collaboration.** LBUSD embraces a team approach that promotes shared learning of best practices and an overall friendly, helpful attitude. Because schools and departments are necessarily interdependent, adults must be able to operate as a collaborative team on which openness and mutual trust are highly valued.

- **Results-focused and results-driven behavior.** There is a clear expectation that all students can and will learn.

- **Data-driven decision-making.** Decisions are not personal but based on data that all accept and understand.

- **The use and interpretation of data are key to improved student learning.**

- **Transparency and mutual learning from mistakes.** The "Long Beach Way" is an analytic culture whereby people dig more deeply to understand *why* interventions are effective. Moreover, the data is available to conduct a thorough analysis.

- **Psychological safety.** Instead of assigning blame, critical problem solving prevails as the operative value. By helping someone work toward a solution, we all become better equipped to sustain improvements at our school. There is a deeply embedded desire to achieve wins but not at the expense of taking risks.

- **Central office operates with a service mentality.** Its role is to serve schools in their efforts to teach kids. Organized in a fairly simple structure (two offices—instruction and support), the district office makes it clear which people are involved and where to solicit assistance.

- **District mainly comprises insiders, but leadership willingly injects outside talent.** LBUSD staff are mostly homegrown leaders and teachers (both a plus and a minus), but there is also a willingness to bring in outsiders to shake up the system when internal skills are not available.

- **Experimentation at the schools is important within defined parameters.** The belief that "one size does not fit all" manifests itself in the improvement practices of research and development.

- **Evaluation matters (both formative and summative).**

The discussion of culture should logically move to accountability. If accountability does not explicitly emerge, instructors may ask: "What is the accountability system at LBUSD? How well does the district achieve accountability?" In addition to what might have emerged in the earlier discussion, the following attitudes and practices that specifically relate to accountability may be noted:

- **The district is results driven at all levels for all people.**

- **Everyone is responsible for performance.** Nobody has an easy ride—for example, principals can be moved if they do not achieve results. The knowledge that there are consequences does not seem to breed a sense of destructive competition among people in the district but instead fosters a culture that promotes teamwork and collaboration.

- **There is a collaborative practice of goal setting carried out at all levels.** There is an expectation that results, not the level of activities, are what count.

- **Data is closely linked to change in instructional leadership.** Data is a tool, and it is expected that it will be used to inform teachers, principals, and other school agents about what to do to improve classroom practice.

- **Competence is expected.** Competencies are defined according to EEEI.

- **Leaders ask themselves, "Would I put _my_ kid in that classroom?"**

- **Regular, mandatory, and focused key-results meetings are held.** While there is a great deal of freedom for principals in this basically decentralized system, there are some non-negotiables that have been created by the district office.

Culture as management practice (25 minutes)

While culture is often seen as a "fuzzy" or a "magic" variable, the purpose of the following discussion is to help participants discover that they can materially influence or shape culture through active management practices. This discussion introduces the themes of differentiation, integration, decentralization, and centralization. Often, the conversation around centralization and decentralization excludes an analysis of the management practices required for effective decentralization to work. In reality, centralization and decentralization are structural considerations. The concepts of differentiation and integration are the management practices that a district must create to effectively manage in a decentralized environment where schools vary considerably in terms of their performance, leadership capacities, and student demographics. A "one size fits all approach," whether centralized or decentralized, will not result in achieving excellence across all schools. District management must create systems and processes that differentiate among the schools according to their needs and other systems, structures, and a culture that integrates all the schools around a coherent strategy that drives results. Getting results with decentralization, rather than requiring less management from the district office, is more about using complex and nuanced management approaches that allow for appropriate freedom at each site. Moreover, it creates common forces such as accountability and sharing best practices that work across the system to create a coherent organization.

Continuing to use culture as a focal point of the discussion and as an entry to this part of the discussion, the instructor might ask, "What specific things does Long Beach do to drive and support their culture? In what ways are they effective or not?"

Decentralization: Decentralized aspects of LBUSD include:

- Site-level decision-making, for example, for resource allocation and professional development

- Curriculum supplemented by other approaches decided at the school level

- High school reform strategy developed by principals (bottom-up)

- Multiple management styles that lead to empowerment of principals

- High school coprincipals given a set of responsibilities, with each pair defining how those responsibilities will be divided

Centralization: Centralized aspects of LBUSD include:

- State-mandated curriculum in literacy

- Universal data systems

- Centralized pool of principal candidates

- Mandated professional development including teacher orientations around the district's essential elements of effective instruction (EEEI) pedagogy

- Mandated coprincipalships at the high school level

Integration: Integrating elements include:

- Mandatory key-results meetings. Outcomes are discussed and results analyzed. This forum provides a common space for dialogue, horizontal integration of information, opportunity for lateral learning, and involvement of multiple school sites in key discussions

- Common messages from the central office that you are accountable, we will supply data and make data-driven decisions, you will receive coaching, and we will support you as necessary

- Branding of the "Long Beach Way" as the accepted behavior in the district

- Common belief that good teaching will lead to improved learning for all students

- Consistent expectations for outcomes (accountability) and shared responsibility for the collective

- Principal rotation across levels and functions, creating a sense that every individual is part of a larger system. The sentiment, "The problems of others could be mine," is known by all. This helps create a desire to solve problems beyond one's immediate zone of responsibility.

- Annual goal-setting process whereby schools collaborate with the district office and receive follow-up visits to analyze progress and determine what assistance is needed. This creates the sense that everyone is working together toward the same objectives.

- Distributed leadership throughout the district office, creating a model of behavior at the school level

- Attention to social network. People are highly valued assets and the glue that hold this system together. The network reinforces the commonly held values across the system of shared leadership, communication, and accountability.

Differentiation: Differentiating elements include:

- Organization by level—elementary, middle, and high schools

- High-performing schools that may have different goals and receive fewer resources and less oversight than their lower-performing counterparts

- Principals' skill and leadership capacities, which help determine the resources they will receive from the central office

- Student demographics, which influence resources received from state and federal sources

- High school principals who have a strong voice in what professional development is needed at their sites and/or level

Examples of how these elements connect include the district's centralized approach to pedagogy (EEEI), which allows for a consistent approach to instruction across the system. Rotating principals from site to site makes this instructional practice common across sites and contributes to the creation of a system-wide view of instruction and success. Another example is that by supplying a centralized system of data, the district reinforces its message that data drives decisions. This provides the fodder for discussion in key-results meetings, where outcomes are analyzed, successes shared, and failures discussed. Differences in application of results or instructional approaches can then be implemented according to the local authority at school sites.

One additional discussion can be around the high school coprincipalship. You can ask, "What is the rationale for coprincipalships at the high schools? What are the strengths and weaknesses

of this approach?" At LBUSD, this structure is seen as a way to address the challenge of scale, to allow for shared leadership, and to help leaders learn new skills. As one participant noted in a class discussion, however, "Co-anything is a little bit tricky." Matching leadership talents is a challenge and requires active and skilled management. Participants can discuss whether this is a good idea, but try to keep them focused on the relevance of this structure to the overall coherence and alignment of the system. For LBUSD, this practice models its emphasis on sharing knowledge and acts as an enabling device to build on individual strengths. It helps both to integrate the system and differentiate by individual leaders' strengths and individual school-site needs.

Participants may notice that there is an unusual longevity of leadership in the district, and the instructor might push them to discuss *why* longevity prevails in Long Beach. The attention to board politics and local power dynamics should surface at this point. The discussion might also include the strengths and potential problems with longevity of leadership.

At this point the instructor might discuss the district's choice to avoid a quick move to small high schools and how this fits with the culture of the district. Unlike many of its contemporary urban districts, LBUSD elected to maintain its large, 4,000-student high schools. Instructors can open this discussion with the query, "At a time when school systems throughout the country are moving to small high schools, in Long Beach, they seem to think big is better. Why?" The ensuing discussion might touch on issues of community pride and identity as a city, as many longtime residents feel fierce loyalty to their high schools. "If the community sees its schools as part of their identity," one person argued, "they will support them." Another participant argued the reason could be summed up as "football," meaning not just the ability to field six football teams (which helps with selection) but also as an example of the high-quality programming a high school of this size can command. The discussion can highlight the potential economies of scale that can be harvested around resources and support but also the complications inherent in any large-scale enterprise. Perhaps most important is the way this decision maps back to the culture. As one participant commented:

> There is only so much available energy in a district at one time. To focus on structural change diverts needed energy from instructional reform. Given that Long Beach has a culture of data-driven decision-making, I would guess that they are waiting for evidence that small schools really can do better before they try to switch over. They want to keep the focus on the classroom.

In-class working groups focused on analysis of individual school district cultures (10 minutes)

Given that the discussion of culture may still have an abstract feel to participant, and has been about the culture of an unfamiliar district, we suggest that instructors convene participants into small groups (dyads or triads) to discuss the culture in their own districts. Some questions to focus discussions are:

1. Name five key characteristics that describe your district's organizational culture.

2. Which actions/tools/levers have to date been most effective in strengthening your organizational culture?

3. What are the two or three most important additional actions/tools/levers you can use as managers to improve the organizational culture of your school district? What will they accomplish, and what are the barriers to implementation?

Before the groups convene, give them the amount of time they will have and tell them that you will want to hear them report out on the third question, namely, the additional actions/tools/levers they feel can impact culture in posi-

tive ways. One quote you can send them off with comes from a principal in the Montgomery County School District in Maryland who asked, "You can't change a school system until there are people in place that have the same belief system. The hard part is, how do you move people to the core beliefs that you want?"[2]

If you are pressed for time, you can ask participants to turn to a neighbor (ideally someone from another district) and talk about these questions for five or so minutes.

Culture reports and embedding mechanisms (13 minutes)

In reporting on their discussions, participants should focus on sharing the means available to leaders for embedding culture. Since it is likely that the instructor will be pressed for time, only a couple of students will probably have the opportunity to report in class. You might suggest to the participants that this exercise was meant to primarily stimulate their thinking as to what they can do when they return to their districts rather than as an opportunity to present. If the class is with nonpractitioners, this time can be used to determine what else LBUSD might be doing to enhance its culture of performance and/or how it might improve on what is already being done.

After the reports, you might ask, "Is culture something that just spreads, like mold? You're not sure how it happens, but all of a sudden it's everywhere. How does it spread?" The point in this discussion is to move the specifics of culture creation and sustainability into a general conversation. This is an opportunity for participants to think of general management actions to use in order to build culture in any organization. Furthermore, it should help them understand that the means are transferable across organizations. Previous participants identified the following mechanisms:

- Decision-making process: Is it top-down or bottom-up? Is it static or dynamic?

- What language do you use?

- Data driven, results oriented . . . how is data used? How is it incorporated? What is measured? Is it universally accessible? Is it transparent? Do people have access to common information?

- Stakeholder involvement: Who is involved? How?

- Hiring and personnel intake: Who gets hired? What roles do they get? How are they trained?

- Accountability: Is performance transparent and/or visible? Is it hidden?

- How is information shared? What is your communication plan? Do you have logos? Short, digestible, clear, powerful, visible messages? Stories?

- Mistakes: How do you deal? Are they errors or learning opportunities? Do you emphasize truth or niceness?

If time permits, instructors might ask, "Are organizational cultures fragile or enduring? What implications does that have for managers?"

Closing (5 minutes)

Instructors can close by sharing a list that Schein outlines in his book, *Organizational Culture and Leadership* (2004), which is included below. Table 1 lists both the primary and secondary mechanisms in the left-hand column, along with some examples from the case in the right-hand column.

- Instructors may also reemphasize two of the major themes of the case:

Table 1

Schein's Primary Embedding Mechanisms	LB Case
What leaders pay attention to, measure, and control on a regular basis	School data, principal performance, relationships
How leaders react to critical incidents and organizational crises	With support, high expectations
How leaders allocate resources	More resources for schools with greater needs, where there are problems, differentiated strategy
Deliberate role modeling, teaching, coaching	Ongoing, EEEI based, stretch assignments
How leaders allocate rewards and status	Based on competence and demonstrated results
How leaders recruit, select, promote, and communicate	Based on competence and demonstrated results
Schein's Secondary Articulation and Reinforcement Mechanisms	
Organizational design and structure	Reporting relationships Clarity Instruction and support units
Organizational systems and procedures	
Rites and rituals of the organization	
Design of physical space, facades, and buildings	
Stories about important events and people	
Formal statements of organizational philosophy, creeds, and charters	

- To create high-performing school districts, many ingredients are necessary. The two we have focused on today are that leaders can create a collaborative culture throughout a public school district that focuses and rewards results. This kind of culture requires deliberate and continuous managerial activities in order to create and sustain it. The second theme is that all of the organizational elements must be coherent—integrated and working together to drive a district improvement strategy. Both are the responsibility of the leadership team. And if these pieces are not in place, it is unlikely that a school district will achieve excellence across its schools.

Notes

1. Instructors wishing to incorporate additional research on organizational culture should consult Exhibit 1.

2. Quoted in "Race, Accountability, and the Achievement Gap (A)," PEL 035.

Managing Schools across Differences

Mercy Corps: Positioning the Organization to Reach New Heights

Overview

This case describes Mercy Corps, a global non-profit organization, and its efforts to achieve and sustain high performance at scale—defined as consistent quality of programming across all of its operating units. Mercy Corps has experienced rapid growth and is now the fifth largest international development and relief agency in the world operating in over 43 countries. Participants should leave this class with a deeper understanding of the complexities of managing for high performance in large multi-site organizations. The case is relevant for leaders and general managers from the nonprofit, for-profit and public sectors.

The case introduces the concept of *differentiation and integration*. This managerial approach is intended to facilitate headquarters' (HQ) ability to provide tailored support for the differing needs and capabilities of its operating units and, at the same time, provide the forces that integrate all of the operating units into a coherent organization. Participants have an opportunity to first diagnose the challenges of managing the or-

ganization to high performance and then analyze and discuss the key roles, structures, functions and culture that are required for success. They then have the opportunity to evaluate Mercy Corps' efforts to date and identify the major challenges facing the agency. Participants will also develop an action plan for case protagonist Steve Zimmerman.

Ultimately, differentiation and integration are a means for achieving and sustaining organizational coherence. *Coherence* refers to the dynamic process by which leaders manage all of the elements of an organization (e.g., culture, resources, systems, structures, and stakeholders) to implement strategy and drive high performance. To introduce students to the concepts of strategy and coherence, the instructor may wish to assign the "Note on the PELP Coherence Framework," PEL–010, as pre-reading. While this note was written specifically for the application of the framework to the public education sector, the concepts discussed are relevant to any mission-driven organization.

This note was prepared by Professor Allen S. Grossman and Researcher Caroline King.

Case Summary

Mercy Corps' mission, developed in 1981, is to "alleviate suffering, poverty, and oppression by helping people build secure, productive, and just communities."[1] The agency's programs fell into three broad categories: emergency relief services, sustainable economic development, and civil society initiatives. As an organization, Mercy Corps is characterized as unbureaucratic and nonhierarchical. Innovation and social entrepreneurship are highly valued within the agency and viewed as the key characteristics that distinguish Mercy Corps from its peers.

The case opens in November 2006 during Mercy Corps' fourth biannual leadership conference in Nepal. The Nepal conference, entitled "Reaching New Heights," marked an inflection point in Mercy Corps' 25-year history. Since 2004, the agency's reputation skyrocketed as a result of its effective responses to major world disasters—notably the Indian Ocean tsunami, Pakistani earthquake and Hurricane Katrina in the U.S. Consequently, Mercy Corps' budget had nearly doubled from $106 million in FY02 to $197 million in FY06 and the agency's opportunities to grow and serve an even larger number of beneficiaries were unprecedented.

First, the case describes the "field," as its country programs are known. Two months prior to the Nepal gathering, Mercy Corps introduced a new program management and reporting structure for the field. The agency divided the world into six regions and named a regional program director (RPD) to lead each region. Each RPD managed 3–6 country programs, each led by a country director (CD). The six RPDs reported to Steve Zimmerman, the newly appointed senior vice president for programs.

The RPDs themselves differ on a number of dimensions (e.g., experience, time with the agency, leadership and management skills) and it is clear that work will need to be done to build a cohesive RPD team. The agency is still defining the RPDs' role and responsibilities—there is an implicit tension over how the role can be supportive, yet exert authority when necessary, without squashing CDs' flexibility. Zimmerman's charge is to help the agency improve its ability to scale quality programming effectively and efficiently, without losing Mercy Corps' entrepreneurial spirit or splintering into six regional "fiefdoms." Thus, Zimmerman's central challenge—and key point of the case—is how to structure and implement the effective HQ-RPD-CD relationships.

The case describes the CD's role, responsibilities and accountabilities. As the senior manager in a country, the CDs enjoy considerable autonomy in designing and executing programs. Four CDs are profiled. As a group, the four offer a microcosm of the inevitable variance among the agency's 43 CDs and countries. CDs differ in terms of years of experience, leadership and management skills, and reputation within the agency. Countries, and in a broader sense regions, present different community needs, operating and political challenges and opportunities for the agency. As a result, as Zimmerman explains, "no two country programs are alike." Thus, Mercy Corps hires CDs for their ability to adapt, innovate and deliver high-quality services.

The case then reviews two discussions during the Nepal conference—(1) the definitions of high-performing organization and social entrepreneurship and (2) the state of Mercy Corps today. We learn that Mercy Corps highly values its entrepreneurial spirit and ability to flexibly respond to the world's most pressing humanitarian crises. On the other hand, we learn that Mercy Corps has rapidly grown and expanded into new alliances and areas of work. Employees are struggling to see how all of the pieces of the puzzle fit together.

The next three sections, "Building Capacity," "Measuring Impact," and "Operational Support," describe the hybrid nature of management functions within Mercy Corps. The agency is neither completely decentralized nor centralized.

Rather, functions are performed by the people with the requisite expertise and capacity and most functions are shared by HQ and field staff. For example, there is a HQ-driven technical support unit (TSU) that provides technical assistance to country programs as needed, but technical staff also works within country programs. Three HQ recruiters help fill field vacancies, yet the primary work to identify and hire new staff is done by field staff. HQ support services (e.g., finance, program operations support) are also differentiated to accommodate the inherent variance in different country program needs.

While we classically think of field units resisting HQ-driven support, Mercy Corps' field staff is asking for greater HQ support. Office in a Box (OiB), the agency's new guidelines for country program operating systems, is a prime example. Prior to OiB, the quality and effectiveness of countries' operating systems (e.g., finance, procurement, etc.) varied quite a bit from country to country. OiB helps to reduce this unwanted variance in quality and the need to continuously "reinvent the wheel." The field welcomed OiB, a form of standardization, as a support and enabler of social entrepreneurship.

Effective performance measurement and management is a pressing challenge for Mercy Corps, and within the international development agency writ large. Impact indicators are emerging, but tend to be only for discrete aspects of programming. Field staff again is pushing HQ for greater support in measuring impact in order to evaluate effectiveness of program delivery and identify innovations that the agency can take to scale in order to deliver on the mission at a higher level.

In closing, Zimmerman discusses his primary managerial challenges:

- Structuring effective HQ-RPD-CD relationships
- Building a strong and cohesive RPD team
- Clarifying RPDs' authority and accountability

- Enhancing strategy development at the regional and country levels
- Strengthening performance measurement and management

Positioning

This case could be used in a wide variety of settings and with different audiences, ranging from experienced managers to graduate students in education, business, or nonprofit management courses.

Learning Objectives

- Introducing the concept that operating units with differing needs and capacities require different kinds and degrees of support from the parent organization and at the same time, regardless of these differences, there must be some aspects of the organization that are consistent across all of these operating units.

- Addressing this challenge requires a sophisticated management approach and cannot be achieved by the historical solutions that tend to focus on structural approaches like centralization or decentralization. An effective response requires a new approach and a different kind of dialogue within the organization that focuses on the enablers of performance.

- Understanding the concept of differentiation and integration and how this approach may fill the current managerial vacuum.

- Understanding that high performance requires that managers act to insure that all the elements of the organization embedded in the Coherence Framework are coherent with each other and the organization's strategy.

Assignment

In preparing to discuss "Mercy Corps: Positioning the Organization to Reach New Heights," HBS No. 9–307–096, participants should read the case and consider the questions below. The "Note on the PELP Coherence Framework," PEL-010, should also be assigned if it has not been read previously. While this note was written specifically for the application of the Framework to the public education sector, the concepts discussed are relevant to any mission-driven organization.

Discussion Questions

1. Do you agree with the definitions of high performance and entrepreneurship on page six of the case? How might you change them? What are the strengths and concerns of a highly entrepreneurial organization?

2. How much of a challenge is it for Mercy Corps to achieve consistent quality across all of its sites? What are they doing well in this pursuit and what concerns you?

3. How does Mercy Corps' headquarters provide the needed support for each of its operating units? What are the variables they need to consider in designing and implementing this support?

4. How should Mercy Corps decide which functions should be performed at the operating unit and which functions should be the responsibility of headquarters? How important is the RPD for success?

Teaching Plan and Analysis

This 90-minute teaching plan is based on an executive education course designed for leaders and managers from the nonprofit, public and for-profit sectors. It is important for the instructor to keep in mind that there is a great deal to discuss in this case and success depends on careful time management. Ideally, this case will serve only as an introduction to the concept of differentiation and integration and an additional case about this subject will be taught to participants to deepen and broaden the participants' understanding and learning.

Summary

I. **Introduction.** The introduction is used primarily to set context for the ensuing discussion and is purposefully short. (2 minutes)

II. **Organizational diagnosis.** During this portion of the discussion, participants are asked to describe Mercy Corps' performance and identify its key success factors. Instructors may begin by asking, "What do you think about how the Mercy Corps conference participants defined a high-performing organization on page 6?" (20 minutes)

III. **Analysis and evaluation: Role of HQ.** This second discussion pasture is aimed at developing participants' ability to analyze the role of HQ in supporting the various country programs, or "the field." This pasture also introduces the concepts of differentiation and integration. Key questions include: "What is the role HQ plays in this success? How good a job do you think HQ is doing at supporting the units?" (25 minutes)

IV. **Analysis of the Regional Program Director (RPD) role.** The third discussion pasture focuses on the role of the RPDs and their importance in Mercy Corps' ability to achieve quality at scale. Instructors should probe participants by asking, "If you were a country director, what would you want from your new RPD? What characteristics or skills would an RPD have to possess to meet that need?" (20 minutes)

V. **Action planning.** The purpose of this conversation is to push participants to develop recommendations and an action plan for Steve Zimmerman. Instructors may begin by asking, "If you were Zimmerman, what would you do over the next 6–12 months?" (20 minutes)

VI. Closing. In the final minutes of the class, instructors might reiterate the major concepts explored during the case discussion. (3 minutes)

Introduction (2 minutes)

The purpose of the introduction is to provide context and we recommend that it be very brief. One suggested opening is as follows:

Every mission driven organization that has more than one site faces a similar set of challenges for achieving high performance across all of its operating units. The challenge often increases with the number of operating units, their dispersion and range of variability in each site's capabilities and the clients served. Typical structural approaches to solving this performance challenge, such as centralization and decentralization, meet with limited success and are often abandoned in favor of a new structural fix. Today, we are going to try to gain insight into other ways an organization and its leadership might think and act when confronting the challenge of building and sustaining a high-performing organization.

Organizational diagnosis (20 minutes)

During this portion of the discussion, participants are asked to describe Mercy Corps' performance and identify its key success factors. Instructors may begin by asking, "What is your reaction to how the Mercy Corps conference participants defined a high-performing organization on page 6 in the case?"

The definition given in the case is:

- Effectively and efficiently serves its target population

- Measures impact

- Systematically learns from its mistakes and successes

A follow-up question might be, "In what way might you modify this definition? Why?"

The instructor might now segue into a more general conversation about Mercy Corp's success to date. A suggested question is, "What

makes Mercy Corps successful?" Participants are likely to mention the following success factors:

- Nimble, flexible, able to adapt to the needs of clients based on the situation on the ground

- High expectations for CDs to deliver and vesting the necessary responsibility to them to get the job done

- Innovative and entrepreneurial behavior rewarded and encouraged at all levels

- Ability to position the organization well with funders

- Strong and stable leadership and management

Since participants are likely to mention entrepreneurship, ask participants to reflect on the definition of social entrepreneurship given in the case. The definition is:

- Spirit of risk-taking; seizing opportunities

- Innovative, flexible, adaptive problem-solver

- Identifies unmet need, designs and implements a new approach in line with the agency's mission and vision for change, gets results

A follow up question might be, "Is there anything that worries you about this entrepreneurial culture at Mercy Corps?" Participants are likely to mention the following:

- Keeping all of the country units driving towards achieving a unified mission

- Maintaining high-quality programs in all countries

- Focus on and rewards for innovation and not on implementation

- Difficulty with measuring sustained performance of individuals or country programs based on impact

The important point of this discussion of high performance and entrepreneurship is *not* the specific definitions, but rather the fact that the organization took the time to explicitly define what it meant by these oft-used terms.

Analysis and evaluation: Role of HQ (25 minutes)

This second discussion pasture is aimed at developing participants' ability to analyze the role of HQ in supporting the various country programs, or "the field." This pasture also introduces the concept of differentiation and integration.

A first set of questions might be, "What is the role HQ plays in this success? What is it about their approach that is an enabler to the country units? What are the constraints to high performance created by HQ under the current system?" This discussion should link how HQ impacts the success factors that participants named in the first discussion pasture.

In terms of the role HQ plays in Mercy Corps' success, participants are likely to mention:

- Program operations support (e.g., proposal development)

- Financial management and recruiting support

- Management support and quality control (e.g., Office in a Box)

- Technical expertise and support (e.g., technical fields, monitoring and evaluation)

- Leadership support and networking (e.g., bi-annual Global Leadership Conference)

- Recognition for high performance (e.g., innovation and leadership awards)

- Inspiring creativity and entrepreneurship

- Designing new structures (e.g., RPD) to support and manage growth

Most of the aforementioned attributes are likely to be judged as enablers of success. Press participants to also mention constraints, which might include:

- Reluctance to put in structures and systems for fear of constraining creativity, which could lead to a higher level of organizational chaos

- Weak impact indicators and performance measurement and management system, which could result in weak or ambiguous accountability

- Broad vision for change which allows wide discretion for program development and implementation creating an assortment of programs rather than a coherent organization

Transition into a discussion about the relationship between HQ and the country units. The instructor might ask, "How good a job do you think HQ is doing at providing the support that the units need for success?" Instructors may ask participants to vote by rating HQ on a scale of 1 (poor) to 5 (excellent) and explain their votes.

Probe participants to unpack the assignment of managerial functions within Mercy Corps by asking, "How does Mercy Corps decide who does what function—HQ, the field or a hybrid?" Some examples are:

HQ	Field	Hybrid
		Recruiting
Design operating guidelines (Office in a Box)		
		Finance
	Strategy development (e.g., country plans)—although may shift to "hybrid" if agency moves to regional strategies	
		Technical support
	Monitoring and evaluation	

The instructor might then ask, "What functions are Mercy Corps performing particularly well? What are your reasons for your conclusion?" For example, recruiting may receive mixed reviews. Many participants will like the involvement of non-HQ people in hiring, but may also feel that HQ staff should play a greater role in ensuring that countries that need extra support with recruiting and hiring (e.g., war torn countries) receive it.

The instructor may also take an HQ example, such as Office in a Box, and ask, "Doesn't this take away some power from units? Does it squash entrepreneurship?" Participants are likely to recall Zimbabwe CD Rob Maroni's comment: "This is exactly what I need. I want to be innovative when I design my programs. I don't want to waste time and energy reinventing the wheel on designing operations systems." Unlike many multi-site organizations, the field units are actually pressing HQ to provide stronger support systems. But, how does an organization know where to draw the line? There may be other functions that could be more codified, like professional development, which could suppress entrepreneurship.

A follow up question might be, "What is it about a country site that may make it better suited to perform a function? How does an organization best answer this question?" The point of this discussion is to help participants understand that functions are identified, discussed in detail and then performed in most cases, by sharing responsibility between the HQ and field, rather than simplistically assigning most functions to the HQ (a centralized model) or to the field (a decentralized model).

If time remains, the instructor might ask, "What is the purpose of the Vision for Change in Exhibit 3 of the case? In what ways is it effective or not?"

Analysis of the Regional Program Director (RPD) role (20 minutes)

The third discussion pasture focuses on the role of the RPDs. Before delving into the RPD structure, start the conversation by setting the RPDs' operating context by asking, "When you think about managing Mercy Corps' 43 country units, how similar or different do you think their needs are? What factors contribute to those differences?"

Based on the CD profiles and other information in the case, participants are likely to respond that the country units have quite different needs. Some of the contributing factors participants are likely to mention include:

- Varying experience and managerial/leadership skills of the CDs

- Country context: stable or in state of upheaval, level of violence, economic conditions, etc.

- Skill set of field staff and the local resources available to train the primarily local country staff

- Different countries operate different programs (e.g., rural economic development vs. civil society strengthening)

- Different donors with different expectations, requirements and relationships with the agency

The instructor can now segue into the RPD discussion by asking, "Given this context of different country needs, if you were a CD, what would you need from your RPD?" Comments may include:

- Tailoring support and allocating resources to meet each country's needs

- Ensuring consistent high-quality program design and implementation

- Differentiating professional development and training to CDs and their staff

- Establishing performance indicators and a system of accountability

- Keeping each country connected to Mercy Corps' vision for change and mission

Subsequent questions might be, "Do you think the RPD structure is well organized? It presupposes that variability among countries is based on geographical regions and common needs/contexts within each region. Is this the best way to organize field management and support, or are there other ways Mercy Corps could think about this challenge?" Participants may propose some of the following alternatives:

- Match RPDs with strong operations management skills (e.g., finance, HR) with CDs that need to strengthen these areas

- Match RPDs with track records as entrepreneurial and effective program managers with CDs that need to strengthen their ability to design and implement programs

- Instead of overseeing a particular geographic region, RPDs could supervise at lease one CD from each region. This reporting structure would ensure that RPDs and CDs interact with colleagues from throughout the world and could increase RPDs' and CDs' connection to the broader global mission of Mercy Corps.

A follow up question might be, "If the current RPD structure were working really well, what should be happening? What would success look like across these six RPDs? What are the managerial mechanisms that will help you achieve success?" "What would you hold the RPDs accountable for and how specifically would you manage this accountability if you were Zimmerman?"

Participants are likely to mention the following:

- Lateral learning and collaboration across regions

- Across regions, RPDs are involved in making decisions to allocate agency resources where they are most needed

- Within a region, CDs are involved in making decisions to allocate regional resources where they are most needed

- High flexibility in designing and implementing programs

- Low variance in program quality and effectiveness of implementation

- The performance of their units in achieving the objectives outlined in the annual country plans

Finally, probe participants to consider the drawbacks to the RPD structure. The instructor

might ask, "What would worry you about this structure?" Responses may include:

- RPDs' roles and responsibilities are not clearly defined—each RPD may interpret his/her own way

- RPDs do not have the authority to allocate resources within their regions

- Communication and coordination among RPDs are ambiguous

- Potential for replication of work and functions across regions (inefficiency)

- May lead to creation of six regional fiefdoms and the difficulty of maintain an organizational culture

If participants bring up the final point, the instructor may consider asking, "Zimmerman and senior leaders are worried about the regions splintering into six regional fiefdoms. What's wrong with having six Mercy Corps if they could all be effective?"

Action planning (20 minutes)

The purpose of this final conversation is to push participants to develop recommendations and an action plan for Steve Zimmerman. Instructors may begin by asking, "You're Steve Zimmerman, committed to success, but wanting to leave the job in 2 years. What suggestions do you have for achieving growth with quality? What would you do over next 6 months to 1 year?"

Recommendations may include:

- Clarify the RPD role and responsibilities

- Structure regular communication among RPDs around key management challenges, such as recruiting

- Create regional discretionary budgets and allow each RPD and their CDs to allocate resources within their region

- Identify promising monitoring and evaluation pilots in the field (e.g., the shared indicators used by Sri Lanka and Indonesia) and field test them in other countries, regions and at the agency level

- Rationalize strategy development process: introduce either an agency-level plan or regional-level plans that would guide the development of country plans

- Build and maintain a strong organizational culture by developing a common set of expectations across countries to achieve results and the means to objectively measure them

- Reward in a public way the implementation of best practices and effective program implementation

- Develop other time saving standard procedures like OiB where appropriate

- Focus on the organization's mission and be sure it is known and integrated into all planning.

- Work to make sure that the Vision for Change is better understood and made more useful as a tool for planning and evaluation

- Insure that management continues to travel frequently to all regions and consider having a global meeting every year instead of biannually

- Communicate to the CDs about the ongoing progress of implementing suggestions from the biannual conference

The Coherence Framework categories (culture, structures, systems, resources and stakeholders) may be useful to explicitly board participants' responses. Alternatively, the Framework can be used implicitly as a guide in asking follow up questions. For example, a follow up question might be, "If Mercy Corps decides to implement a particular recommendation (the instructor might choose one from the list provided by the student), what else in the organization has to change to insure [the recommendation] is effective for driving high performance across all regions and countries?"

Closing (3 minutes)

In the final minutes of the class, instructors might reiterate the major concepts explored during the case discussion and draw parallels to other sectors. These might include:

- Regardless of what kind of mission-driven organization you represent, you have experienced the same problems as Zimmerman. Our discussion has revealed the complexity of managing multi-site organizations to high performance. We have tried to understand how an organization can retain and encourage productive entrepreneurial behavior at the operating units and at the same time insure consistent quality. Notice how we did not fall into the classic debate over centralization versus decentralization but tried to focus all of analysis and recommendations on what would drive high performance across the organization. The managerial approach that we are recommending to achieve this end is differentiation and integration.

- We have seen how critical the role of the RPD is for success and the care that leaders must put into their selection, development and oversight. And, we have also seen the importance of quality performance data to facilitate the management of a multi-site organization.

We will continue this conversation in our discussion of other cases and the specific challenges you are facing in your sector.

Notes

1. For additional background information, see "Mercy Corps: Global Social Entrepreneurship" HBS No. N9–303–079.

Managing the Chicago Public Schools

Overview

This case describes efforts to manage for high performance at scale in the Chicago Public Schools (CPS), the nation's third-largest public school system in 2006. It is one of a series of cases developed by the HGSE/HBS Public Education Leadership Project (PELP) to describe for school leaders, executives, and graduate students the challenges and realities of leading and sustaining large-scale organizational improvement in an urban public school district.

"Managing the Chicago Public Schools," PEL-033, was written as a "fan" case, one that lays out many issues for participants and instructors to discuss. The case introduces the concept of *differentiation and integration,* a managerial approach emerging in public school systems that couples *differentiated* treatment of schools, which have varying needs and capacities, with efforts to *integrate* the work of all schools and the district office around an improvement strategy to create a coherent high-performing organization. Participants have an opportunity to diagnose the circumstances in the 617-school district that drive CPS leadership to manage through differentiation and integration in their pursuit of high performance. The discussion will enable partici-

pants to evaluate the district's actions to date; analyze key roles, structures, and functions that facilitate effective differentiation and integration; and identify major challenges.

A key concept in the case is achieving and sustaining organizational *coherence,* which, as articulated by PELP, refers to the dynamic process by which leaders manage all of the elements of an organization (e.g., culture, resources, systems, structures, and stakeholders) to support effective strategy execution. To introduce students to the concepts of strategy and coherence in a public education setting, the instructor may wish to assign the "Note on the PELP Coherence Framework," PEL-010, as pre-reading.

Participants should leave this class with a deeper understanding of the complexities of managing for high performance at scale in large multisite organizations, particularly urban public school districts.

Case Summary

The case is set in the 2005–2006 school year, the district's fifth year under the leadership of Chief Executive Officer Arne Duncan. After summarizing key reforms and results under Duncan, the case provides an overview of the district.

This note was prepared by Professor Allen S. Grossman and Research Associate Caroline King.

Readers understand that the district is large (with 617 schools, CPS is the third-largest school system in the country), is organized into 24 geographic "areas," and serves a diverse and largely poor student body. Wide performance gaps exist among schools. Seven categories of schools operate within the district. The categories are distinguished by school academic performance, federal or state law, or district policies. Descriptions are provided for all seven categories in the case.

The case then follows CPS leadership's efforts during 2005–2006 to manage for high performance in every school. Their actions are guided by a theory of action which is articulated at the beginning of the school year—namely:

- Improved student learning requires improved instruction.

- Schools are the unit of change for instructional improvement, and principals are the leaders of that change.

- Area and central offices provide critical support for instructional improvement and differentiate that support based on performance and need.

The case describes the actions that the district takes beyond structure to enact this theory of change during the school year. The participant has the opportunity to analyze how these actions are used to both differentiate among schools and integrate the schools and district into a coherent organization. District actions fall into three major categories: (1) setting clear expectations, (2) providing effective and targeted support to schools, and (3) creating consistent accountability mechanisms.

In order to *set clear expectations,* the district defines an ultimate district goal to "graduate all students prepared for college and beyond." To measure progress toward that goal, the district establishes system-wide 2010 outcome goals (e.g., 70% of students enter first grade ready to read, 50% of 11th graders meet or exceed state

standards; see case). Every school (except charter schools) receives differentiated annual performance targets; schools at different performance levels are expected to improve at different rates. If every school meets its targets, the district will accomplish its 2010 goals. CPS creates a process and template (known as "School Improvement Plan for Advancing Academic Achievement" or SIPAAA) to help each school diagnose its strengths and weaknesses and design its own plan and budget to raise student performance. The nontraditional schools (charter, contract, performance) sign five-year performance contracts with the district and undergo annual reviews.

CPS takes four steps to *provide effective and targeted support* to schools. (See the case for details on each of the following steps.)

1. The district differentiates treatment of schools based on performance and need.

2. The district clarifies the role of Area Instructional Officers (AIOs) who have managerial responsibility for schools within the area structure.

3. The district takes steps to provide schools with better student data and information technology.

4. CPS reorganizes the central office in an attempt to provide better service and support to schools.

Lastly, the district attempts to *create more consistent accountability mechanisms.* CPS designs a high school scorecard to measure and rank high schools on 17 indicators of academic and non-academic indicators. The district also revamps its accountability system in favor of a streamlined probation policy.

In closing, the case sets up the challenge of communicating and managing in a way so that everyone in the district—not just senior leaders—understands the district's strategy and feels accountable for achieving the 2010 outcome goals.

Positioning

This case could be used in a wide variety of settings and with different audiences, ranging from experienced school leaders to graduate students in education, business, or management courses. As a fan case, it can be used at the beginning of a course or module to lay out issues of managing multisite organizations, strategy execution, and leadership. If used after "Mercy Corps: Positioning the Organization to Reach New Heights," participants will notice many parallels.

Learning Objectives

By design, this case provides an overview of the many and varied parts of a school district. It can be used as a vehicle for teaching lessons about leadership, change management, strategy development, and systemic coherence. Potential learning objectives include:

- Understand the rationale for differentiated treatment of schools within a broader strategy to improve performance districtwide.

- Identify various dimensions along which a district may choose to differentiate its relationship with schools—e.g., performance, capacity, governance structures, legal requirements, and demographics.

- Understand the integration mechanisms that district leaders might use in a decentralized environment to tie schools and the district office together into a coherent organization.

- Diagnose the system capabilities and culture required to effectively execute differentiation and integration and explore potential design choices and tradeoffs.

- Develop an appreciation for the complexity and intensity of managing a set of differentiating and integrating functions in a decentralized environment.

Assignment

In preparing to discuss "Managing the Chicago Public Schools," PEL-033, participants should consider the questions below. The "Note on the PELP Coherence Framework," PEL-010, should also be assigned if it has not been read previously.

Discussion Questions

1. Why does Chicago have different categories of schools—e.g., contract, performance, and autonomous management and performance (AMPS)?

2. What are the key roles that the district should play across these schools? Why?

3. What is your assessment as to how well the district is filling its role in relation to the various categories of schools?

4. How important are the Area Instructional Officers (AIOs), and what are the key challenges to their effectiveness?

Teaching Plan and Analysis

This 80-minute teaching plan is based on an executive education course designed for the PELP inaugural cohort of urban public school leadership teams.

Summary

I. **Introduction**. (5 minutes)

II. **Contextual analysis.** During this portion of the discussion, participants are asked to identify the circumstances that led to the creation of the seven school categories, as well as to analyze the challenges that are embedded in managing this diverse portfolio of schools. Instructors may begin by asking, "What is the district trying to achieve by having seven categories of schools?" (20 minutes)

III. **Analysis and evaluation: Role of the district.** This second discussion pasture is aimed at developing participants' ability to analyze the role of the district by applying the PELP coherence framework. In addition to developing participants' familiarity with this conceptual tool, this pasture provides an opportunity to evaluate how coherent (or not) the district's activities are with the district's strategy and with one another. This pasture also introduces the concepts of differentiation and integration. Instructors may begin by asking, "What are the specific actions that the district is taking to integrate the work of all schools and central office departments?" (30 minutes)

IV. **Analysis of the Area Instructional Officer (AIO) role.** The third discussion pasture focuses on the role of the AIOs. Instructors should probe participants by asking, "Given the district's theory of change, how and why are the AIOs important?" (20 minutes)

V. **Closing.** In the final minutes of the class, instructors might reiterate the major concepts explored during the case discussion. (5 minutes)

Introduction (5 minutes)

The instructor can begin class by outlining the purpose of the case in the context of the course. One sample opening follows:

Today we are going to explore the complexities associated with managing a 617-school district for high performance. We will explore the roles of district and school leaders in creating a system of schools. We will try to understand which aspects of the district's strategy to improve student achievement should be differentiated in response to different school needs and capacities, and which aspects should be consistent across all schools to integrate the schools and the district into a coherent organization.

The case opens with a quote from Chicago's Mayor Daley asking, "Can we do a better job of teaching not just in a few schools but in every school?" In a district striving for high performance, we would instead ask, "How can we lead and manage the district so that we can do an excellent job of teaching in every school?"

Throughout our discussion, keep in mind the district's theory of change. (Prepare the following on a side board:)

- Improved student learning requires improved instruction.

- Schools are the unit of change for instructional improvement, and principals are the leaders of that change.

- Area and central offices provide critical support for instructional improvement and differentiate that support based on performance and need.

As we analyze each of the district's actions, we'll consider, "What is CPS trying to achieve? How does it map back to the theory of change?" Let's get started.

Contextual analysis (20 minutes)

The class begins with an analysis of the circumstances that led to the creation of the seven school categories, as well a diagnosis of the challenges that are embedded in managing this diverse portfolio of schools. As mentioned above, an instructor might open the conversation by asking, "What is the district trying to achieve by having seven categories of schools?" Through discussion, participants should identify the following issues, which can be captured on the first center board and side boards.

Overall, the purpose of this initial analysis is for participants to figure out the rationale for differentiating treatment of schools. The instructor will want to be sure that participants identify what the district is trying to achieve by differentiated treatment of schools, the internal and external forces driving differentiation, and the various dimensions along which CPS differentiates.

Likely responses to the question, "What is the district trying to achieve by having seven categories of schools?" include:

- Scale decision-making—having categories makes it easier to identify school needs and manage 617 schools.

- Target resources to low-performing schools.

- Offer students and parents greater performance transparency and help facilitate school choice.

- Deal with size and scope of 617-school district. (This type of comment leads to an interesting followup question: "Is there a different theory of organizational coherence in a large district?" Even though increased district size logically points to increased complexity, participants should understand that managing for coherence around a strategy is an essential and universally important concept regardless of the size of the district. However, the means used to achieve organizational coherence may differ from district to district depending on size, strategy decisions, or other district characteristics.)

The above responses largely reflect internal drivers for different categories of schools. The instructor should probe participants to also consider the external forces driving differentiation in CPS. These include:

- Federal No Child Left Behind Act mandating districts to restructure chronically low-performing schools

- State law authorizing creation of charter schools

- Mayor Daley's pledge to replace chronically low-performing schools with 100 new schools by 2010 ("Renaissance 2010")

- The Gates Foundation's support for the creation of small high schools

While the instructor will want to avoid spending too much time defining each of the seven categories of schools (which are fully described in the case), the instructor should help participants identify the various dimensions of differentiation by asking, "What dimensions does CPS use to differentiate treatment of schools?" The dimensions are:

- Performance (High—AMPS; Low—Probation, Restructuring)

- Structure (Charter, Contract, Performance)

- Capacity (High potential principals given AMPS status)

Having identified these various dimensions of differentiation, help participants tease out the complexity of managing these schools for high performance by asking, "What challenges do you see for trying to manage this portfolio of schools?" Likely responses include:

- Overlapping categories (e.g., restructuring and probation)

- Given that each school selects its own curriculum, how can the district office effectively support schools to improve instruction?

- The situation is so complex as to make it not understandable by managers and external stakeholders

- AIOs have large caseloads (~18–44 schools); some areas are largely low-performing, some are largely high-performing, some are mixed. How does the district provide professional development to AIOs that enables them to differentiate support to schools in a way that is coherent with the district's strategy?

Analysis and evaluation: Role of the district (30 minutes)

The purpose of this pasture is to analyze the role of the district. Specifically, the discussion should enable participants to evaluate how coherent (or not) the district's activities are with the district's strategy and with one another. This pasture also introduces the concepts of differentiation and integration. The instructor should prepare on the board the categories of the PELP coherence framework.

We suggest opening this pasture by asking participants to identify the district's key activities during 2005–2006 using the elements of the PELP coherence framework: structure, resources, systems, culture, stakeholders, and environment. Having spent time on the rationale for differentiating among schools in the first pasture, focus this pasture on the district's integrating mechanisms. Instructors may begin by asking, "What are the specific activities that the district launched to integrate, or create organizational coherence across, the work of all schools and the district office? What is the intended impact of each of these activities?"

Instructors should direct participants to describe the action and indicate which framework category the action represents. Record responses under the appropriate framework category, although some actions could easily be under more than one category and almost all will affect multiple categories. Probe participants to evaluate whether or not they think the activity mentioned was coherent with the district's theory of action and all of the activities in progress. Actions that may come up (their sequence is not important) include:

Culture: Participants will likely identify measures that CPS leadership enacted in order to shift the culture in CPS to one of results and performance The 2010 district outcome goals establish common expectations across the district, the 617 schools, and all central departments. The goals send a message that everyone's work—from principals, teachers, and district managers alike—should be focused on the achievement of these goals (see Exhibit 7 in the case to see the district's 2010 outcome goals). Additionally, clarifying the role of the AIOs and reorganizing the district office ("flipping the pyramid," as Duncan says) reflect an organizational attitude of serving and supporting schools in order to ensure their success. This culture of service and support emphasizes results over the assertion of managerial authority often evident in public bureaucracies, including CPS in the past. The creation of the autonomous management and performance schools indicates a culture and organization that rewards high per-

formance. The creation of the high school scorecards reflects a culture that is results-oriented and in which performance issues are transparent and expected. The decision to adapt the high school scorecards for elementary schools indicates a culture that enables innovation and organizational learning.

Resources: Steps were taken to build the capacity of the AIOs to support instructional improvement in schools. The clarification of the AIO role removed any expectation that AIOs should be involved in school operation issues. Along with the monthly AIO coherence meetings, the new quarterly progress meetings for AIOs with Barbara Eason-Watkins can be viewed as a mechanism to build the capacity of AIOs to (a) assess schools' strengths and weaknesses based on performance data, (b) make decisions about how to allocate area resources and time, and (c) provide differentiated support to principals based on individual school needs and in service of achieving the district's outcome goals. The design of the School Improvement Plan for Advancing Academic Achievement (SIPAAA) planning process tools (e.g., "Five Fundamentals of a Great School" rubric) helps build the capacity of school leadership teams to diagnose strengths and weaknesses based on performance data. The instructional support options provide a menu of supports (resources) to schools, seemingly facilitating their ability to develop more effective action plans to improve student achievement.

Systems: On the systems side of the organization, the school scorecards introduce a common set of outcome goals that will, for the first time, be used to track the performance of all categories of schools operating in Chicago and to rank each school in each category (see Exhibit 11 in the case to see a sample scorecard). The introduction of the benchmark assessments in reading and math are another mechanism to provide common performance measures across all schools that could ideally result in greater collaboration both within and among schools. The district's investments in the IMPACT system should help district managers and schools to more readily access relevant performance data, facilitate schools' access to curriculum and instruction supports, and streamline reporting requirements. This should encourage people throughout the district to use data to gain knowledge and to design improved instruction to students.

Structure: The discussion might begin around the tradition of local control in CPS, which is a very noticeable feature about this district. Participants may note that the district is subtly moving from a highly decentralized state in which every school makes its own curriculum, instruction, and budgetary decisions to a more centralized district in which district managers are attempting to bring more consistency across schools. In order to introduce the concept of differentiation and integration, ask a follow up question such as, "Is the district moving from decentralization to centralization? Isn't it preferred to have a decentralized organization?" The instructor should allow participants time to wrestle with the nuances of this question. The instructor should help participants understand that the district's activities signal the development of a new management model for how to create coherence within a decentralized organization, and that decentralization does not mean that the district office should not actively manage schools. It means that managers must rethink their role and that successfully managing in a decentralized environment necessitates integrating mechanisms, many of which should be brought out during this discussion pasture.

In order to help participants tease out the unique role that the district is trying to play, consider asking, "Is this integrating role important, or necessary? Who should play this role—schools or district managers?" Participants with experience in school districts or multisite organizations should be able to understand that inte-

grating functions—sharing best practices, providing common expectations and performance measures, etc.—would be fairly difficult for schools to implement on their own; district leaders have an incentive and the ability to add this value to the system. The case protagonists, as well as class participants, continue to wrestle with the question, "How do we manage this complex system and still retain a bias toward decision-making at the school site?"

The creation of the field-based business service centers (BSCs) reflects the district's desire to provide more effective, timely, and tailored operations support to schools. The BSCs should also help "pick up" any operations support that AIOs were formerly providing to schools. The central office reorganization, particularly the explicit articulation of different school "customers," is coherent with the district's theory of action to provide differentiated service and support to all of the various categories of schools.

Stakeholders: The school scorecards facilitate transparency around performance for all stakeholders. The mayor strongly influences the district's strategy and activities, as evidenced by the launch of Renaissance 2010. Participants may mention that the teachers' union seems relatively weak, which gives district and schools greater leeway. Stakeholders—from teachers and principals to parents and community organizations—are likely to resist some of the districts' perceived efforts to wrest local control away from schools.

Environment: Understanding the CPS operating environment is critical for understanding the district's activities. The federal NCLB law requires CPS to "restructure" chronically low-performing schools; however, what is notable is the district's proactive stance toward this requirement. Instead of leaving schools on their own to design restructuring plans or taking a one-size-fits-all approach towards restructuring schools, the district designed a menu of solutions based on assessments of each school's strengths and weaknesses, leadership capacity, prior interventions already in place, etc. State law authorized the creation of charter schools in the district. Again, the district has taken a proactive stance toward charter schools, viewing them as part of the district rather than stand-alones, and as a source of friendly competition to drive improved performance across the district, rather than as an invention to punish the district by usurping students.

Analysis of the Area Instructional Officer (AIO) role (20 minutes)

The third discussion pasture focuses on the role of the AIOs. Review the recent AIO role clarification: AIOs are expected to spend 70% of their time working with principals to improve instruction, 30% developing and supporting new principals, and 0% on operations. Instructors might open up the conversation by asking, "Given the district's theory of change, how and why are the AIOs important?

Participants are likely to conclude that the AIOs are critical to the successful execution of CPS's strategy for the following reasons:

• AIOs hold the key position for both providing differentiated support to schools and ensuring consistency and coherence across the district.

• AIOs are the agents for ensuring the success of systemic reforms (as opposed to principals who drive school-level reforms).

• AIOs are a "choke point" in the system—they look up (to senior leaders), down (to principals), and ideally, across (to other AIOs).

• AIOs are the key to driving the district's theory of change. If schools are the unit of change and principals are the drivers of that change, then principals need to be effectively developed and supported by the AIOs.

Probe participants further by asking, "What challenges do you see with this role?" Comments may include:

• Scale—with 24 AIOs, it is easy for each AIO do his/her own thing.

• Not clear how to differentiate support to the mid-tier schools, the majority of the district.

• Accountability for AIOs is unclear.

• There is likely to be considerable inconsistency of capabilities and performance across AIOs.

Having acknowledged the critical importance of the AIOs, logical follow up questions to pose might be, "Do the AIOs have a doable job? Consider the number of schools an AIO supports (ranging from 18–44), the varying performance levels and categories of schools, etc."

Participants within the public education sector—particularly from large school systems—who are familiar with large spans of control, are likely to perceive the AIOs job as challenging, but "doable." Participants from the for-profit sector are more likely to conclude that the AIOs' span of control is too large and that their primary charge to "improve instruction" is too vague to make the job "doable." All participants are likely to recommend that AIOs should be provided with regular professional development (e.g., instructional improvement, leadership/management skills, etc.), opportunities to extend their professional learning, and cross-functional support from throughout the district office.

Other suggested lines of questioning include, "What characteristics would you look for if you were hiring the AIOs? How should the AIOs be held accountable?" Record responses on the board under the relevant heading—characteristics or accountability.

In terms of characteristics, responses are likely to include: proven principal with track record of improving instruction and raising student performance, effective communicator, and strong leadership skills. Participants will probably acknowledge that the 20+ AIOs represent a range of capabilities and therefore, careful thought should be put into AIO assignments to best match an AIO's strengths with an area's needs.

Recommendations for strengthening accountability of AIOs may include: clearly defined expectations, and performance reviews (currently nonexistent) that include principals' perspectives and rewards (or sanctions) based on the performance trends in the area.

Closing (5 minutes)

In the final minutes of the class, the instructor might reiterate the major concepts explored during the case discussion. A suggested closing follows:

1. This case shows a new way to view the traditional debate around organizational design/management in school systems, which has typically been dichotomized as centralization vs. decentralization. Differentiation and integration is a much more nuanced concept and approach, and actually requires greater managerial capability to execute than a centralized "command and control" environment. The district's activities signal the development of a new management model for how to create coherence within a decentralized organization. Managing into a decentralized environment in a coherent way necessitates differentiating and integrating mechanisms. However, we (and the case protagonists) continue to wrestle with the question, "How do we manage this complex system with a bias toward decision-making at the school site?"

2. The middle-management tier—the AIOs—is critical. District managers have to develop a deeper understanding of the role and how to recruit, retain, and support these key managers. Historically, school districts have not spent a significant amount of time understanding this critical role, preferring instead to focus on the role of the principal.

To achieve excellence at scale, it is imperative that both roles be performed well.

3. This case introduces the concept of *emergent strategy*. District leaders do not always have the time or luxury to design a complete strategy from day one. More likely, strategy is iterated over time, and in the case of CPS, is developed to bring coherence across a set of activities that might otherwise appear ad hoc or being pursued in isolation. CPS is trying new things (e.g., the school scorecards), spreading what works and making adjustments to the strategy along the way.

The STAR Schools Initiative at the San Francisco Unified School District

Overview

The purpose of this case is to reveal the managerial mechanisms by which a leader can support continuous improvement of student outcomes in chronically low-performing schools. It is one of a series of cases developed by the Public Education Leadership Project at Harvard University to illustrate for school leaders, district administrators, and graduate students the complexities of leading and sustaining large-scale organizational improvement in an urban public school district.

"The STAR Schools Initiative at the San Francisco Unified School District," PEL-039, focuses on one critical component of SFUSD's district improvement strategy, which provided low-performing schools with additional resources and services. It seeks to illustrate that the degree of effective decentralization among school sites will be a function of organizational culture, utilization of data, and a set of processes/procedures that enable integration.

A key concept in the case is achieving and sustaining organizational *coherence*. This refers to the dynamic process by which leaders manage all of the elements of the organization (e.g., culture,

resources, systems, structures, and stakeholders) to support effective strategy execution. To introduce students to the concept of organizational coherence in a public education setting, the instructor should assign the "Note on the PELP Coherence Framework," PEL-010, as a prereading.

Case Summary

In this case, Chief Academic Officer Christine Hiroshima contemplates her team's understanding of the strengths and weaknesses of the district's strategy to address underperforming schools, which is called the "Students and Teachers Achieving Results," or STAR, Initiative. The case opens with a description of the district's strategy from 2000 to 2006, called "Excellence for All," which focused on raising academic achievement for all students, the equitable allocation of district resources, and accountability for results.

The case details the origins of and rationale behind the STAR Initiative, which sought to address common challenges facing struggling schools. It describes the district's historical at-

---

This note was prepared by Lecturer Stacey Childress and Research Associate Tiffany K. Cheng.

tempts to address underperforming schools, both mandated by court order and by the state of California. Readers also understand how district leadership sought to apply lessons of past reforms to the STAR Initiative design.

The case then outlines how STAR schools were selected and the ways in which the district subsequently supported these schools (e.g., with funding and additional personnel). The leadership team identified common performance barriers and created five centrally funded positions for each site, including an instructional reform facilitator, long-term substitutes, parent liaisons, advisors, and learning support consultants. Other instructional resources and district supports are identified and implemented as well.

The remaining part of the case documents the challenges and achievements of the first few years of implementation, including lessons learned and adaptations to various roles and processes. Managing differences, striving for consistency, and managing complexity are ongoing managerial issues facing the leadership team.

The case concludes with a description of new challenges, as the district faces political unrest, shrinking enrollments, and decreased funding. Hiroshima and her team wrestle with questions about the future of the STAR Initiative and resource allocation.

Positioning

Overall, this case could be used in a wide variety of settings and with different audiences, ranging from experienced school leaders to graduate students in business, management, or education courses. It was written to be used in the capstone case series at the conclusion of a three-year PELP executive education program for teams of school district leaders. In addition to fostering discussion about the role of leadership in an urban public school setting, this case intends to offer readers an opportunity to consider how struggling schools can be supported for continuous improvement.

Learning Objectives

This case purposefully examines SFUSD's strategy implementation efforts to offer readers an opportunity to consider a number of educational leadership issues. Potential learning objectives include:

- **Deepen understanding of PELP coherence framework.** Students will learn to apply the conceptual framework through a discussion of how a district's elements (its structures, systems, resources, stakeholders, and culture) can be brought into coherence with a district-wide improvement strategy that ultimately changes school-level practices.

- **Illustrate how intervention strategies become more refined over time when the practice of reflecting and measuring success is institutionalized.** This case provides students with several concrete examples of how SFUSD applied lessons from previous reforms and tracked ongoing efforts in order to understand the connections between student achievement and their strategy.

- **Develop proficiency for identifying, building, and managing a multisite organization.** This case illustrates levers that can be used to influence school sites collectively (e.g., district strategy providing data, oversight, and accountability) and individually (e.g., customized interventions, etc.) in order to achieve high performance throughout the system.

- **Illustrate that managing a decentralized system is difficult and requires tight control of integrating mechanisms.** One of the central themes explored in this case is SFUSD's ability to support schools with varying student populations, resources, and leadership capacities. Students will build their analytical skills and be able to identify which managerial mechanisms are critical to maintaining appropriate integration and differentiation across schools successfully.

Assignment

Before class, participants should read "The STAR Schools Initiative at the San Francisco Unified School District," PEL-039, and consider the questions below; the "Note on the PELP Coherence Framework," PEL-010, should also be assigned if it has not been read previously.

Discussion Questions

1. What is the districtwide strategy in San Francisco? Assess the degree to which the STAR Schools Initiative is coherent with the districtwide strategy.

2. Evaluate the process the SFUSD team used to design and implement STAR. What worked well in the process? Why? What could have gone better?

3. What are the key elements of STAR that allow for differentiation between schools? Which elements are designed to achieve integration across schools? What are the strengths and limitations of the various elements of the intervention?

4. Has the program been successful so far? What is your evidence? What advice would you give the San Francisco team about STAR going forward? Be specific.

Teaching Plan and Analysis

This 90-minute teaching plan is based on an executive education course designed for the capstone session for PELP's inaugural class of urban public school leadership teams. The teaching plan can be modified to suit a 75-minute or 120-minute session if necessary.

Summary

I. **Introduction.** (2 minutes)

II. **Diagnosis.** During this portion of the discussion, participants are asked to identify the common characteristics of STAR schools in 2001. Instructors may begin by asking, "Before we jump into an analysis of the STAR Initiative and its fit with SFUSD's overall strategy, let's make sure we have a common understanding of what the 40-plus STAR schools have in common. If you were to visit 10 of the 40 over the course of a week, what would you see?" (10 minutes)

III. **Analysis and evaluation: STAR Initiative design.** This discussion pasture is aimed at developing participants' ability to analyze the district's design and planning process. Instructors can ask participants to evaluate the process the leadership team used to develop the STAR Initiative. "Did the team ground their strategy in a theory about how low-performing schools improve? Was there a balance between involving old and new decision makers, as well as old and new ideas? How would you evaluate the team's decision about pace?" (15 minutes)

IV. **Evaluation: STAR Initiative implementation.** In this discussion block, instructors can ask students, "How well are the various pieces of the STAR Initiative working together? Is the district successfully managing the mechanisms that result in appropriate differentiation and integration across schools?" (30 minutes)

V. **Evaluation: Student performance.** Instructors should direct participants to the data in the case's exhibits and ask, "How well is the STAR Initiative working? What results has the intervention achieved?" (10 minutes)

VI. **Recommendations.** "What advice would you give Hiroshima and her team about improvements to STAR, specifically to deal with the variability across STAR schools?" (10 minutes)

VII. **Reflection and transition.** If this case is being used to set up the race, achievement, and accountability cases on Montgomery County Public Schools (see PEL-043, PEL-044),[1] the instructor can pull back from the programmatic details of STAR and ask, "Much of the conversation and data in San Francisco is based on the race or ethnicity of students. How do you react to that? Exhibit 2 shows that most STAR schools have high poverty rates—would this be a better way to frame the conversation and intervention?" (10 minutes)

VIII. **Closing.** In the final minutes of class, instructors can reference specific moments in the discussion to highlight learning objectives. (3 minutes)

Introduction (2 minutes)

Before class, the instructor should write on the side board the district's goal, strategy, and theory of action. Then, the instructor can begin class by outlining the purpose of the case in the context of the course or module. One sample opening follows:

Today, we are going to discuss the STAR Initiative in San Francisco Unified School District. Throughout this module, we have analyzed district improvement strategies in terms of its connection to the district's goal and theory of action to understand whether systems achieve organizational coherence. I have written up what San Francisco's goal, strategy, and theory of action are on the board for us to consider as we discuss this case. The case describes the STAR Initiative as one of the key components of San Francisco's larger reform component, "Excellence for All." As we discuss the case, continue to think about whether the STAR Initiative seems to be in coherence with this overall strategy. We are going to move quickly in order to understand the case and its implications for school and district-level leadership. Let's get started.

Diagnosis (10 minutes)

The class begins with a diagnosis of the conditions common to STAR schools. As previously mentioned, instructors can open the conversation as follows: "Before we jump into an analysis

of the STAR Initiative and its fit with SFUSD's overall strategy, let's make sure we have a common understanding of what the 40-plus STAR schools have in common. If you were to visit 10 of these 40 schools, what would you see?" This is an opportunity for participants to see themselves as district leaders facing real challenges within a set of low-performing schools. In the past, participants have identified the following characteristics:

- **Demographics.** STAR schools largely comprise African-American/Latino students and represent disproportionate numbers of students from low-income, minority backgrounds when compared to district demographics.

- **Teachers and principals.** STAR schools have high levels of turnover that prevent stability and creation of a positive school culture and young, inexperienced teachers and principals with varying leadership capacities.

- **Instructional practice.** STAR schools display little to no collaboration among teachers and low-level instruction (in the previous SFUSD case, report revealed evidence of "dumbed-down curriculum"); perhaps there are a number of teachers and principals nearing retirement who are resistant to change and disinvested in the school community.

- **School climate.** STAR schools show low parental engagement, student behavior problems, buildings in disrepair, and so on.

Analysis and evaluation: STAR Initiative design (15 minutes)

In this analysis, participants should focus on the process through which SFUSD's leadership team developed the STAR Initiative. Instructors can ask participants, "Did the team ground their strategy in a theory about how low-performing schools improve? Was there a balance between involving old and new decision makers, as well as old and new ideas?" This is an opportunity for students to analyze the ways in which the SFUSD leadership team incorporated lessons from past reforms and generated new ideas in designing the district's intervention program. Past participants point to the team's prioritization of providing specific, school-based support to teachers and principals, as well as the multi-year design of the program improvement strategy, as evidence that the new reform effort did in fact build on previous learning. In addition, the mix of insiders and outsiders involved in designing the strategy reflected the leadership's value of collective input.

Instructors can move the discussion further by asking students, "How would you evaluate the team's decision about pace?" The instructor should note that this strategy element will be referenced and explored in depth later in the session. However, for the purposes of this initial analysis, it should be made known that the leadership team began planning in June of 2001 and rolled out the new initiative in fall 2001. Decisions and actions about hiring, planning, capacity, and so on had to be made within this three-month period.

Evaluation: STAR Initiative implementation (30 minutes)

Instructors will want to focus this discussion pasture on SFUSD's differentiated treatment of schools and its efforts to integrate simultaneously the work of all schools around the STAR improvement strategy. In order to help participants tease out the various nuances of the strategy, consider asking: "How well are the various pieces of the STAR Initiative working together? Is the district successfully managing the mechanisms that result in appropriate differentiation and integration across schools?"

It may be helpful to structure this discussion as follows:

Integrating Elements across All Schools:

- **Weighted student formula.** All schools in SFUSD received funding through a centralized resource allocation method that calculated funding amounts based on a series of

"weights" (i.e., language status, SES, mother's educational attainment, etc.).[2]

- **Academic planning process.** Every school in SFUSD completed an annual academic plan based on prior-year performance data.

- **Principal evaluation.** Principals at all schools were required to create management/leadership plans to meet academic targets and the academic planning priorities.

- **Walkthroughs.** To ensure accountability and monitor schools in their pursuit of improvement, cross-functional teams from various central office departments conducted a series of visits throughout the academic year.

- **Reporting structure.** STAR and non-STAR principals reported to one of five assistant superintendents.

Differentiating Elements across All Schools:

- **Additional funding.** STAR schools received an additional per student allocation from central office.

- **Additional school personnel.** Central office fully funded a total of five additional positions at each STAR school (instructional reform facilitator [IRF], long-term substitutes, parent liaisons, advisors, and learning support consultants).

- Increased oversight of principals. STAR leadership met with principals to help them understand the connection between their students' academic data and their strategy for the year.

- Increased oversight of core curriculum implementation: In STAR schools, teachers were required to have blocks of uninterrupted time for language arts and mathematics instruction.

Integrating Elements across All STAR Schools:

- **Additional resources.** All STAR schools received supplemental funding and school personnel.

- **Central office supports for IRFs.** All IRFs received the same professional development and attended central office meetings with other IRFs twice a month.

Differentiating Elements across All STAR Schools:

- **Variation in IRF role.** Depending on the specific conditions at the school (i.e., student needs, teacher skill and knowledge, principal style and capacity, etc.), IRFs performed a variety of functions from school to school.

As the discussion winds up regarding the STAR Initiative's integrating and differentiating elements, instructors should focus participants on the critical role of the IRF. Overall, the main point of this phase of the class is to discuss how the IRF is both an integrating and differentiating mechanism and the effect this has on STAR schools across the district. Instructors can ask students, "What about this works well? What could be changed to make it more effective?" The STAR Initiative is designed in such a way that a school's ultimate success depends on the IRF role. If the IRF is utilized to support critical needs in an effective manner, then the particular school will likely improve. For example, in some schools, IRFs focused on instructional improvement activities and worked with teachers to determine professional development needs based on student performance data. In others, IRFs took responsibility for administrative duties involving discipline and schoolyard monitoring. Instructors can push this point by probing students: "Thus, is the implementation and ongoing refinement in this area all it could be? Should the central office take a stronger position about whether IRFs should focus on instructional improvement versus administrative duties? What would be the consequences of such a stand?"

After additional consideration of the district's role and its management of the intervention strategy, instructors should ask students to consider: "Why do the weaknesses in the STAR Initiative exist?" Answers will likely focus on the speed of implementation. Some participants may express their belief that the district should have spent more time planning to increase consistency in the quality of implementation. The instructor can ask these participants, "If you think they should have waited, what time period seems appropriate? What would you have done during that time?" In the past, some participants have argued that managing a school district for improvement requires a willingness to enact a strategy in order to learn which of the new components elicits desired behavior and outcomes and make adjustments along the way.

Evaluation: Student performance (10 minutes)
Here, the instructor can ask participants to consider, "How well is the STAR Initiative working?" Instructors can point to case Exhibits 2a, 2b, and 9 to discuss what SFUSD's leadership team is producing. Over a five-year period, there is substantial improvement in some schools, with African-American, Latino, and English language learners enrolled in STAR schools outpacing their non-STAR district counterparts on the whole. However, the results across STAR schools are inconsistent and show that there is wide variability between schools. Twenty-eight out of 44 schools met API growth targets, which suggests that there is a connection between the variance in IRF behavior and uneven school performance outcomes. While there was some focused reflection and response on the part of the district's leadership (e.g., categorizing schools as "STAR," then "Intensive STAR," and finally "Dream Schools"), the district allocated additional resources and support to these schools without a concerted management strategy to ensure that all would meet performance targets. It is important to force students to consider the student-level data in Exhibit 1 separately from the school-level data in Exhibit 2. Instructors can ask those who would have waited longer before implementing, "How much of the gain in Exhibit 9 would you be willing to trade off for

more planning time?" Instructors will want to emphasize that the data reflects the progress of five years, which means that waiting to implement the STAR Initiative might have led to lower gains at the end of 2006.

Recommendations (10 minutes)

Having acknowledged the uneven performance of STAR schools under the district's improvement strategy, instructors should ask participants for explicit recommendations: "What advice would you give Hiroshima and her team?" Some suggestions will focus on the discovery of the accidental pipeline for developing teacher and principal leadership in IRFs and address ways to exploit and expand this growing cadre of instructional leaders. Others will emphasize the importance of spreading this intervention to non-STAR schools that are struggling to bridge achievement disparities among racial/cultural groups.

Reflection and transition (10 minutes)

If this case is being used as a setup for the Montgomery County schools cases, the instructor can pull back from the programmatic details of STAR and ask, "Much of the conversation and data in San Francisco is based on the race or ethnicity of students. How do you react to that? Exhibit 2 shows that most STAR schools have high poverty rates—would this be a better way to frame the conversation or intervention?" After several comments on both sides of this argument, the instructor can show the data in Exhibits 1 and 2 of this teaching note. Here, the data dramatically shows that the performance disparities in SFUSD do not break by socioeconomic status but by race. In San Francisco, the challenge is to accelerate the performance of African-American and Latino students while continuing to raise the top level of performance.

The instructor can close this discussion and set up the Montgomery County cases by saying, "In the next session, we will examine a district that framed the achievement gap discussion in

terms of poverty for a number of years. Now, the community is facing the need to focus on race as a variable in a direct way despite its aversion to discussing school achievement in these terms. Come prepared for an important discussion about the concrete steps the district is taking to address this difficult issue."

Closing (3 minutes)

Instructors can close this session by emphasizing that the STAR Initiative offers an opportunity to consider the complexities facing urban school districts working to address the various needs and existing capacities in schools with diverse student populations. As a managerial case, it is of note that the San Francisco leadership team's actions differentiate and integrate simultaneously by delineating roles and responsibilities to specific members of the organization. However, district leadership must continue to confront the issues of race productively in order to achieve equity for its students.

Notes

1. If the STAR case is not being used to set up the Montgomery County cases, the remaining 10 minutes can be added to the recommendations section.

2. For more information about the weighted student formula, please see "Pursuing Educational Equity: Aligning Resources at San Francisco Unified School District," PEL–005.

Exhibit 1
SFUSD Achievement Data by Income Subgroups

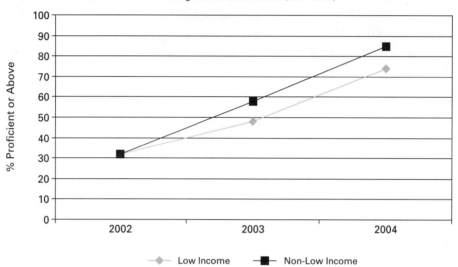

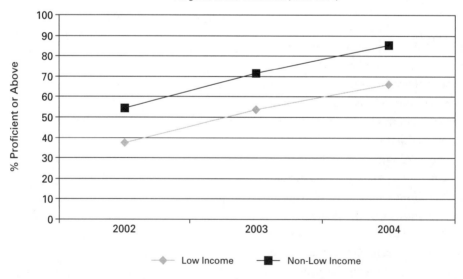

Source: California Department of Education

Exhibit 2
SFUSD Achievement Data by Racial/Ethnic Subgroups

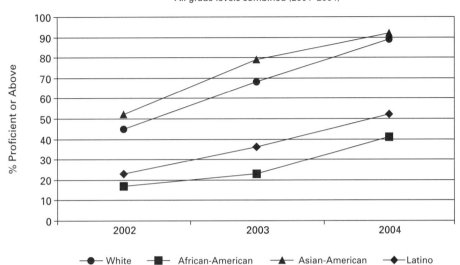

SFUSD Students Scoring Proficient or Above on State Mathematics Exam

All grade levels combined (2001–2004)

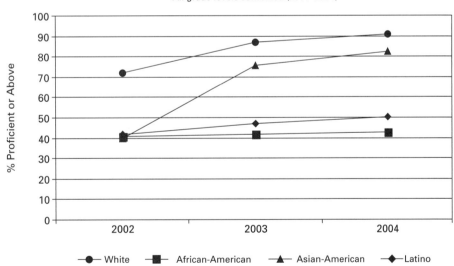

SFUSD Students Scoring Proficient or Above on State Reading Exam

All grade levels combined (2001–2004)

Source: California Department of Education

Race, Accountability, and the Achievement Gap Case Series (A) and (B)

Overview

These cases were developed by the Public Education Leadership Project at Harvard University to demonstrate one school district's effort to address issues of race while seeking to eliminate the district's minority student achievement gap. This case series is designed to facilitate discussions among school leaders, executives and graduate students about the challenges and realities of leading and sustaining large-scale organizational change in urban public school districts.

The first case entitled, "Race, Accountability, and the Achievement Gap (A)," PELP No. 035, overviews Montgomery County Public Schools' history of race relations and the minority student achievement gap. It highlights key district developments to combat the achievement gap leading up to the summer of 2005. The (A) case is designed to facilitate discussions about the connections between race and the achievement gap in addition to the sensitivity people experience when talking about race, racism, and the achievement gap. The (A) case be-

gins and ends with MCPS leadership's decision to reexamine issues of race and institutional barriers impeding the success of African American and Hispanic students. It prompts participants to develop an action plan for the district to deal with issues of race and the achievement gap.

The second case entitled, "Race, Accountability, and the Achievement Gap (B)," PELP No. 036, begins where the (A) case ends with the actions MCPS leadership took during the school year following the summer of 2005. The case walks through MCPS leadership's use of data to identify racial inequities in student performance and their attempts to integrate strategies to close the achievement gap into the district's overall strategic operations. The (B) case is also accompanied by a video of white Superintendent Jerry Weast speaking explicitly about race and the achievement gap at the first administrators meeting of the 2005–2006 academic year. The case allows participants to analyze the actions MCPS leadership took and discuss the communication challenges when attempting to deal with issues of this nature.

This note was prepared by professors Karen L. Mapp and David A. Thomas and Research Associate Tonika Cheek Clayton.

Case Summaries

Race, Accountability, and the Achievement Gap (A)

The (A) and (B) case series details Montgomery County Public Schools' efforts to address issues of race in district policies, practices and behaviors. To give the reader context, the (A) case provides background on Montgomery County Public Schools, its history of race relations, and its attempts to systemically address the minority student achievement gap. It includes student performance data that shows the achievement gap and how district performance has changed over the past few years. Next, the case overviews a wide range of reactions of teachers and administrators to whether or not the district's achievement gap is related to issues of race. Key relevant changes to district policies, procedures and professional development efforts that took place prior to 2005 are also covered. Finally, the case highlights several school-based initiatives spearheaded by teachers and principals to close the gap without direct assistance from central office.

The case ends in the summer of 2005 with case protagonist Deputy Superintendent Frieda Lacey reflecting on how to effectively tackle race and equity issues in addition to successfully making it a priority throughout the school system.

Race, Accountability, and the Achievement Gap (B)

The (B) case chronicles the actions of MCPS leadership following their decision in the summer of 2005 to focus on race and removing institutional barriers that impeded the achievement of African American and Hispanic students. It details MCPS' utilization of data, research and technology to employ tactics aimed to improve the performance of African American and Hispanic students within the school system.

The case also describes the leadership team's communication challenges with regards to ex-

plicitly discussing race and the achievement gap. An excerpt of Superintendent Jerry Weast's speech to administrators one month into the timeline of the case shows the effect of Hurricane Katrina on the timing and dialogue of the school district's efforts. In addition, the case delves into uncomfortable leadership team meeting moments when issues of race were brought to the forefront and team members debated whether or not terms like "institutional racism" or "institutional barriers" should be used publicly.

Finally, the case outlines MCPS leadership team members' efforts to create a data-driven accountability system focused on improving minority student achievement.

Positioning

This case series may be used for a wide variety of audiences to facilitate discussions about an organization's effort to explicitly address issues of race as part of an overall strategy to improve performance. Given the sensitive nature of discussions on race, the case facilitator should exercise judgment when deciding on when to teach the case series during a course. It helps if the class has already built a respectful learning community in which group norms have been established and participants generally feel comfortable expressing opposing viewpoints.

It is important that the facilitator be transparent about the difficulty in discussing issues of race and equity. The instructor should encourage participants to engage in an open-minded debate without attacking an individual because of a particular viewpoint. Also, the instructor should actively seek to solicit feedback from all races and backgrounds and avoid allowing one particular group to dominate the discussion. Prior to the class discussion, it may be helpful for the facilitator and participants to read the following references:

Robin J. Ely, Debra E. Meyerson, and Martin N. Davidson, "Rethinking Political Correctness," *Harvard Business Review OnPoint,* September 1, 2006.

Glenn E. Singleton and Curtis Lindon, *Courageous Conversations about Race: A Field Guide for Achieving Equity in School,* Thousand Oaks, CA: Corwin Press, November 2005.

The teaching plan outlined below assumes that the (A) and (B) cases will be taught in two separate 90-minute sessions on the same day, consecutive days, or weeks apart. Nevertheless, this teaching plan may be modified so that the case series is taught in one session. For example, instead of asking participants to read the (B) case after the (A) case discussion, the instructor may summarize the (B) case to participants, show the video footage of Superintendent Jerry Weast, and commence the "leadership discussion" outlined in the (B) case teaching plan and analysis.

Learning Objectives

Potential learning objectives include:

- **Effective diversity initiatives are embedded in an organization's overall strategy.** This case allows participants to consider ways in which an organization can incorporate strategies to eliminate racial and class inequities into its overall strategy. Often times, organizations assign a few persons or a department to handle the diversity work without embedding the work into the overall execution of the strategic plan. MCPS not only used diversity trainings in its attempt to close the achievement gap, but also focused on how to systemically eliminate racial inequities through changing district policies, analyzing data, and focusing on outcomes.

- **What leadership is needed to address race and equity issues.** In most professional settings, race and class inequities are extremely difficult to address openly. This case gives participants an opportunity to identify what kind of leadership is necessary when dealing with race and equity issues in professional and public settings.

Assignment

(A) Case

Students should read the "(A) case" and be prepared to answer the following questions:

Discussion Questions

1. Evaluate Montgomery County Public Schools' efforts to "raise the bar" and "close the gap" between 1999 and 2005.

    a. What has been their strategy?

    b. How successful have they been in making meaningful progress?

2. Based on the data in the case, should Frieda Lacey and Jerry Weast be alarmed and feel MCPS' efforts are inadequate to close the gap?

3. What are the most significant obstacles to accelerating their district's efforts to close the gap?

4. To what extent are race and racism significant issues in the case?

5. What is required for a district to effectively address the racial achievement gap?

6. Develop an action plan for Lacey, Weast and MCPS' executive team. Be as explicit as possible about what and how they should approach the problem.

(B) Case

Students should read the "(B) case" and be prepared to answer the following questions:

Discussion Questions

1. What additional strategies were put in place after the July retreat? How successful were they?

2. What are the differences between the initia-

tives in the A and B case? Evaluate the success of these additional efforts.

3. What challenges and obstacles did district leaders face in these additional attempts to create systemic change to close the achievement gap?

4. What skills and competencies are required to lead an initiative where issues of race and class are addressed?

Teaching Plan and Analysis—(A) Case

This teaching plan is based on an executive education course designed for the school district administrators and affiliates. It assumes that the corresponding (B) case will be taught subsequently during a separate 90-minute session. This teaching plan can be modified to suit a 75-minute or 90-minute session.

Summary

I. **Introduction.** The discussion will begin with participants sharing their beliefs and perceptions of the achievement gap. To begin, the instruction may say, "When you think of the achievement gap, what comes to mind? What are the central reasons for the gap?" (5 minutes)

II. **1999: Weast comes to MCPS.** This brief section allows participants to briefly explore the historical context of MCPS and the achievement gap. Key questions posed are: "What is important to understand about MCPS' context especially as it relates to closing the gap? What is the appetite for going directly at issues of race?" (5 minutes)

III. **Raise the bar, close the gap.** This section gives participants an opportunity to critique Weast's major reform efforts to date. Key questions posed are: "Is it different from Success for Every Student? What does "raise the bar, close the gap" mean?

What value proposition is Weast making to the community? What do we have to do to get there?" (10 minutes)

IV. **What is the strategy?** During this segment, participants will discuss the pros and cons of MCPS' current strategy. The instructor should push participants to discuss how the achievement gap relates to each component of the strategy. Key questions posed are: "What are the key components of MCPS' strategy? What does this have to do with the racial achievement gap? What is the implicit theory about race and closing the achievement gap? What are the embedded assumptions about it?" (15 minutes)

V. **Let's give MCPS a grade: A—B—C—D.** This discussion time gives participants an opportunity to critically think about MCPS reform efforts and assess their effectiveness. They instructor may ask, "What grade would you give MCPS on their efforts to close the achievement gap based on the case?" It may be helpful for the instructor to show slides of performance data as a quick reminder before the vote. The discussion should begin with participants who gave the lowest grade, especially if the discussion of MCPS has been mostly favorable up to this point. The instructor may ask, "Why the low grade? What mistakes have they made? What has been critical?" (10 minutes)

VI. **Challenges: Concerns.** In this segment, participants will evaluate the challenges facing MCPS leadership as they attempt to employ strategies to close the achievement gap. Key questions posed: "How concerned should Lacey and Weast be? Do they need to turn up the heat? Why? What are the major obstacles? Where is the key leverage point?" (10 minutes)

VII. Decisions. During this time, participants can evaluate the school-based efforts to close the achievement gap. The instructor may begin the discussion by saying, "What do you make of what's happened in the schools presented in the case?" Follow-up questions posed are: "What have you learned about closing the gap in this system? What do the school-based examples from the case tell us?" (10 minutes)

VIII. Action plans/Small groups discussion/Closing. The instructor may decide to divide the participants into groups of 2–4 people to develop concrete action steps for the MCPS leadership team. Key questions posed: "What should they do going forward? What should Lacey and Weast do? How explicit should they talk about race? What groups should MCPS focus on?" In closing, the instructor should distribute the (B) case and assignment questions. (25 minutes)

Introduction (5 minutes)

The case analysis will begin by briefly discussing participants' perceptions and beliefs about the achievement gap. The instructor may begin by posing the following questions: "When you think of the achievement gap, what comes to mind? What are the central reasons for the gap?" Participants may point to societal dynamics, school systems, student backgrounds, or other reasons. Since it is possible to dedicate a full session to the causes of the achievement gap, it is important that the instructor emphasize that the case discussion will focus on how a school system can build the capacity to close the achievement gap, noting that it is important to understand its environmental context. After participants briefly discuss their views on achievement gap causes, the instructor can shift the conversation to the case subject by saying, "Today's session is not about the theory of the achievement gap. It is about the reality of at-tempting to close it. How do we create the capacity to close the achievement gap?"

1999: Weast comes to MCPS (5 minutes)

To provide context for the case discussion, participants can briefly discuss the historical background as it relates to the achievement gap leading up to the moment when Weast arrives at MCPS. Key questions posed are: "What is important to understand about MCPS' context especially as it relates to closing the gap? What is the appetite for going directly at issues of race?"

The discussion may bring out the school district's changing demographics, past attempts to address the student achievement gap even before Weast arrived, and the characterization of the Montgomery County community as progressive-minded. Since more minorities are entering the school district at such a rapid pace, there is increased pressure on MCPS leadership to close the achievement gap and to live up to the district's reputation of consistently meeting high performance targets. Past initiatives under Superintendent Paul Vance targeting the achievement gap suggest that there is an appetite for addressing the issues but that there is somewhat of a reluctance to single out African-American and Hispanic students explicitly as part of the overall strategy.

Raise the bar, close the gap (10 minutes)

Next, participants can discuss the positives and negatives of Weast's "raise the bar, close the gap" efforts. Key questions posed are: Is it different from Success for Every Student? What does "raise the bar, close the gap" mean? What value proposition is Weast making to the community? What do we have to do to get there?

The "raise the bar, close the gap" (RBCG) effort under Weast endeavored to improve performance of the highest performing students while simultaneously improving the overall performance of minority students who represent the low end of the achievement gap. To accomplish both goals simultaneously, MCPS must improve the overall performance of students on the low end of the achievement gap at an even faster rate assuming that the performance bar is steadily rising. The reform's dual message confronts the achievement gap which is a serious problem for the administration, but also speaks to affluent, influential MCPS stakeholders who worry that low-performing schools will take resources away from high-performing schools.

The instructor may want to take some time to reflect on the critical tasks MCPS employed to make RBCG work. Critical tasks included defining the problem (red/green zone performance), maintaining a strategy in which everyone wins, and using equity as design principle. Instead of focusing on equity of resources across schools, Weast focused on equity of outcomes.

What is the strategy? (15 minutes)

During this segment, participants will debate the merits and negatives of MCPS' current strategy using supportive evidence from the case. Key questions posed are: "What are the key components of MCPS' strategy? What does this have to do with the racial achievement gap? What is the implicit theory about race and closing the achievement gap? What are the embedded assumptions about it?" Participant responses may include but are not limited to the following:

- **Differentiation and integration.** One key component of MCPS' strategy was to differentiate managerial treatment and resources across schools. MCPS poured more resources and funding into red zone schools (low-performing schools with disproportionate numbers of minority students) in an effort to improve overall minority student performance. Although many reforms were also rolled out to even schools in the green zone, it was unclear if strategies specific to addressing the achievement gap were really implemented at green zone schools, which catered to a smaller number of minority students.

- **Setting high standards.** Weast hoped to create an internal demand for high-performing students in middle and elementary schools by setting high school targets high. By standardizing grades and tests across all high schools, MCPS eliminated a system that institutionalized low expectations of minority students.

- **Data-driven decision-making.** MCPS used data effectively to define and monitor the minority student achievement gap down to individual students, to identify barriers for minority student performance, and to execute the district's overall strategy. Often times, teachers and principals don't have access to timely data that they can use to differentiate instruction down to the individual student. .

- **Stakeholder buy-in.** Public relations is an integral piece of Weast's strategy to keep key stakeholders involved and happy with the reform's progress. This political capital is important when it becomes necessary for Weast to tackle issues, such as race and equity, in the face of community/stakeholder resistance.

- **Focus on data.** The focus on data is integral to MCPS' execution of the district's overall strategy. MCPS administration used data to define the problem, to identify barriers to student performance and to develop strategies for performance improvement.

- **Staff development.** Building organizational capacity through professional development was another key component of RBCG reform efforts. Weast's administration created the staff development teacher (SDT) role as a means to disseminate reform efforts at a fast pace across the school system. In addition, Weast started a diversity training division to focus specifically on achievement gap strategies. Nevertheless, diversity training offerings were limited and mostly voluntary for SDTs only. Since only a few SDTs took full advantage of the diversity trainings, the effectiveness of the diversity training process and structure was questionable.

Let's give MCPS a grade: A—B—C—D (10 minutes)

After participants discuss MCPS' strategy and student performance evidence from the case, write grades A, B, C, and D, on the board. Then the instructor can remark: "There are lots of data in the case. Here is a friendly reminder—[show a few slides of the data]. What grade would you give MCPS on their efforts to close the achievement gap based on the case?"

Then, the discussion should shift to criticisms from participants who gave MCPS a "C" or "D." Key questions posed: "Why the low grade? What mistakes have they made? What's been critical?"

This segment gives participants an opportunity to think critically about MCPS actions. Some participants may remark that there is no coherent strategy to change the culture of low expectations down to the classroom. Much of the diversity training that administrators deem to be effective in combating achievement gap issues is voluntary and mostly administered to staff development teachers. Moreover, the key change agents at the school level, the community superintendents and staff development teachers, vary widely in their adoption of practices designed to address achievement gap issues. Some participants may point out that the leadership focuses mainly on performance but does not adequately address teacher expectations of minority students. Others may ask if achievement gap strategies focused primarily in the red zone will extend to the green zone, noting that case Exhibit 10b indicates that minorities in the red zone appear to be improving at a faster pace than minorities in the green zone. Also, some may oppose the red/green zone categories for fear of perpetuating negative stereotypes of minority students. Finally, there is no accountability sys-

tem in place to ensure that achievement gap efforts are implemented or working.

Challenges: Concerns (10 minutes)

Next, participants will evaluate the challenges MCPS faces in their attempt to close the achievement gap and make suggestions about the areas in which the action plan should focus. As participants discuss the challenges that MCPS must address, the instructor will note on the blackboard the key design requirements that are needed in the action plan. Key questions posed: How concerned should Lacey and Weast be? Do they need to turn up the heat? Why? What are the major obstacles? Where is the key leverage point? To what extent is this about race?" In the past, participants mentioned the following challenges and action plan design requirements (not an exhaustive list):

Challenges:

- There is a general lack of accountability throughout the school system as it relates to the minority achievement gap.

- Low expectations of minority students are widespread but often not acknowledged.

- Opinions about whether or not race plays any role in the achievement gap vary widely across stakeholders.

- There are many inconsistencies in adoption and implementation across community superintendents and staff development teachers.

- There is uneven buy-in across district and school-level leaders for the various achievement gap initiatives.

- Only 15% of staff development teachers are minorities.

- Racism is part of the fabric of the community but largely goes unseen.

Design Requirements:

- Leadership must have hard conversations about race and expectations in order to figure out the appropriate actions that will work.

• There needs to be consistency in achievement gap efforts across the system.

• There must be a transfer of learning mechanism down to the classroom.

Decisions (10 minutes)

The discussion then moves to the school-based initiatives to close the achievement gap. The instructor may start by saying:

What do you make of what's happened in:

• **Westland Middle School.** Green zone— throw out on-level classes for English

• **Piney Branch Elementary.** Red zone –Focus on Math A for minority students

• **Newport Mill Middle School.** Red zone – Predictive assessments—posting kids names and performance status

Follow-up questions posed are: "What have you learned about closing the gap in this system? What do the school-based examples from the case tell us?" The school-based examples show that hard conversations about race and the achievement gap have already penetrated down to the classroom level at some MCPS schools. It is important to note that the school principal played a critical role in pushing the initiatives forward in each of the school examples. Participants may suggest that the district allow the local school experiments to drive some of the next steps for the overall system. Other schools could potentially learn from the mistakes and successes of schools that have already tried to tackle issues of race and the achievement gap by developing their own practices.

Action plans/Small groups discussion/Closing (25 minutes)

Next, the instructor may divide the participants into small groups of 2–4 people to discuss what specific action steps MCPS should do going forward. The instructor may give the participants 5–10 minutes to discuss action plans before debriefing with the larger group. Key questions

posed: "What should they do going forward? What should Lacey and Weast do? How explicit should they talk about race? What groups should MCPS focus on?"

After 5–10 minutes of small group discussion, the instructor may ask participants to share their ideas with the whole group.

In closing, the instructor should distribute the (B) case and corresponding study questions.

Teaching Plan and Analysis—(B) Case

This teaching plan is based on an executive education course designed for school district administrators and affiliates. It assumes that the corresponding (A) case will be taught previously during a separate 90-minute session. This teaching plan can be modified to suit a 75-minute or 90-minute session.

Summary

I. **Introduction.** The instructor may begin by saying: "We ended the (A) case with Frieda in August of 2005 wondering if the achievement gap strategies put in place were gaining any traction. And wondering how MCPS could hold itself (administrators, principals, and teachers) accountable for the work and what could the senior leadership staff do to make a difference. Where are we when the (B) case opens?" (5 minutes)

II. **Describe MCPS' strategy in the (B) case.** In this section, participants get the opportunity to evaluate the actions MCPS took following the 2005 summer retreat. The instructor may begin the discussion by asking, "What new strategies did the district employee after the summer retreat?" The instructor may use the PELP Coherence Framework to outline the actions executed by MCPS leadership on the blackboard. (30 minutes)

III. **September 29th meeting.** During this

segment, participants will have an opportunity to evaluate a case scenario in which race is explicitly discussed during a leadership team meeting. Key questions posed: "What happened at the meeting on the 29th? What happened next? Did the heat go up or stay the same? Post Sept. 29th? Were there some specific strategies designed to improve accountability?" (15 minutes)

IV. **Recommendations.** Participants can make recommendations and discuss things they would have done differently from MCPS leadership. Key questions posed: "What's working, not working with this approach? What were the challenges/push backs? Do you have any recommendations?" (10 minutes)

V. **Leadership discussion.** During this discussion period, participants will explore what it takes to lead a productive conversation about race to ultimately address the achievement gap. Key questions posed: "What does it mean to lead in this work on race? What does it look like? Do we have any examples in the case that jumped out at you? What is the leadership team doing that's different?" (30 minutes)

VI. **Closing.** The instructor may review the big ideas from the learning objectives and thank participants for engaging in a difficult case discussion.

Introduction (5 minutes)
The case analysis begins with a brief reminder of where the participants finished at the end of the (A) case. The instructor can begin class by saying, We ended the (A) case with Frieda in August of 2005 wondering if the achievement gap approach put in place was gaining any traction. And wondering how MCPS could hold itself (administrators, principals, and teachers) accountable for the work and what could the se-

nior leadership staff do to make a difference. Where are we when the (B) case opens?

Describe MCPS' strategy in the (B) case (30 minutes)
Then the discussion shifts to what new actions were taken during the (B) case. Key question posed: What new actions did the district employ after the summer retreat? How would you evaluate their effectiveness?

The instructor can use the PELP framework to capture the student responses. Participants may make the following observations about the actions MCPS leadership took (not an exhaustive list):

Culture: In the first administrator's meeting of the school year, Weast explicitly spoke about racial inequities in society and in the school system referencing the aftermath of Hurricane Katrina. He also made it clear that closing the achievement gap and eliminating barriers for African American and Hispanic students to achieve was a high priority for MCPS. Thus, principals learned early on in the school year that the district focus has shifted more towards racial inequities and closing the achievement gap. Also, MCPS leadership team worked together to try to determine the best language to use when speaking about issues of race throughout the district.

Systems: MCPS leadership decided to review course enrollment data disaggregated by race even at the elementary grades. Analysis of the new data compelled leadership to shift its focus to providing more minority students access to rigorous courses. MCPS administrators also developed school improvement targets and school monitoring calendars to share accountability between district and school leadership. In addition, Lacey created M-Stat, a system focused mainly on eliminating institutional barriers that hindered the success of African American and Hispanic students. M-Stat gave community superintendents the opportunity to look at data across schools and work together on developing solutions based on best practices and research. Also, the HAPIT tool was developed to help principals identify students with high performance potential who may have been overlooked.

Resources: Since the four-person diversity team had limited capacity to conduct diversity training sessions throughout the year, the department created online modules that could be administered at schools without district personnel. This could potentially extend the diversity team's reach. Nevertheless, it does not address the fact that a small group of SDTs repeatedly utilized the diversity department while others don't use them at all. Thus, the extent to which the modules will extend beyond the usual SDT groupies is questionable. The administration also increased efforts to recruit more minorities into leadership positions at the district level.

Stakeholders: MCPS leadership solicited feedback from students and board members in seeking to better understand race and equity issues within the school system.

September 29th meeting (15 minutes)
Next, the instructor can move the discussion to the September 29th meeting to give participants an opportunity to discuss the case scenario in which race is explicitly discussed in an executive leadership team meeting. Key questions posed: "What happened at the meeting on the 29th? What happened next? Did the heat go up or stay the same *post* Sept. 29th? Were there some specific steps designed to improve accountability?"

This is an opportunity for participants to reflect on what it is like to have a difficult conversation about race and equity in a professional setting. The instructor should focus the discussion on how Lacey handled the situation and what she could have done differently to change the outcome. Participants may notice Lacey's unwillingness to compromise the achievement

gap agenda combined with her deliberate attempts to make other members of the leadership team feel more at ease while openly discussing the tough issues. Lacey's group began to build in accountability for community superintendents and principals through M-Stat and the school monitoring calendars.

Recommendations (10 minutes)
During this segment, participants will critique the action steps presented in the case and discuss the changes they think should be made. Key questions posed: "What's working, not working with this approach? What were the challenges/push backs? Do you have any recommendations?" Past participants made the following comments:

Challenges:

- Difficult conversations about race still not happening throughout most of the school system

- Low expectations of minority students have not been adequately addressed.

- Unclear how to foster a shared responsibility among principals.

- Still inconsistencies across community superintendents.

- Community Superintendents and principals may feel as if they are being micromanaged.

Sample Recommendations:

- Require diversity training for all staff development teachers.

- Focus on improving math instruction.

- Use pedagogy to drive the discussion on diversity.

- Market major changes and successes as part of the district's strategy.

Leadership discussion (30 minutes)
During this segment, participants will discuss what it takes to lead a productive dialogue about

race to ultimately address the achievement gap. Key questions posed: What does it mean to lead in this work on race? What does it look like? Do we have any examples in the case that jumped out at you? What is the leadership team doing that's different? Past participants highlighted Donna Graves and Frieda Lacey for their courage and willingness to directly take on issues of race despite internal and external resistance to explicitly discuss the issues. Other participants pointed to school teachers and principals who took risks to adopt unproven strategies to close the achievement gap based on their experiences and beliefs.

Next, the instructor should show case participants video excerpts of Superintendent Jerry Weast's speech about the parallels of Hurricane Katrina to the school system. Then the instructor may ask, "What does it take to do this work? What kind of leader/team? If Jerry was a Black man would the same speech have been received differently?"

At this time, participants may debate issues such as the racial representation or the race candor needed to lead this kind of effort. Opinions on this topic will probably vary widely depending on racial background and experiences.

Closing

Following the leadership discussion, the instructor may wish to check temperature of the class by saying something like, *"How is everyone feeling?"* After hearing some responses, the instructor may wish to follow-up by saying, "I'm sure this case has raised some issues for you that we need to think about more. It may have been hard for some folks but we need to regularly talk about these issues."

In closing, the instructor may review the big ideas outlined in the learning objectives and repeat exceptional participant comments that pushed everyone's thinking during the discussions.

Sustaining High Performance over Time

Meeting New Challenges at the Aldine Independent School District

Overview

The "Meeting New Challenges at the Aldine Independent School District" case illustrates the challenges of managing for improved student achievement in a dynamic urban public school district setting. It is one of a series of cases developed by the HGSE/HBS Public Education Leadership Project (PELP) to describe for other school leaders, executives and graduate students the challenges and realities of leading and sustaining large-scale organizational change in an urban public school district.

The case examines the Aldine Independent School District (AISD)'s efforts in 2005 to sustain and accelerate significant increases in student performance achieved during the preceding decade. The case highlights the school district's managerial challenges posed by higher state standards, performance gaps within AISD, and the district's historically decentralized approach towards the implementation of reforms at the school level. Students can engage in a robust discussion of how to effectively lead and manage systemwide reform and continuous im-

provement efforts over time. The case also provides an opportunity for students to analyze the importance of effective leadership and develop an understanding of how the relationship between a leader and his/her subordinates facilitates (or hinders) organizational effectiveness. Finally, the case introduces the concept of "differentiation" as a managerial approach through which mangers exert more or less control over direct reports based on capacity, performance, and function. In public education, this strategy has often been dichotomized as centralized versus decentralized management; however, a more nuanced perspective depicts managerial actions along a "loose-tight" continuum.

A key concept in the case is achieving and sustaining *coherence,* the dynamic process by which leaders manage all of the elements of the organization (e.g. culture, resources, systems, structures, and stakeholders) to support and drive effective strategy execution. To introduce students to the concept of organizational coherence in a public education setting, the instructor should assign the "Note on the PELP Coher-

---

This note was prepared by professors Allen S. Grossman and Stacey Childress and Research Associate Caroline King.

ence Framework," PEL-010, as a pre-reading if students have not yet read it.

Case Summary

Near the end of her fourth year as Superintendent, Nadine Kujawa is confronted with the greatest challenge of her 41-year career with AISD. From 1994–2001, Kujawa had been the chief architect of curriculum and instruction reforms that had achieved remarkable gains in student performance across the district's increasingly diverse and low-income student population. While slightly less than 50% of students passed the Texas Assessment of Academic Skills (TAAS) in 1994, nearly 90% met state standards by 2002. The district also closed a significant achievement gap during the same period (see Case Exhibit 4). However, when Kujawa assumed the helm at AISD in the fall of 2001, she found herself driving a redoubling of efforts in anticipation of a considerably more challenging state assessment, the Texas Assessment of Knowledge and Skills (TAKS), which launched in 2003. Under the new test, student achievement dropped sharply and a sizeable achievement gap reemerged (see Case Exhibit 7).

A specific example of the management challenge facing Kujawa is the stagnating fifth grade reading scores in AISD. The fifth grade reading dilemma highlights Kujawa's leadership challenge as she ponders what it would take to regain high levels of academic achievement in AISD—continuing to improve the longstanding practices that had brought the district success in the past or rethinking significant aspects of her managerial approach?

As background, the case describes the historical and demographic changes that have shaped AISD into a predominantly minority and low-income mid-sized urban school district by 2005. Then, summaries of the Texas assessment and accountability system and the district's re-

form efforts from 1994–2004 give the reader context on the challenges facing AISD and Kujawa.

It is helpful for the instructor to be aware of the debates regarding the use of high-stakes tests for accountability in public education and over the significant disparities in the rigor of state assessments.[1] While Texas was criticized throughout the 1990s for having relatively low state standards, in 2003, the state significantly upgraded state standards and introduced the more rigorous TAKS assessment. In fact, in December 2004, Achieve[2] hailed Texas as the only state in which the higher education system had adopted the state high school exam (11th grade TAKS tests) as the statewide college placement exam to date, and one of the few states to require all students to complete a college preparatory curriculum unless an exemption is requested by parents. However, state standards, assessments, and accountability systems are continually changing, so instructors should guide these types of comments back to the broader questions of how success is defined in public education.

The case outlines the district's strategic planning and evaluation processes, and management structure and roles are described. The district is organized into five sub regions, called "verticals," each comprised of a high school and its feeder schools and led by an area superintendent. In essence, each vertical operates as a mini school district, which presents both challenges and opportunities for systemic reform efforts as becomes evident throughout the case. Horizontal structures are grade-level supports, such as program directors who lead curriculum development. School management, resource allocation, and instructional supports are also explained.

The following two sections describe the evolution of the district's curriculum and instruction reforms and human capital management strategy, respectively.

The case then shifts to Kujawa's assessment of AISD's performance in light of the 2005 TAKS results. Four primary challenges are presented: (1) strengthening instruction, (2) managing performance gaps across the five verticals, (3) balancing accountability and organizational learning, and (4) addressing the low fifth grade reading scores. For each challenge, the case summarizes the current state from the perspective of Kujawa and other district leaders, as well as the district's responses to date. This section should facilitate ample student diagnosis of the district's key managerial challenges.

Finally, the case ends with Kujawa deliberating over her next steps and the potential impact of managerial actions on the entire organization.

Positioning

This case could be used in a wide variety of settings and with different audiences, ranging from experienced school leaders to graduate students in education, business, or management courses. It can be used at the beginning of a course or module to lay out issues of managing multi-site organizations, strategy execution and leadership.

Learning Objectives

There are four intended learning objectives for this case analysis and discussion:

- **Organizational coherence.** Help students develop an appreciation for the value and complexity of managing for coherence as a dynamic and constant leadership task.
- **Differentiation.** Explore the concept of "differentiation," the relative degree of autonomy that managers should afford direct reports depending on capacity, performance, and function. Enable students to understand that "loose" does not mean under- or poorly-managed, but represents a more nuanced management approach as opposed to "tight," or more centrally controlled.

- **Role of multi-site managers (area superintendents).** Analyze the role of the managers tasked with managing and supporting principals.
- **Leadership.** Give students an appreciation of the requisites of effective leadership and management at all levels of the organization.

Assignment

In preparing "Meeting New Challenges at the Aldine Independent School District," PEL–030, students should consider the questions below; the "Note on the PELP Coherence Framework," PEL–010, should also be assigned if it has not been read previously.

1. How coherent are the elements—culture, systems, structures, resources, and stakeholders—of Aldine Independent School District with its strategy?

2. Based on your analysis in question 1, what changes, if any, would you recommend to Kujawa as she faces new challenges?

3. What are the strengths and weaknesses of Kujawa's management approach to area superintendents and principals?

4. How has Kujawa handled the fifth grade reading problem? What should she have done differently and what should she do now?

Teaching Plan and Analysis

This 90-minute teaching plan is based on an executive education course designed for the PELP inaugural cohort of urban public school leadership teams.

Summary

I. **Opening: Discussion of and vote on AISD coherence.** (5 minutes)

II. Diagnosis of coherence in AISD.
(20 minutes)

III. Vote on AISD performance and analysis of its strengths and weaknesses.
(25 minutes)

IV. Analysis of area superintendent role.
(20 minutes)

V. Evaluation of Kujawa's leadership and recommendations. (15 minutes)

VI. Closing. (5 minutes)

Opening: Discussion of and vote on coherence in AISD (5 minutes)

Open class with a brief discussion of the concept of coherence in public education based on students' reading of the assigned pre-reading.

Suggested questions: What is your definition of coherence in public education? What is its value? What does it look like? Is it difficult or easy to achieve- and why?

Before delving into a diagnosis of AISD's relative coherence, it is recommended that the instructor take a vote in order to "read" what the class thinks about AISD. Given the absence of clear and agreed upon measures of success in public education, it is quite plausible that students will have divergent evaluations of the coherence of AISD. The instructor should be prepared for strong disagreement, especially if students are current or former educational practitioners.

Suggested vote set-up: Where is AISD in terms of coherence (i.e., management of organizational elements to support implementation of strategy)? You can suspend your consideration of student performance for the moment. Record the class's votes.

How coherent is AISD?			
1	2	3	4
Completely incoherent			Very coherent

Diagnosis of coherence in AISD (20 minutes)

Segue into a diagnosis of coherence in AISD. What reflected coherence (or lack of) to you?

To start the discussion, it may be helpful to ask who voted "1" and select two-three people to elaborate on the rationale for their vote. Record students' responses using the five elements of the PELP coherence framework as categories, which should be written on the board before class. Note whether the response indicates coherence (+) or incoherence (−) Ask for two responses from people who voted "2" or "3." By now, people who have voted "4" should be sufficiently eager to share their comments, which you should invite. The instructor might then encourage any student to defend her position in light of the preceding opinions put forth by colleagues.

Vote on AISD performance and analysis (25 minutes)

In anticipation of potential strong reactions among students, it is recommended to again poll students on their evaluation of AISD's performance (improved student achievement) before diving into an analysis.

Suggested vote set-up: How well is AISD performing with respect to improving student achievement? Is this a high-performing district, or, is AISD underperforming? You may consider mentioning that AISD qualified as a finalist for the Broad Prize for Urban Education in 2005 and 2004,[3] an accepted signal of high performance to many in the public education sector. Record the class's votes.

How is AISD performing?			
1	2	3	4
Very low			Very high

Again, it is difficult to predict how students will vote. Some students may look at the district's results on the Texas state assessments from 1994–2002 (see Case Exhibit 4) and feel convinced that AISD became a highly successful district as 90% students from all ethnic/racial groups met state standards. Others may take issue because of the perceived low quality of the Texas state assessment used during that time period (the TAAS), the district's flat and unimpressive results on the SAT and Iowa Test of Basic Skills (see Case Exhibit 6), or the decline in student performance from 2003–2005 under the more rigorous TAKS assessment (see Case Exhibit 7). The instructor should be prepared for anything from heated debate to relative consensus, particularly dependent on students' depth of familiarity in the public education sector. The instructor may wish to comment that this debate reflects the lack of clear performance metrics for defining "success" in the sector.

Invite comments from participants who voted "1" or "4," asking for their rationale and recording responses on the board. It is important that the instructor push students to justify their claims of how AISD is performing with evidence from the case. To promote debate and dialogue, ask students if they agree or disagree with their colleagues.

It is particularly interesting to note the relationship between the first vote on coherence and this vote on performance. Taken together, the results of the two votes may be surprising (majority 4s for coherence, majority 1s for performance) or consistent (majority 4s for coherence, majority 4s for performance). If participants vote 4 in both votes, the instructor should be asked how AISD can continue to get even more coherent or achieve even higher levels of performance.

The comparative votes will help the instructor think about the rest of the class. In a PELP executive education program designed for district leadership teams, participants voted that AISD's coherence was very high but its performance as mediocre. This helped emphasize a key learning in the remaining case discussions of how structure, no matter how well planned and executed, must be married to effective leadership and management. This is a particularly important point in the public education sector that continuously focuses on structure as a key instrument of change without usually acknowledging that a change in structure absent effective leadership and management will usually not achieve the desired improvements. This point can be made regardless of the way the relative votes turn out. If students vote four on both dimensions, then the instructor can ask, How important was effective leadership and management in achieving such a high rating in both areas? The instructor can still pursue the line of inquiry around how Kujawa could do even better in the last discussion section.

Analysis of area superintendent role (20 minutes)

Building upon the performance discussion, move into an analysis of the role of the area superintendents in AISD. Ideally, participants will identify the role of the area superintendents, and their relationship with the superintendent in the prior analysis of why they evaluated AISD as performing well or underperforming. If not, the instructor should surface this topic and point out its curious absence. It may be helpful to use the following framework as a way to more easily picture and diagnose the relationship between Superintendent Kujawa ("team leader") and her five area superintendents ("team"), and the relationship between the superintendent ("team leader") and each of the five area superintendents ("team members").

Suggested Diagram:

Team Leader

Team

Team Members

Suggested Questions:

What should Kujawa's relationship with the five area superintendents look like in order to improve student performance districtwide? Ask participants to consider her relationship with the team, as well as each of the individual team members.

What does it really mean, on the ground or operationally, for a leader to hold people accountable for results? Is Kujawa effective in this role?

What is working well in these relationships in AISD, and what needs to be improved?

What are the implications of how these relationships play out on student performance?

What characteristics would you look for when hiring an area superintendent?

Students may bring up the fact that AISD is populated with leaders who have on average been in the district for a long time. The instructor might ask the advantages and disadvantages of this phenomenon. Students my also bring up the implications of "the Aldine way" of allowing people at all levels to apparently decide if, when, and how they will adopt best practices in their areas of responsibility.

Evaluation of Kujawa's leadership and recommendations (15 minutes)

Start this discussion by introducing the concept of loose-tight management. "Tight" refers to actions that are firmly controlled by managers (often the central office in a school district) for a number of reasons, including maintaining consistency of expectations or implementation, as a response to weak capacity, or as a strategic choice to control specific functions, such as hiring. "Loose" refers to actions over which individuals (e.g. principals or teachers) maintain a relatively high degree of autonomy. Referring to a Loose-Tight continuum, ask participants to point where they would place AISD along the continuum, with their rationale. Record each response with an "X" on the continuum.

The intended insight of this discussion is that a district can achieve coherence at any point along the continuum as long as leadership is carefully selecting which things are "loose" and which are "tight" (e.g. is hiring done by the central office, individual schools, or a hybrid approach?) and effectively managing implementation.

Finally, ask for recommendations about how Kujawa could be a more effective leader. It is helpful to push the students to provide specific examples of how their recommendation would play out in AISD.

Recommendations might include:

- Redefine strategic goals
- Create a sense of urgency for higher results
- Use information to drive performance in a more real-time frame
- Rotate area superintendents
- Shorten accountability period for area superintendents and principals

Closing (5 minutes)

Given that the AISD case surfaces a number of important managerial concepts, the instructor may wish to end class by summarizing three main ideas:

1. A high degree of coherence is necessary for high performance, but not sufficient. For example, even the most fabulous race car needs a highly skilled driver to win NASCAR. Coherence is not static. Effective leaders, managing for high performance must constantly read the organization's position and adapt responses to the changing needs and circumstance. Coherence is a journey, not a destination.

2. The paradox of morale in organizations. The AISD illustrates that organizational culture sets the tone for expectations and accountability. "The Aldine way" may have been an

effective way of operating in the district, but it may have been holding the district back from achieving higher results. Kujawa may be stuck in her own culture. Effective leaders can ratchet up the pressure to perform and actually improve morale.

3. "Loose" does not equate to under- managing. It actually requires a more sophisticated and nuanced skill set. Leaders must have reliable and timely information. They must know when and how to exert pressure when data reveals that performance is not up to par and be able to read the data for future problems. For example, which classroom requires a more highly-skilled teacher in order to facilitate high levels of student learning: an open classroom in which students can choose among multiple activities or a regimented classroom in which students are sitting in rows and engaging in the same activity at the same time? Balancing the loose-tight continua is one of the most challenging managerial approaches to execute effectively.

ban Education is an annual award that honors urban school districts that demonstrate dramatic gains in student achievement while reducing achievement gaps among ethnic groups and between high-and low-income students. The winning district receives $500,000; four finalist districts each receive $125,000. All money goes directly to college scholarships for graduating seniors. See www.broadfoundation.org.

Notes

1. For a general overview of standards, accountability, and assessments in public education, consult *Education Week*'s Website, http://www.edweek.org/rc/issues/.

2. Created by the nation's governors and business leaders at the 1996 National Education Summit, Achieve, Inc., is a bipartisan, non-profit organization that helps states raise academic standards, improve assessments, and strengthen accountability to prepare all young people for postsecondary education, work, and citizenship. See "Do Graduation Tests Measure Up? A Closer Look at State High School Exit Exams," June 2004, and "The Expectations Gap: A 50-State Review of High School Graduation Requirements," December 2004, available fromhttp://www.achieve.org.

3. The Broad Foundation is a Los-Angeles-based venture philanthropy established in 1999 by Eli and Edythe Broad. The Foundation's mission is to dramatically improve K-12 urban public education through better governance, management, labor relations and competition. Established in 2002, the $1 million Broad Prize for Ur-

Long Beach Unified School District (A): Change That Leads to Improvement (1992–2002)

Overview

This case is the first in a two-case series developed by the HGSE/HBS Public Education Leadership Project (PELP) that focuses on organizational change efforts at the Long Beach Unified School District (LBUSD) from 1992–2004. This series was created to describe for school leaders, managers of nonprofit organizations, and graduate students the challenges and realities of leading and sustaining large-scale organizational change in an urban public school district.

The (A) case provides readers with an opportunity to evaluate the leadership of LBUSD, Superintendent Carl Cohn from 1992–2002, and to complete a retrospective analysis of a long-term change effort. By showcasing the challenges of creating strategic organizational coherence in a public school district, participants can evaluate what they consider to be the key success factors and remaining hurdles facing LBUSD. An important intent of this case is to capture the complexity and difficulties of this district-wide school reform that is not begun

with a master plan, and requires constant evaluation and revision along the way. It helps leaders recognize that while real change may be slow, significant progress can be made in urban school districts that many might consider unfixable.

Instructors can use the (A) case on its own, or in concert with a (B) case, "Long Beach Unified School District (B): Working to Sustain Improvement (2002–2004)," PELP No. 007. The sequel concentrates on the challenges facing Cohn's successor Chris Steinhauser from 2002–2004, including high school reform, leadership transitions, and decreasing enrollment in tougher economic times.

Case Summary

The (A) case highlights the results of reform efforts that took place during Cohn's ten years as LBUSD superintendent. Set in 2002, the case opens with newly-appointed LBUSD Superintendent Christopher Steinhauser reflecting on the legacy of his predecessor. When Cohn was appointed superintendent in 1992, many challenges faced the Long Beach community includ-

---

This note was prepared by professors James Austin, Allen S. Grossman, and Robert B. Schwartz and Research Associate Jennifer M. Suesse.

ing growing diversity, economic adversity, and threats to public safety. The city rallied together to address these issues, providing Cohn and his leadership team with what they interpreted to be a mandate for change in the public school system.

Cohn and the Board began by fostering a new type of governance relationship that implemented day-long retreats structure in which large-scale "Board initiatives" directing the school reform strategy were developed. These initiatives included the adoption of a mandatory K-8 school uniform policy, standards-based instructional reform, and the development of a partnership with local institutions of higher education, each of which are described in the case. Cohn and his team also worked to transform the role of the central office, by linking departments more closely with classroom-level instruction. The case describes Cohn's leadership style and philosophy in general and for each of these initiatives.

The case illustrates how one school district attempted to use multiple management levers for organizational improvement in service of improved student achievement, and can be used to highlight what it takes to initiate and sustain change across a complex public school system.

Positioning

This case could be used in a wide variety of settings and with different audiences, ranging from experienced school leaders to graduate students in business, management, social enterprise or education courses. It was written to be used in a case series in the PELP executive education program for school leaders. In addition to fostering discussion about the role of leadership in an urban public school setting, the Long Beach case series intends to offer readers a chance to integrate theories of organizational coherence and change. This is a "fan case," which touches on many issues relevant to leadership including modeling behavior, setting a clear agenda, en-

gagement of stakeholders, and mixing understanding with toughness.

Learning Objectives

The (A) case focuses on Carl Cohn's leadership and the implementation of a series of initiatives at LBUSD. The Long Beach story provides a good vehicle for teaching about institutional capacity for organizational change and organizational coherence. Objectives include:

- **Organizational coherence.** Provide participants with the understanding that the elements of an organization, culture, resources, systems, structure and stakeholders, must be coherent with each other and an improvement strategy to create a high performing organization and spread excellence across all units.

- **Change management.** Deepen participants understanding of the obstacles and opportunities for change, and to identify key success factors in the change process.

- **Leadership.** Reveal the importance of leadership and demonstrate that outstanding leadership is not about charisma but about practices that can be learned and improved.

Assignment

Students should read "Long Beach Unified School District (A): Change that Leads to Improvement," PEL No. 006. We recommend that the "Note on the PELP Coherence Framework," PEL-010, also be assigned if it has not been read previously. If instructors choose to use the (B) case, it should be handed out after the discussion of the (A) case. As mentioned earlier, the (A) case can be used alone to discuss the implementation district reforms as well as the realities of leading and sustaining large-scale organizational change.

Discussion Questions

1. What were Cohn's strengths and weaknesses as a leader?

2. What is your assessment of Cohn's reform initiatives at LBUSD? What was he trying to accomplish with each?

3. What lessons can we learn LBUSD about managing change in an urban public school district?

4. What could derail the improvements after Cohn leaves?

Teaching Plan and Analysis

This 80-minute teaching plan is based on an executive education course designed for the PELP class of urban public school leadership teams. The teaching plan can be modified to suit a 75-minute or 90-minute session.

Summary

I. **Introduction.** (3 minutes)

II. **Consideration of success.** How successful was LBUSD by the end of the case? (10 minutes)

III. **Leadership.** What kind of leader was Carl Cohn? (15 minutes)

IV. **Analysis of organizational change.** What is your evaluation of LBUSD's progress? (30 minutes)

V. **Sustainability.** What are the barriers to sustaining change at LBSUD? (10 minutes)

VI. **Reflection.** What can we learn about changing urban public school districts from LBUSD? (12 minutes)

Introduction (3 minutes)

The instructor can begin class by outlining the purpose of the case in the context of the course. One sample opening follows:

As you know, one purpose of this course is to examine how to build leadership capacity in school districts at all levels. Today, we would like to discuss the case of Long Beach Unified School District under the direction of Carl Cohn. We will examine the role of a school leaders and the importance leadership plays in building and sustaining organizational change. Before we begin our discussion, let me remind you that this is not a "best practice" case study, but rather an opportunity to look inside an organization—with all its freckles and warts. We would encourage you to be critical in your evaluation of the district's efforts to lead and sustain organizational change, as well as to dig deeply for lessons learned.

Consideration of success (10 minutes)

In this next discussion pasture, instructors may wish to transition using the following:

Before we start the discussion, I would like to get your assessment of the progress that the district made under Cohn. I have put a scale on the board from 1—district made little or no progress to 5—district made outstanding progress. Let me see a show of hands for each number from 1–5.

Why did you vote as you did?

The purpose of this vote and subsequent discussion is to get a sense of how participants evaluate LBUSD's progress by the end of the case. While most of the participants will vote 4 or 5, some will also vote 3. Even those who voted 4 will surface criticism about the district and Cohn. This short conversation will allow people in the class to feel comfortable criticizing aspects of what has been done at LUBSD and model in class that this is NOT intended to be a puff piece for the district. The instructor should first call on any 3s and then a couple of 4s before allowing any 5s to speak.

After getting out a few comments, the instructor might also ask at this point, "How do we judge success? Should our evaluation be based on absolute performance or on rate of improvement?"

A debate should emerge about how success should be defined in public education. The point can be made that defining the parameters of success could be one aspect of leadership. Some participants will feel that the LBUSD story during the Cohn era represents an astonishing success story. They will point to increased coherence of the system, rising test scores, decreasing violence, and community involvement. Others worry that even with the improvements mentioned above, LBUSD is not improving quickly or dramatically enough to qualify as a "success." Additionally, during Cohn's tenure, the achievement gap among races did not improve. Some might also feel that without Cohn's visionary leadership, the changes instituted during his tenure will not outlast him.

This discussion around sustainability and performance could also lead to a debate regarding performance metrics in public education. Some participants feel that such metrics would improve districts' service to students, while others might argue that no meaningful metrics can be devised. As an instructor, you could lead a discussion about what might constitute a meaningful measurement.

One caution for the instructor is to be careful not to allow this discussion to spin out of control. The intention here is to put a frame around the following discussion and pose questions rather than arrive at definitive answers. Many participants had not really thought about the fact that with a general absence of a definition for success, it is the role of leadership to establish one for the district and communicate this definition both internally and externally. Otherwise, leadership is setting themselves up for continuous criticism for not doing enough.

Leadership (15 minutes)

The purpose of this discussion is to understand that outstanding leadership is about a set of practices that can be learned and not about charisma. In fact, it is mentioned at the end of the case that Cohn was not charismatic. Many believe that leadership is about a set of personal attributes rather than practices that can be learned. This discussion should disabuse the participants of that idea.

An instructor can invite responses by asking the following:

What kind of leader was Carl Cohn? Give specific examples to support your observation. They can be positive or negative. What impact did his actions have on the various stakeholders in the district?

In this first discussion, we suggest that instructors spend time discussing Cohn's individual leadership, which will help set up the next larger discussion of the overall impact of the changes that took place during his tenure. In general, Cohn's leadership practices modeled the culture he wanted to establish throughout the district—collaborative, learning, kids first, etc. Some of Cohn's leadership practices include:

- Collaborate with the stakeholders to include in the change process from unions to the Board to local universities.

- Commitment to recruiting and retaining skilled central office leadership.

- Overall consistency and coherence of actions. Cohn did not embrace the latest fad but stayed focused on execution. At the same time, he was willing to modify if something was not working.

- Allowed others to lead and apparently get credit for success.

- Respectful of the culture of having people from Long Beach lead yet at the same time willing to bring in outside talent.

- Unwavering in his commitment to doing what is best for the kids.

- Collaborative and at the same time tough. He was not afraid to employ the use of the "non-negotiables," that is, items which were not subject to discussion or debate. Some feel that this tactic was an important key to his success. He forced discussion and debate around issues of implementation rather than on whether the initiative should be kept in place. Others felt that this approach did not allow sites enough control and had a top down feel.

- Some will question whether or not LBUSD can sustain his vision once he is gone. Despite his humility, is he a heroic leader?

Finally, it is important to emphasize leadership as a practice that can be developed over time, rather than a set of personal characteristics or attributes from which one acts. The instructor might go out of the case at this point for a few minutes and ask, "To what degree do you feel leaders are natural and are successful because of personal attributes and to what degree do you believe that leadership is a set of practices that can be learned?" This has the potential to unleash a lively debate among participants. The point is that some leaders may be naturals but most leaders must learn the leadership practices that result in success.

Analysis of organizational change (30 minutes)
We suggest completing an analysis of the case using the elements of the PELP Coherence Framework, starting with the element of culture. This is the opportunity for participants to dig into how the various changes made during Cohn's tenure at LBUSD were related to each other and helped drive the district's improvement strategy. We have found that the use of the Coherence Framework makes it easier for participants to understand the meaning of a coherent organization and helps them organize their thoughts in an area that may otherwise feel vague. Finally, the framework provides a graphic way to portray the interrelationship of activities in a complex system that is a school district. As the instructor lists the activities under the elements, the following points should be noted. Most activities could be entered under more than one element. For example, the change in governance might be considered by some as

structural but we have put it under a change in an existing system. More importantly, is that the participants begin to understand that Cohn's changes complemented each other and were all intended to drive improved teaching and learning in the classroom. There were few if any initiatives or random activities that were introduced because they were popular at the time or a donor was providing money to implement the activity. Finally, Cohn tried to make changes that were based on research. For example, he did not follow the move to small schools because data that this change would improve student performance did not exist.

One question that can be used to begin this discussion is: "What specific organizational changes or initiatives accounts for the progress made by LBUSD?" (The following list and discussion is representative rather than exhaustive. Participants may identify others they consider important. There is no set of "right" answers. The objective is to get students to understand how deliberate Cohn and his team were in managing the district. They did not just have good ideas, but they also understood that a constant focus on improving implementation was critical for their success, which for them was defined as improved student performance.

Culture:

- **"Kids come first" attitude that permeates the central office and schools.** By focusing on learning outcomes for kids, instead of compliance, many of the adults in the system felt empowered to act. Cohn and LBUSD's leaders push each other on behalf of the students to make strategic choices about what needs to be done. These decisions are rather independent of outside pressures e.g., how they manage growth, the historic choice to desegregate the schools voluntarily, mandatory uniform policy, and choosing to adopt standards early.

- **The "central office exists to serve the schools."** This approach differs significantly from many school districts, where the central office is often characterized by its command and control philosophy and considered by many, particularly at the school level, as a barrier rather than enabler of teaching and learning. By redefining the role of the central office as one of service, Cohn and his team were able to focus energy and resources on improving the schools.

- **Tolerance for ambiguity and risk.** This contributes to an atmosphere of psychological safety[1] and makes it okay for people to experiment and possibly fail.

- **Commitment to a stable organization,** with long-term thinking and willingness to sequence actions and take one project at a time. With so many long-time employees in the district, there is a lot of history and institutional memory. Participants may disagree about whether this is an advantage or a disadvantage.

- **"Iowa by the sea" mentality of Long Beach** may worry participants because it could promote insularity and lead to complacency, and resistance to change. It could also promote a culture of niceness where you do not criticize the person you have lived and worked with for decades.

Structure:

- **Organizing by levels instead of geography.** This change promoted consistency across schools in curriculum and management. It also provided greater focus to assistant superintendents who could now manage one category of schools rather than an entire K–12 system. They could more easily improve their capabilities as instructional leaders when focused on one level of school.

- **Reorganization of research and special education.** By hiring Winters, Elliott, and the others on the central office team, Cohn acquired the talent that enabled him to delegate much of the power and decision-making authority to his team. This distributed power structure coupled with the shared values and a commitment to teamwork allowed individual team members to restructure their own departments in innovative ways. The team structure also encouraged lateral learning and the transfer of best practice, as meetings welcomed active cross-pollination of ideas, innovation, and experimentation. The case describes specific innovations that were made in the research and special education areas including the integration of regular teachers into the special education department.

- **Establishment of early literacy institute.** This fostered understanding and development of necessary teaching capacity at the elementary level.

- **Uniforms.** In addition to the objectives described by Cohn in the case for uniforms, their introduction sent a number of important symbolic messages. The district was taking charge and while students were their focus, adults were making decisions. Schools were not primarily a social center but a place where work was going to get done. Cohn was willing to be bold and think outside the box since this was the first mandatory uniform policy in the country.

An area that might emerge during this discussion is the ongoing question for multi-site organizations, including school districts, of how to balance tensions between the headquarters and the individual sites. Participants can debate about how decision rights and authority should be distributed in LBUSD. Some might feel that Cohn and the central office team have too many "non-negotiables," while others might feel that they are "too loose" with principals. They can also discuss whether or not it is appropriate to treat different sites differently.

Systems:

- **Testing ideas.** Before rolling initiatives out across the district, a system of pilot testing, evaluation, and modification became the norm. The commitment to uniforms serves as a good example of this system. By testing an idea first, Cohn was able to utilize resources more carefully and get early buy-in. He also signaled that learning was to take place to improve on the implementation of any idea. Finally, he demonstrated that if an idea did not work, it could be stopped before a major commitment of resources.

- **Human capital management.** LBUSD had a history of rotating teachers and principals in and out of the central office, which functioned as a vehicle for lateral learning and dissemination of knowledge. Both central office workers and site-leaders would learn from working with each other. Moreover, this created a culture of loyalty to the system of LBUSD as a whole, rather than fostering individual site-based fiefdoms. Like many other districts, however, LBUSD was facing a large number of retirements and was struggling to develop a pipeline for new leadership.

- **Training and development.** The case hints that LBUSD has a promotion system that brings people up through the ranks, often providing personnel with early-career promotions based on perceived or demonstrated capabilities. Also, there was a willingness to hire outsiders like Lynn Winters and Judy Elliott to assist with solving hard problems.

- **Governance.** By reorganizing the relationship between the central office and the school board, Cohn tried to use the Board as a substantive resource, taking charge of what is often a purely political process/relationship. He wanted the Board to become an asset instead of a liability. Together Cohn and the Board restructured the use of their time by instituting quarterly retreats, short semimonthly meetings, a structure for committee work, and a custom of extensive preparation preceding votes. This led to a number of unanimous "board initiatives," which were driven by a common agreement of the bottom line. The group also supported organizational coherence by not championing and then moving from one good idea to the next good idea. They recruited members to maintain a high quality of Board membership and used the structure to facilitate strong relationships with the union.

- **Information systems.** Using data to drive decision-making relied on a number of systems implemented by Winters, Cohn, and others. Overall, LBUSDF used information to identify problems, develop responses and target support. They also invested in professional capacity in the central office. Winters and her team taught teachers and principals how to use data, and the case described how the training involved an iterative process as lead people internalized an understanding of how to use data. Winters' research shop also modified information systems based on feedback from schools, and valued user-friendliness and quick turnaround so that the research office could be responsive to schools. This encouraged a sense of involvement by all personnel regardless of where they were placed.

Resources:

- **Allocation based on the need of the school.** While all schools could receive assistance if requested, it was known that the schools in most need had priority.

- **Consistent pedagogy.** The district's ongoing commitment to the Essential Elements of Effective Instruction (EEEI) helped build a consistent language across schools and programs.

LBUSD continued to build the capabilities of all of its teachers, principals, and leadership to use EEEI more effectively.

- **Standards-based curriculum.** The description of middle school reform illustrates that everything cannot be learned at once, as the leaders had a willingness to sequence their actions and think long-term about the capacity necessary to offer a standards-based curriculum.

- **Partnerships.** Finally, the Long Beach case illustrates an ongoing commitment to partnerships with the higher education community. The joint work with the city's colleges and university's allowed faculty access to information that led them to develop the standards for instruction.

Stakeholders:

- **Strategic involvement of stakeholders** is another important aspect of the Long Beach story. Many participants look at Cohn and say that he was able to look across the spectrum to get all the parties involved in improving LBUSD. He sought intellectual resource, guidance, and validation from a variety of stakeholders, including the board, union, and parents.

- **Sharing of credit.** Cohn was comfortable having others receive credit for ideas that he may have generated and promoted. Calling these "Board Initiatives" may have reduced the spotlight on him and given the credit to the board. That was okay with Cohn whose primary concern was getting the work approved and implemented.

Environment:

- **Able to influence his operating environment.** While it is likely that there will not be much time to discuss the players in the environment in any detail, it is worth noting that Cohn brought in the universities as allies, did not succumb to pressures to introduce the lat-

est fad from funders, and was able to influence legislators when it came to facilitating the mandatory uniform policy.

Leading change: Throughout the above discussion, participants will be discussing the aspects of LBUSD that changed as a result of the reform strategy selected by Cohn, the Board, and the leadership team. We suggest weaving throughout this analysis a discussion of change leadership, and one question to raise when the uniform policy is mentioned is: "Why start with uniforms?" This can lead to an interesting discussion about how to sequence change efforts, and can also foster a debate about whether or not change at a public school district should take place slowly (what Rosabeth Moss Kanter calls a "long march") or quickly, with "bold strokes."[2]

Finally, the case writers wish to note that a quote was included in the case to give instructors the option of having a debate about the personal side of leadership. The quote from Principal Debbie Stark poses the question of how much of this change was as a result of Cohn's personality. Some LBUSD insiders felt that Cohn was responsible for much of the improvement. Instructors can take this as an opportunity to discuss the "great leader" syndrome. Much of what the Cohn era legacy reinforces is Cohn's team approach to leadership (distributed leadership): consensus-based governance, introducing standards and data into the classroom, and the cooperation between schools and the central office. He was not a charismatic leader, but he was extremely effective in creating and empowering a leadership team.

Sustainability (10 minutes)
Once you feel that the class discussion has surfaced an understanding of the variety of changes and the connections between them, it is time to move the discussion to reflect on whether or not these changes will outlast Cohn. If instructors plan to use the (B) case, this will set up the following discussion.

One way to transition if you will not use the B case is to ask, "If you were Cohn's leadership coach, what recommendations would you give to him to improve?" Or, if you plan on using the B case, you can pose the question, "If you were Chris Steinhauser, what would be your biggest priorities?" We suggest giving participants 3–5 minutes to talk together with their neighbors, in "buzz groups," about either one of these questions. The instructor might also include one of the following questions in the subsequent discussion depending on whether she will use the B case or not:

- What do you see as the greatest threats for the positive changes not lasting beyond Cohn's tenure?

- Given the relative success of LBUSD, if you were Steinhauser, how fast and far would you move?

Also, while much of this analysis has focused on the strengths of what worked (or started to work) in Long Beach, it is essential to note that the district faces a number of critical challenges including an ongoing achievement gap, the struggle to bring meaningful reform to the high schools, the implementation of state mandated Open Court curriculum in the elementary schools, and a change in union leadership. Also, like so many other districts, they face a state budget crisis, declining enrollment, and accountability pressures.

Reflection (12 minutes)

At the conclusion of the class, give participants some time to reflect on what they have learned about leadership, strategic coherence, and organizational change. Some questions you could ask to stimulate this discussion are:

- What takeaways do you have for your own leadership or your team from this case?

- What are the principal obstacles that you face in your own work?

- Why is this work so hard to do?

Notes

1. See Amy Edmondson, "Psychological Safety and Learning Behavior in Work Teams." *Administrative Science Quarterly* 44, no. 4 (1999): 350–383.

2. These ideas were first introduced in chapter 14 of R. M. Kanter, B. Stein, and T. D. Jick, *The Challenge of Organizational Change: How Companies Experience It and Leaders Guide It,* New York: Free Press, 1992. Chapter 6 of R. M. Kanter, *Confidence: How Winning and Losing Streaks Begin and End,* New York: Crown; London: Random House, 2004, provides further elaboration.

Exhibit 1
Master List of Change Topics

Establishing sense of urgency

- How were crises/needs and opportunities sensed?

- Explain source and level of dissatisfaction

- Baseline realities & environmental factors

- Governance & role of board. . .

- Union relationships

Forming guiding coalition

- How did it get started?

- How were people chosen to participate?

- Group membership

- Formation

Vision

- What was vision? Is LBUSD an example of kaleidoscope thinking?

- How vision was created

- What was the model/strategy for achieving it?

Communicating vision

- By what process did change unfold?

- How did it spread?

- Inspiring elements: destination, dream, prize, target, message, first step.[c]

- What new behaviors were necessary?

Empowering others to act

- How were obstacles—systemic, structural, cultural—removed?

- How were risk taking and experimentation encouraged?

- Need to show some screw ups and the consequences

- What level of delegation?

- What were costs involved with change? (e.g. changes in power, required competencies, networks of relationships, reward systems, identity)

- What forces drove this action? (backers & supporters)

- Professional development?

Short-term wins

- Was there early success? If so, what?

- Who/what was involved? How were they recognized? How was working team nurtured?

- Feedback mechanisms? What signals, symbols and rewards?

- Management by exception?

Consolidating improvements, more change

- How change was sustained? What did the "difficult middle" look like?

- How did it expand across organization?

- If trying to let 1000 flowers bloom, how to distinguish between good variations and bad variations?

Institutionalized (what is now in place)

- What changed?

- What is strategy for today?

- What is aligned? What is not?

- HR (including hiring policies)

Larger themes

- Role of standards

- How did LBUSD become data-driven?

- How to characterize the speed of change?

Source: This list of change topics and questions was compiled from a series of notes including "Leading Change" by Michael Beer, HBS No. 9–488–037; "Moving Ideas into Action: Mastering the Art of Change" by Rosabeth Moss Kanter, HBS No. 488–002; "Leading Change: Why Transformation Efforts Fail" by John P. Kotter, HBR #95204; and "Leadership for Change: Enduring Skills for Change Masters" by Rosabeth Moss Kanter, HBS No. 304–062.

Long Beach Unified School District (B): Sustaining Improvement during a Leadership Transition (2002–2004)

Overview

This case is the second in a series developed by Harvard University's Public Education Leadership Project (PELP) that focuses on organizational change efforts at the Long Beach Unified School District (LBUSD). This series was created to describe for school leaders, executives, and graduate students the challenges and realities of leading and sustaining large-scale organizational change in an urban public school district.

The (A) case, "Long Beach Unified School District (A): Change that Leads to Improvement (1992–2002)," PEL-006, provides students an opportunity to evaluate the leadership of LBUSD Superintendent Carl Cohn and to complete a retrospective analysis of a long-term change effort at a large urban public school district. The (B) case follows the progress of Cohn's successor, Christopher Steinhauser, in his first two years as LBUSD superintendent. It concentrates on the challenges of following a legendary leader from the time Cohn left in 2002 through 2004. Steinhauser is faced with a number of

changes including leadership transitions at the top levels of the district, high school reform, and decreasing student enrollment in tougher economic times. He must manage these changes and at the same time continue the district's improvement in student performance. Steinhauser must decide what to keep from Cohn's tenure and what should be changed to deal with a changing environment.

While instructors can use the (A) case separately, the (B) case was not written to stand alone. Rather, it can serve as the basis for a discussion of how to build on and sustain organizational change and improvement discussed in the (A) case during a leadership transition. The (B) case also updates students interested in following the district's progress over time.

Case Summary

Set in 2004, the (B) case opens with newly appointed LBUSD Superintendent Christopher Steinhauser reflecting on his first two years in office. The first section briefly summarizes the

This note was prepared by professors James B. Honan and Allen S. Grossman and Research Associate Jennifer M. Seusse.

legacy Steinhauser inherited from Cohn, which is described in more detail in the (A) case. Then, the case describes how the political and financial landscape has shifted. It outlines the change in student enrollment, which began falling in SY03, and highlights the challenges presented by California's budget shortfalls. The next section describes the changing membership on the LBUSD School Board (historically, a very stable group), a strained relationship with the Teacher's Association of Long Beach (TALB), and a number of retirements from the central office. The case also describes Steinhauser's initial efforts to address these challenges.

Next, the case updates ongoing instructional reform efforts. At the elementary school level, the district's 59 schools were working to become more self-sufficient and to rely less on district office support. LBUSD's middle schools sought to institutionalize some of the reforms from the Cohn era. Steinhauser felt his mandate was to focus on high school reform. The case provides some background on the high school work by describing the "Every Student, Every Day" plan and goals. While still in its early stages, the reform effort has shown some positive results, with all high schools meeting their statewide performance targets in SY03.

The case closes with a few district officials reflecting on Steinhauser's leadership. District leaders also discuss the transition from Cohn to Steinhauser. At the conclusion of the case, Steinhauser looks ahead to the future.

Positioning

This case could be used in a wide variety of settings and with different audiences, ranging from experienced school leaders to graduate students in education, business, or management courses. It was written to be used in the PELP executive education program for school leaders. The Long Beach case series offers readers a chance to integrate theories of organizational coherence and change following a series of cases and lectures detailing organizational coherence, human capital management, and resource allocation.

Learning Objectives

The (B) case focuses on the transition of leadership in a large public school system. It provides a vehicle for teaching about leadership transitions, change management, and systemic coherence. Learning objectives include:

- **Leadership transition.** Provides insight into the challenges of succeeding an iconic leader. Helps students understand the linkage among leadership, management, and improved student outcomes.

- **Change management.** Refines participants' understanding of obstacles and opportunities for change and identifies the key success factors in the LBUSD change process.

- **Change over time.** Provides insights into the challenges new leaders face in sustaining organizational change and improvement efforts over time by not only building on a foundation of success but also having a willingness to change.

- **Organizational coherence.** Integrates concepts and frameworks introduced earlier in the program. The case provides understanding of the forces and factors that enable or impede coherence. Instructors can use the PELP strategic coherence framework for analyzing the current LBSUD structure and provide insight into the change and improvement process.

Assignment

As previously stated, students should have read and discussed "Long Beach Unified School District (A): Change that Leads to Improvement," PEL-006, before reading "Long Beach Unified School District (B): Sustaining Improvement during a Leadership Transition (2002–2004)," PEL-007.

Discussion Questions—(B) Case

1. How tough are the current challenges facing Steinhauser and LBUSD? Can you assign a degree of difficulty to each?

2. If you were Chris Steinhauser, how would you know what to change and what to leave the same?

3. In what ways has Steinhauser changed the district's strategy from the Cohn era? What does Steinhauser and his leadership team have to do to optimize his chances of success?

4. What are the leadership challenges that Steinhauser faces in succeeding an iconic leader?

Teaching Plan and Analysis

This 80-minute teaching plan is based on an executive education course designed for a PELP class of urban public school leadership teams. The teaching plan can be modified to suit a 75- or 90-minute session.

Summary

  I. **Introduction.** (5 minutes)

 II. **Analysis of organizational performance to date.** (20 minutes)

III. **Risks and opportunities facing Steinhauser.** (40 minutes)

IV. **Reflection: What can we learn from this to apply to our own work?** (15 minutes)

Introduction (5 minutes)

The instructor can begin class by outlining the purpose of the case in the context of the course or program. The instructor may begin by reflecting on the challenges of the intergenerational nature of leadership work. She might remind students that leaders and leadership teams must decide how or whether to build on the work of their predecessors and also decide how

and what organizational strategies to pass on to their successors. The instructor may then describe the key elements of the leadership transition that occurred in LBSUD when Chris Steinhauser succeeded Carl Cohn. Building on prior discussion of the (A) case, instructors can also call attention to key elements of LBUSD's district-wide strategy including the concept of "non-negotiables," commitment to cross-functional/data-driven decision making, and its relationship to elements of the PELP strategic coherence framework (stakeholders, resources, culture, systems, and structure).

Analysis of organizational performance to date (20 minutes)

After the introduction, one way to begin the analysis is to have participants assess the current performance status of LBUSD at the beginning of the (B) case. An effective way to tee up this conversation is to ask students, "How would you plot LBUSD's organizational performance at Steinhauser's point of entry on a basic graph of organizational performance over time?" Ask students to vote, "Do you think LBUSD is at point A, B, C, or D on the graph below?" (To improve the flow of the discussion, the instructor should draw the graph and include the letters on the board before the start of class.)

Graph A: Organizational Performance

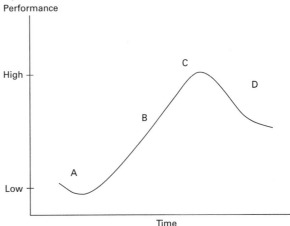

Source: Casewriters.

Instructors can anticipate a range of responses that include:

Point A: "They are at the early stages of an improvement cycle."

Point B: "They are making steady progress but still have a long way to go."

Point C: "They have nearly reached a relatively high level of performance and should attempt to resist declining organizational outcomes."

Point D: "They made good progress but are sliding backwards and losing ground."

After the vote, the instructor should call on a participant who voted for A and then one who voted for D. This polarity of opinion should promote a lively conversation. After allowing for some back and forth from participants with these two positions, the instructor should open the conversation to participants with other perspectives. The instructor should push the participants to articulate their specific reasons for making their selection as to the progress of the district. The instructor can also ask how the students' assessment of LBUSD's organizational performance connects to the strategies that were described in the (A) case.

Risks and opportunities facing Steinhauser (40 minutes)

The instructor should then ask students, "What are the greatest risks and opportunities facing Steinhauser and his leadership team at the beginning of the (B) case? What do you think is keeping him up at night?" Among the *risks* that might be identified are:

- Following a "legendary" and popular leader can create a dynamic where everyone compares the new leader's actions with what Cohn might have done. Any changes can be perceived as going against Cohn and even considered by some as disrespectful to Cohn's legacy.

- Working with a new school board has all sorts of unpredictable dimensions, some of which could undermine Steinhauser's ability to be effective. Many considered the partnership of the board with Cohn as a key to his success.

- Coping with budget cuts, central office retirements, and a strained relationship with TALB can be difficult.

- Sustaining prior reform and improvement efforts and at the same time determining what should be modified in a complex system can be daunting. While LBUSD is successful in many respects, not everything is working as well as it should. Little progress has been made in closing the achievement gap. Steinhauser must decide if all previous efforts should remain in place and must work with a leadership team that put most of the strategies in place. They understand the current strategies but could also be more resistant to change.

Potential *opportunities* students might identify are:

- The chance to build on prior success. Steinhauser is not taking over a failing district, often the case for a new superintendent, so he can immediately focus on building from a strong foundation rather than having to disrupt the entire organization.

- Capitalizing on the prior learning and knowledge that an "insider" can bring. Steinhauser does not have to get to know everyone and prove that he is committed to LBUSD and its students' improvement.

- The general sense of hope and potential for future strategic direction that a new leader can foster.

- The potential progress available to an organization that already has a certain amount of strategic focus.

The instructor might ask after the risk and opportunity discussion, "How might the organizational culture in LBUSD help or inhibit Steinhauser with the risks and opportunities you have identified?" It is our experience that most students will identify the culture of collaboration, results, and focus on children as a positive force for dealing with both risks and opportunities. Some will point out that the culture also has a closed feeling in that so many in the district are homegrown and insiders. This could make it more difficult for Steinhauser to bring in new ideas and people.

Evaluate the strategy: Having outlined the main risks and opportunities facing the LBUSD leadership team, the instructor should then ask students, "Identify and evaluate the key aspects of the strategy that LBUSD is pursing in the (B) case in order to bring the district to the next level of improvement. In what way does it differ from the (A) case strategy?" Among the items students will likely point to are the focus on high schools, administrative promotions that were announced and reorganization efforts Steinhauser undertook, the implementation of the Baldrige performance standards, and the various instructional reforms that were pursued. The instructor should ask students to assess the potential impact of these actions and whether they agree or disagree with Steinhauser's choices and sequencing. Deciding what to build on and what to change is a source of interesting debate. The instructor may use the PELP strategic coherence framework to organize student responses.

Given the obvious priority of focusing on high school reform, it can be useful for the instructor to engage students in a discussion of the particular role that high school Assistant Superintendent Margaret Webster has been asked to play in the overall instructional reforms within LBUSD. The instructor might tell students, "Speculate as to what it might actually be like to be in a situation like Webster's, with high expectations for results and performance coming from multiple directions."

Predictions: The instructor could then ask students to speculate as to the outcomes that might result for LBUSD from the strategies and initiatives being pursued by Steinhauser and his leadership team. The instructor can ask the students to list some of the things that Steinhauser and his team might hope to "pass on" to the next generation of leaders at LBUSD. Participants may identify the following: a clear vision based on prior organizational accomplishments, "cutting edge" work based on data and research, successful high school reform strategies, knowledge about optimal resource use that facilitates instructional improvement, and a cadre of leaders capable of implementing organizational change. The instructor might then ask, "What might you do if you were Steinhauser to ensure that these important elements are passed on to your successor?"

Reflection: What can we learn from this to apply to our own work? (15 minutes)

Toward the end of the class, give participants some time to reflect on what they have learned about leadership, organizational coherence, and organizational change. Some questions you could use depending on the mix of participants could include:

- What have you learned from these LBUSD cases about your personal leadership?

- What are the key obstacles that you face in your own organizational change and improvement work?

- Why is organizational coherence so hard to achieve and sustain?

- What are the key considerations you and your leadership team must focus on in order to successfully "pass on" effective improvement strategies to your successors?

About the Editors

Stacey Childress is a Lecturer at Harvard Business School, where she developed and teaches an MBA course called Entrepreneurship in Education. She is a cofounder of the Public Education Leadership Project, a joint initiative of Harvard's graduate schools of business and education. She has authored more than twenty case studies on education enterprises, and is a coauthor, with Richard F. Elmore and Allen S. Grossman, of the bestselling *Harvard Business Review* article, "How to Manage Urban Districts" (November 2006).

Richard F. Elmore is the Gregory R. Anrig Professor of Education Leadership at the Harvard Graduate School of Education. He is on the faculty of the Public Education Leadership Project, jointly run by Harvard's graduate schools of business and education. His most recent publications are *School Reform from the Inside Out: Policy, Practice, and Performance* (2004); *Building a New Structure for School Leadership* (2000); and *When Accountability Knocks, Will Anyone Answer?* (coauthored with C. Abelmann, 1999).

Allen S. Grossman, the MBA Class of 1957 Professor of Management Practice at Harvard Business School, is a faculty cochair of the Public Education Leadership Project, a joint project with the Harvard Graduate School of Education, whose mission is to enhance the quality of leadership and management in urban school districts. Grossman previously served as chief executive officer of Outward Bound USA, where he cofounded a comprehensive school reform model, Expeditionary Learning, implemented in over 130 public schools.

Susan Moore Johnson is the Pforzheimer Professor of Teaching and Learning at the Harvard Graduate School of Education, where she served as academic dean from 1993 to 1999. She studies and teaches about teacher policy, organizational change, and administrative practice. Johnson is a faculty cochair of the Public Education Leadership Project. She is also director of The Project on the Next Generation of Teachers, which examines how best to recruit, support, and retain a strong teaching force over the next decade. She is the author of *Finders and Keepers: Helping New Teachers Survive and Thrive in Our Schools* (2004).

Permissions

Premises and Practices of Discussion Teaching, by C. Roland Christensen

Adapted and reprinted by permission of Harvard Business School Press. From *Education for Judgment: The Artistry of Discussion Leadership,* by C. Roland Christensen, David A. Garvin, and Ann Sweet, Boston, MA 1992, pp. 15–34. Copyright © 1992 by the Harvard Business School Publishing Corporation. All rights reserved.

Teaching Notes

Taco Bell, Inc. (1983–1994): Using the Case with Education Administrators

Copyright © 2006 by the President and Fellows of Harvard College. Harvard Business School teaching note 5–307–083. The teaching note was prepared by Lecturer Stacey Childress and Research Associate Tonika Cheek Clayton as an aid to instructors in the classroom use of the case "Taco Bell, Inc. (1983–1994)," 9–398–129. Reprinted by permission of Harvard Business School.

Bristol City Schools (BCS)

Copyright © 2007 by the Public Education Leadership Project at Harvard University. Used with permission.

Pursuing Educational Equity at San Francisco Unified School District

Copyright © 2006 by the Public Education Leadership Project at Harvard University. Used with permission.

Southwest Airlines: Using Human Resources for Competitive Advantage (A): Using the Case with Education Administrators

Copyright © 2007 by the Public Education Leadership Project at Harvard University. Used with permission.

Reinventing Human Resources at the School District of Philadelphia

Copyright © 2006 by the Public Education Leadership Project at Harvard University. Used with permission.

Staffing the Boston Public Schools

Copyright © 2005 by the Public Education Leadership Project at Harvard University. Used with permission.

NYPD New: Using the Case with Education Administrators

Copyright © 2006 by the President and Fellows of Harvard College. Harvard Business School teaching note 5–407–056. The teaching note was prepared by Lecturer Stacey Childress and Research Associate Tonika Cheek Clayton as an aid to instructors in the classroom use of the case "NYPD New," 9–396–293. Reprinted by permission of Harvard Business School.

Learning to Manage with Data in Duval County Public Schools: Lake Shore Middle School (A)

Copyright © 2004 by the Public Education Leadership Project at Harvard University. Used with permission.